War, Culture and Society, 1750–1850

Titles include:

Richard Bessel, Nicholas Guyatt and Jane Rendall (*editors*)
WAR, EMPIRE AND SLAVERY, 1770–1830

Alan Forrest and Peter H. Wilson (*editors*)
THE BEE AND THE EAGLE
Napoleonic France and the End of the Holy Roman Empire, 1806

Alan Forrest, Karen Hagemann and Jane Rendall (*editors*)
SOLDIERS, CITIZENS AND CIVILIANS
Experiences and Perceptions of the Revolutionary and Napoleonic Wars, 1790–1820

Karen Hagemann, Gisela Mettele and Jane Rendall (*editors*)
GENDER, WAR AND POLITICS
Transatlantic Perspectives, 1755–1830

Marie-Cécile Thoral
FROM VALMY TO WATERLOO
France at War, 1792–1815

Forthcoming:

Michael Broers, Agustin Guimera and Peter Hick (*editors*)
THE NAPOLEONIC EMPIRE AND THE NEW EUROPEAN POLITICAL CULTURE

Alan Forrest, Etienne François and Karen Hagemann (*editors*)
WAR MEMORIES
The Revolutionary and Napoleonic Wars in Nineteenth and Twentieth Century Europe

Leighton S. James
WITNESSING WAR
Experience, Narrative and Identity in German Central Europe, 1792–1815

Catriona Kennedy
NARRATIVES OF WAR
Military and Civilian Experience in Britain and Ireland, 1793–1815

Kevin Linch
BRITAIN AND WELLINGTON'S ARMY
Recruitment, Society and Tradition, 1807–1815

War, Culture and Society, 1750–1850
Series Standing Order ISBN 978–0–230–54532–8 hardback
978–0–230–54533–5 paperback
(*outside North America only*)

You can receive future titles in this series as they are published by placing a standing order. Please contact your bookseller or, in case of difficulty, write to us at the address below with your name and address, the title of the series and the ISBN quoted above.

Customer Services Department, Macmillan Distribution Ltd, Houndmills, Basingstoke, Hampshire RG21 6XS, England

From Valmy to Waterloo

France at War, 1792–1815

Marie-Cécile Thoral
Senior Lecturer, Modern European History, Sheffield Hallam University, UK

Translation by

Godfrey Rogers

palgrave
macmillan

First published 2011 by
PALGRAVE MACMILLAN

Palgrave Macmillan in the UK is an imprint of Macmillan Publishers Limited, registered in England, company number 785998, of Houndmills, Basingstoke, Hampshire RG21 6XS.

Palgrave Macmillan in the US is a division of St Martin's Press LLC, 175 Fifth Avenue, New York, NY 10010.

Palgrave Macmillan is the global academic imprint of the above companies and has companies and representatives throughout the world.

Palgrave® and Macmillan® are registered trademarks in the United States, the United Kingdom, Europe and other countries.

ISBN 978–0–230–25287–5 hardback

This book is printed on paper suitable for recycling and made from fully managed and sustained forest sources. Logging, pulping and manufacturing processes are expected to conform to the environmental regulations of the country of origin.

A catalogue record for this book is available from the British Library.

A catalog record for this book is available from the Library of Congress.

10 9 8 7 6 5 4 3 2 1
20 19 18 17 16 15 14 13 12 11

Printed and bound in Great Britain by
CPI Antony Rowe, Chippenham and Eastbourne

Contents

Acknowledgements

I wish to express my gratitude and thanks to the Arts and Humanities Research Council, which funded the research project 'Nation, Borders, Identities: The Revolutionary and Napoleonic wars in European Memories,' in which I worked as a postdoctoral research fellow at the University of York from 2006 to 2008. Their funding allowed me to carry out the research necessary to write this book. I also benefited hugely from working with the members of this international project, in Berlin (Karen Hagemann, Etienne François, Ruth Leiserowitz, Kirstin Buchinger-Schäfer, Wolfgang Koller, Lars Peters, and Maria Schultz), and in York where I could enjoy long and fruitful exchanges with Alan Forrest, Jane Rendall, Richard Bessel, Catriona Kennedy, and Leighton James. I am also indebted to Michael Broers and Alan Forrest, who kindly accepted to read the whole manuscript through several times. Their precious comments and ideas are greatly appreciated. Many thanks to both of them. At Palgrave, special thanks to Michael Strang and his assistant, Ruth Ireland, for their kind, competent, and efficient collaboration. Many thanks as well to the Musée du Louvre and the Réunion des Musées Nationaux for allowing me to use the picture of *Napoleon on the battlefield of Eylau* by Antoine-Jean Gros for the cover jacket, to Godfrey Rogers for the impeccable translation of the manuscript, and, lastly, to all the members of the Department of History, International Relations and Politics at Coventry University where I enjoyed working in a friendly and congenial atmosphere for 2 years, and to all my colleagues of the Department of History at Sheffield Hallam University.

Outside of work, I wish to thank my dearest ones for their constant and invaluable support.

Introduction

The Revolution that began in 1789 produced a far-reaching political, social, religious, and cultural upheaval in French society. The radical and comprehensive changes made in the early months and years by France's new rulers set up a shock wave that affected countries across Europe. In fact it soon became clear that a root and branch reconstruction of French society on fundamentally new bases – the image of the 'tabula rasa' – was not possible in practice. But although numerous elements from the ancien régime survived the turmoil and came through the revolutionary era intact, the existing foundations of society were seriously undermined. It was during the Revolution narrowly defined (1789–1799) and the Consulate and the Empire that the contours of modern France first emerged: abolition of the society of legally defined estates, establishment of civil rights for all, moves towards national unification (creation of administrative departments and a single system of weights and measures), and introduction of a more rational system of public administration for the country as a whole.

The transformations were not limited to the civil, political, and social spheres: they also affected the army and military affairs. 'The Revolution was war,' observed Jean-Paul Bertaud in 1979. 'For eight years, with rifle raised and pike erect, the Frenchman was a combatant.'[1] The reference to 8 years of continuous conflict is explained by the chronological limits of his study (1792–1799). But the peace that followed the signing of the Treaty of Amiens on 27 March 1802 was short-lived. From May 1803 France was again at war, and would remain so for a further 11 years, with an interruption during the First Restoration. Thus the French declaration of war on Austria on 20 April 1792 in fact committed the nation to more than 20 years of war. Faced with a coalition of European powers united against the young Republic, the revolutionaries came up with an original solution to the double imperative of defending the territory of France and the new political values of the revolution: they called upon the citizenry to form a truly national army. By breaking with old-established practices and the monarchical tradition of mercenary armies, and relying instead on an army of citizen soldiers, France entered the era of political and military modernity. Recruitment was voluntary in the early years, but before long a shortage of soldiers led to the introduction of conscription. Initially an exceptional measure, it became systematic after 1798 and the passing of the Jourdan Law, and as such was continued and indeed intensified during the Consulate and Empire.[2] The revolutionary and Napoleonic wars were the first national wars in which the combatants were drawn directly from civilian society. The result was an unprecedented tightening of the bond between the civilian and military worlds, between war and nation.

That the conflict would have consequences for the very foundations of French society was inevitable given its sheer scale, duration, and geographical extent (the whole of continental Europe and beyond in the campaigns in Egypt and Saint-Domingue); its far-reaching impact on civilian society and trade; and its forcible involvement of hundreds of thousands of young Frenchmen in year after year of interminable war. Several generations of young and not-so-young men underwent their baptism of fire during this 20-year period. Between 1800 and 1815, a total of 1.5 million conscripts, equal to 7 per cent of the population of France, were enrolled in the army and sent off to war.[3] Through the conscripts' experience and what it represented, countless French families also discovered the reality of the war. They did so at different moments and in different ways: receiving news of the front from sons, husbands and fathers; reading the battle accounts – of questionable reliability – published in the press; hearing the wild rumours that circulated; or experiencing higher prices, the scarcity of colonial products, and the unwelcome changes to ways of life and patterns of consumption and diet. They faced the demands of the war effort – through requisitioning, forced loans, higher taxes, and financial crises – welcomed new opportunities offered by army supply and speculation, or suffered the adverse consequences of the naval war and blockade, the decline of maritime commerce and the string of bankruptcies among major merchants and shipowners.

Directly or indirectly, therefore, on the battlefield and within families, the war that started in 1792 and only really ended in 1815 impinged on the whole of French society. How did the French people experience these long years of conflict? How did they perceive, understand, analyse, assimilate, and transmit the ever-changing and frequently indescribable reality of the war? How were they able to 'stick it', to withstand and get through a time of crisis in the history of France and, more importantly, in their personal history, in their own lives? How did they come through it? Were they affected – physically but also mentally – by the experience, by the sights they witnessed or by their own actions? It is to these questions that this book attempts to provide some elements of an answer. The scale of the subject and the limits of space made it necessary to restrict the field of study: my main focus is the experience of soldiers, though civilians form the subject of the Chapters 6 and 7.

The theme of this book is the first-hand experience of French soldiers and civilians during these conflicts. Seen through their eyes and using their testimony, a picture gradually emerges of the reality in the field, the limited but deeply human vision of their daily existence, the nature of combat as it was for the combatants themselves. In addition to this social and cultural reading of soldiers' lives, the present study is also the occasion to take a new approach to human experience, to assess the place of the revolutionary and Napoleonic conflicts in the evolution of the art of warfare, and the elements of modernity which made them the first example of 'total war'.

The expression 'total war' used first in connection with the Great War was frequently employed in the period immediately before the Second World War, notably in the book by Ludendorff published in 1936. It is widely used today in social and political science as well as in historical studies on the conflicts of the twentieth century, and for this reason it is worth trying to define it more precisely. The concept of total war, though somewhat vague, is useful and convenient to describe the new art of warfare that developed in Europe at the beginning of the modern period. No consensus definition exists; however, some historians tried to identify its main features. According to Jeremy Black, total war is defined by 'the intensity of struggle, the range (geographical and/or chronological) of conflict, the nature of the goals, and the extent to which civil society was involved in war, not only as victims but also because of an unprecedented mobilisation of the resources of societies in order to permit a pursuit of war that was, at once, more intense and more extensive than hitherto'.[4] Jean-Yves Guiomar had already resorted to some of these categories of definition, but had paid more attention to the political dimension of total war. According to him, it is based on four main criteria: the mobilization of an entire civilian society and its resources (human, economic, etc.) for the war effort; the blurring of the dividing line between civilians and military or combatants and non-combatants (notably in levels of battlefield violence and the treatment of enemy and prisoners); the desire to exterminate the enemy, demonize him, and accentuate his 'otherness'; lastly, the merging of politics and war.[5] Our study will combine these two definitions when assessing the character of the revolutionary and Napoleonic wars.

The first historian to emphasize the importance of the revolutionary and Napoleonic wars in the evolution of the western art of warfare was John U. Nef. Writing at a time (1949) favourable to reflection on the nature of war, he saw the revolutionary and Napoleonic wars as marking the transition from the 'age of limited war' under the ancien régime to 'a new concept, total war', 'a massacre as not seen since the Thirty Years War' in continental Europe.[6] This idea of a far-reaching transformation of warfare after 1792 was later taken up by other historians: Albert Soboul in 1959,[7] Gunther Rothenberg in 1980,[8] John Lynn in 1984,[9] Roger Chickering in 1999,[10] and most recently David Bell in 2007.[11]

It would be impossible to list all the studies conducted on the revolutionary and Napoleonic wars during the last 200 years. Most of these works, however, treat the subject from a fairly narrow perspective (biographies of famous generals, descriptions of battles) or take the approach of traditional military history. The renewal operated in the historiography of the two world wars of the twentieth century,[12] and to a lesser extent in that of the Franco-Prussian War of 1870–1871,[13] completely ignored the great conflict with which the contemporary period in Europe opens. A few historians, however, notably Alan Forrest in *Napoleon's Men*[14] and David Bell in *The First Total War*,[15] have pioneered a renewal in the historiography of these conflicts. The former studies the letters written by soldiers, both for their content and for their style and the conditions in which they were produced, while the latter analyses the wars in the light of highly modern concepts like that of total war. Arguing its thesis with style and conviction, David Bell's seminal work treats this theme at a macro-political and macro-cultural level, showing how, between the mid-eighteenth and early nineteenth centuries, changes in the collective representation and imagination of war – perception of the army and soldiers, relations between soldiers and civilians, militarism and militarization of society, civilian perceptions of war, aesthetics of war, relation between war and politics – engendered 'a new culture of war'. In this cultural history of war the author skilfully analyses the relations between war and politics and between war and collective representations, but does not, despite a few references to accounts by contemporaries of the events, attempt to study and analyse in-depth the actual experience of combatants – which is no criticism of the book since that was not its intended purpose.

The present work's claim to originality lies in proceeding from the viewpoint, perceptions, vision, and experience of the actors involved in the events: the men who lived through these wars, faced up to death and disease, fought in the mud and on the seas, struggled against the adverse economic consequences of the conflicts. This is not another book about the role of the revolutionary and Napoleonic wars in the evolution of the art of warfare: its subject matter is the everyday human experience of the participants in the war, and specifically the aspects touching on combat and battle.

One challenge in preparing this study has thus been to give due weight to sources written in the first person – 'autobiographical narratives' – to get an idea of how these wars were perceived and experienced by the main actors involved. With a few exceptions – as when administrative documents of civil or military origin are used to provide additional information – the raw material for our research was penned by the combatants themselves or by civilians who lived through the events.

Alan Forrest has demonstrated the importance of personal narratives as a historical source for the study of collective psychology and mentalities, and above all the close, intrinsic relationship between such first-person writings, actual experience, and its transcription. The various types of personal narratives – letters, diaries and journals, memoirs and reminiscences – are 'the most immediate conduit we have to the thinking and mentality of those involved, and the most personal, in that they reflect the experience of individuals rather than the goals of army administrators or the public, self-image of political leaders... personal narratives are just that: the story of an individual's experience or his later memory of it, along with occasional reflections on that experience, either at the time or in succeeding years'.[16]

These sources derive coherence from the common status of their authors: all were actors in or witnesses of the events they relate. But the homogeneity and simplicity of these sources are more apparent than real, and their use presents real difficulties for the historian. For this reason a more detailed presentation of them is in order.

The three main categories of private writings used in the present study are the personal correspondence of the soldiers, their *carnets de route* or diaries and journals, and lastly their memoirs. While these three sources are complementary, they are not at all interchangeable. Like any historical source, they must be subjected to a detailed epistemological critique and used with a certain caution.

Letters written by soldiers and officers are precious sources of information because of when and how they were written. These letters were written at the centre of events, on the edge of a battlefield or in breaks during long marches; they provide direct living testimony, often naïve and sometimes quite detailed, of day-to-day existence in the war. Sending and receiving letters assumed immense importance for men who had been torn from their homes. Letters were an important, if not the most important link they retained with their family, as well as with the world of civilians and with the region they came from. That is why in so many of their letters they enquire after the health and doings not just of parents and loved ones but of simple acquaintances, and about what was happening in the region and in the rest of France (the price of bread, state of the harvest, numbers conscripted from the village, etc.). What Carine Trevisan has observed for letters from the First World War combatants has a more general relevance and applies equally to letters from soldiers in the revolutionary and Napoleonic wars (and indeed in any war): the wartime letter, written by someone not used to putting pen to paper, a 'non-writer', was intended above all as a means of maintaining contact with civilians, with what she calls the world of 'people living normal lives', a point of added importance given the impression many soldiers had of being cut off from the rest of humanity.[17] The arrival of the mail was awaited impatiently, and when, as often happened, delivery was disrupted, due to unsafe roads and convoys or broken communications, the likely result was a stream of complaints together with increased levels of anxiety and the severe form of homesickness known as *mal du pays*.[18]

Written primarily to sustain social ties, and intended for an audience of family and friends or, during the Revolution, of clubs and political societies, soldiers' letters were almost invariably and necessarily subject to a degree of self-censorship, which suggests the limits of these documents as sources for historical study. Postal censorship of the kind that operated in France during the First World War was also practised during the revolutionary and, particularly, Napoleonic wars. But it did not reach anything like the same technical sophistication or effectiveness, and soldiers' letters from this period cannot be suspected of having been subjected to official filtering. Some letters were strongly critical of the war or the conduct and decisions of the high command and yet were delivered nonetheless.

But if official censorship was light, self-censorship – the deliberate omission of certain subjects and details from correspondence – was widespread among soldiers of all ranks. The reasons were not military but personal, chiefly the desire to spare the feelings of parents and loved ones. The same is probably true for all wars and all soldiers, and in this sense the phenomenon is more anthropological than historical. Rémy Cazals and Frédéric Rousseau have observed similar behaviour among the French *poilus* of the Great War.

> In correspondence to his family, Eugène Bayle carefully suppresses any expression that could make them anxious on his behalf. His main purpose is not to inform but to maintain a link with close family and friends, without alarming them. Soldiers know that their own morale depends on that of their loved ones. Thus in their regular correspondence with them they make no mention of any episodes or anxieties likely to cause them distress. On the other hand, reassuring expressions of their good state of health abound, part of a seemingly compulsory ritual.... Tacitly, each party elaborated a fiction in which little or nothing was said about the real war. Much of the time a comedy intended to sustain the morale of both parties was played out in the correspondence...[19]

Soldiers and officers could have other reasons, too, for omitting or minimizing particular aspects of the war: a fear of not being understood or believed by civilians who knew nothing of the war and daily life in the army; the sheer impossibility of verbalizing particular scenes; a belief that not everything was fit to be told (accounts of drunkenness, relations with women, or pillage, for instance); the difficulty of writing down and putting into words certain feelings or traumas, or admitting to actions where there was a sense of shame and guilt (about stealing, killing). Soldiers did not say everything in their letters, far from it, and while some letters are rich and informative, others disappoint by a content that is repetitious and dull, banal and monotonous, limited to a few details about the writer's health to reassure close family and friends, or a few bare facts about the latest military operations. Letters from volunteers during the Revolution, in particular, tend to be full of ready-made republican and patriotic formulas taken from Jacobin propaganda, sometimes repeated in identical form in letters from several soldiers of the same regiment. This was especially likely to happen when illiterate soldiers had their letters written for them by a soldier who acted as public writer for several of his fellows and used the same formulas over and over again. But providing allowance is made for the limitations of these documents, even the simplest letters can supply valuable information about the men's daily existence, experience and perceptions, and about how this was communicated and transmitted to their loved ones and to the civilian world at large. Studied for what they omit or forget to say, for what is absent or left unsaid, as much as for their content, the letters supply many insights.

Unlike their letters, soldiers' diaries and journals, their *journaux de marche* and *carnets de route*, were not intended to be read in their original state and so were not written for a direct or immediate audience. As daily accounts of the author's private opinions, feelings, and state of mind, they have affinities with the literary genre of the intimate journal. In some cases they also resemble travel literature in that they give precise indications of places visited and distances covered and descriptions of the regions the soldiers passed through. In theory the soldier would write them up each day to produce a written record of that or the previous day's activity. In practice, however, men and officers could seldom keep up a daily journal for weeks or months at a time; in most cases entries were spaced further and further apart as the journal progressed. Consequently, writers would sometimes lump together several days or even several weeks in a single paragraph.[20] But this was unavoidable: excluding the periods of intense activity, such as when preparing for and fighting major battles, their monotonous and repetitious military existence commonly did not provide enough material to write a daily account. Though some stuck scrupulously to the rule of daily writing and produced journals with a succession of short entries, others opted to group their entries together.

The factual information contained in soldiers' diaries and journals permits an accurate and detailed reconstruction of the everyday existence of combatants on such questions as itineraries, distances covered daily and modes of transport, type of accommodation, number of days bivouacked or encamped during a single campaign, food or lack of it, climate. Like their letters,[21] soldiers' diaries and journals are an important source because they are contemporary, written either during events or in the days or weeks immediately following. And like the letters, therefore, they frequently possess spontaneity, with a narrative that is an immediate response to events, not composed or reconstructed at a later date as with war memoirs, and thus offer valuable insights into the nature of the daily experience of war as it felt at the time.

Another significant advantage of diaries and journals over letters is that they are more complete and have a greater frankness of tone and content. As a rule they are free of self-censorship. Apart from a few campaign diaries produced and sent to families to supplement letters, which resemble correspondence, soldiers were not selective about what they put down in their journal or notebook, since in theory they were not writing for a public. As Rémy Cazals and Frédéric Rousseau stress in relation to soldiers' writings from the Great War, 'The few words jotted in a letter to his wife or mother are not the same as those set down in a soldier's war diary. The style of expression is not at all comparable.'[22] A desire to dissimulate or play down certain aspects of the war was even less likely given the important place the journal often had in the life of the soldier. It was several things at once: a constant companion and a prop to morale, a familiar ritual, a way of preserving routine and countering anxiety and *mal du pays*, an outlet and a therapeutic device (putting them into words could help to overcome certain fears, anxieties, stress reactions). With the journal there was also a strong element of personal commemoration, as many authors were aware and explicitly recognized. The journal was the written record of all that its author saw, heard, did and learned in the course of what the majority of these young men felt was not merely the most momentous event in their own existence but also part of history, a true testimony of which it was their responsibility to record and pass on to civilians of their own and future generations. The journal produced with this in mind often served as the raw material when the author came to write up his personal memoirs after the war.

This second category of source forms a useful complement to the first. Because he is not writing to be read by others, or at least not immediately, the author can employ a degree of frankness in his journal not possible in letters to close family, allowing him to discuss a range of subjects he is unable to write about in his correspondence. But this also has a disadvantage: because he is not writing the journal for a public, the author will tend to leave long gaps between writing up his account, whereas letters written to keep in touch with close family and friends are usually written at close intervals.

The use of diaries and campaign journals as a historical source is not without problems, similar to those associated with letters. The author has no distance from the events he is describing, and his account may well contain numerous errors and approximations, and repeat uncertainties (not necessarily acknowledged) and rumours. In addition, the viewpoint is necessarily limited to that of the writer's personal experience. Often the horizon is narrowly circumscribed, so that soldiers' journals and diaries, like their letters, are highly subjective. This makes them of questionable value as a source for a historical study of the revolutionary and Napoleonic wars from a factual standpoint. But provided we keep in mind the inherent shortcomings of the *journal intime* as a literary genre, journals and diaries are an invaluable source for a cultural analysis of the human experience of those involved.

The third type of personal narrative used as a source for this study takes the form of memoirs written by soldiers about their role in the wars. Unlike the two previous categories, memoirs are not directly contemporary with the events they describe, but are, as their name indicates, written up after the event. The time that elapses between the events and the writing is not always long, and some soldiers wrote up their memoirs, often at the request of their family, shortly after they returned to civilian life. In the majority of cases, however, memoirs were written several years or even decades after the end of the war, generally towards the end of the author's life. A number of memoirs were published in the Restoration and July Monarchy, especially after the return of the Emperor's ashes and the rise of the Napoleonic legend. The output of memoirs rose sharply during the Second Empire – the wars and conquests made this a period propitious to recollecting Napoleonic glory – but most of all during the Third Republic, for reasons related to politics and publishing, and to a context of rising military tension that foreshadowed an imminent large-scale war. Publication of memoirs on the revolutionary and Napoleonic wars peaked in the years 1880–1900.

The outpouring of memoirs by former soldiers on the revolutionary and Napoleonic wars reflects a new phenomenon, one confirmed in subsequent conflicts (the Mexican and Crimean wars, the Franco-Prussian War, and the two world wars). This was the birth of a new literary and publishing genre, the personal literature of war, with the proliferation of personal accounts of events felt to be 'historical' as soon as they occurred, and the transition from the 'aristocratic memoir' of the ancien régime, written exclusively by nobles and prominent figures, to the 'democratic memoir' of the modern period, produced increasingly by ordinary individuals.[23] This trend, as Damien Zanone has shown, was linked to broader structural changes occurring in the nineteenth century, with the new taste for history and the development of the 'scientific' study of history, the onset of Romanticism, and the exaltation of the individual (encouraging anyone who had witnessed or taken part in an important event to give his own interpretation of the facts). Related to this was the nineteenth century's passion for civilian and military memoirs written by public figures but also by unknown individuals or indeed by forgers (who concocted or fabricated fictitious memoirs, some of them written on a 'production line' by professional writers for specialist publishers of this type of literature).[24] Publishers in the nineteenth century responded to the public's appetite for memoirs and to the potency of the Napoleonic legend by asking survivors of the revolutionary and Napoleonic wars to write their memoirs, while towards the end of the century the same reasons often led descendants of veterans to dig out unpublished manuscript memoirs and send them to publishers.

The large number of soldiers' memoirs on the revolutionary and Napoleonic wars form a key source for the present study, both by their quantity – far more plentiful than letters or, in particular, diaries and journals – and because of their quality. While letters, diaries and journals are frequently repetitious, factual, or dull, memoirs, by contrast, have been revised, worked over and improved by their authors. And because those authors have both the time for writing, not always the case in wartime conditions, and a critical distance, the final result is a carefully crafted testimony with a greater degree of reflection and introspection, and analysis by the author of his situation and perception of events at the time. Although they must be used with care, the fact that memoirs were written at a much later date is not grounds for dismissing them as a source for studying experience in these wars: they are not primary sources but narratives reconstructed after the event. The elements in each narrative have necessarily been sifted and selected; and facts may have been distorted to obscure some less than glorious exploit by the author or to highlight an act of bravura. This degree of subjectivity, however, is certainly not peculiar to memoirs but characterizes all accounts written in the first person, including letters and diaries, and has to be accepted by the historian wishing to use this type of source to reconstitute the cultural history of these wars. Although these sources present definite shortcomings for a factual or material study, they are indispensable for the historian trying to reach an understanding of how events were experienced and perceived by contemporaries.

A further criticism of memoirs as a source, this one specific to the genre, relates to the long delay in writing about events and the risk of faulty recall when authors reconstitute their memories of the past. It seems to me that this risk, though real, is nonetheless fairly slight for two reasons. In the first place, numerous medical studies have shown that although memory is selective and unreliable, any traumatic events are recorded and stored intact: fighting in a war is unquestionably a momentous and traumatic event in the life of any individual. In addition, while these memoirs were indeed often written many years after the event, this was usually done with the aid of contemporary documents kept by the former soldier, particularly letters and campaign diaries – material sources that contributed substance and detail to the memoir. A possible third argument is that memory may fail over matters of fact like dates and places, thus accounting for the errors and half-truths common in memoirs, but that for recollecting emotions, feelings, perceptions it is generally highly reliable. This legitimizes the use of memoirs by the historian for studying not the material reality of the wars themselves but the perception and experience of the wars among the soldiers who fought in them. It is for these reasons that I decided that memoirs written by contemporaries (without any cut-off date in the nineteenth century) should be included among the sources used for this study.

The aim here is to use the writings of those present at the time, principally though not exclusively soldiers, to analyse the significance of the revolutionary and Napoleonic wars and their position in the evolution of the art of warfare in the West. The book is divided into chapters in which key aspects of day-to-day experience during the wars are examined: physical experience, in the form of wounds, disease, and medical care; psychological experience, the emotional reactions to battle and death; combat on land and also in naval warfare; levels of troop morale and the sources of cohesiveness and group unity; relations between civilians and soldiers as these are mediated by diaries and letters; and the impact of the war on the economy and on the daily life of civilians.

1
Battle Experience

From the time of the French Revolution, the literary and artistic representations of war, and more specifically of battle, had undergone an important transformation. Starting around 1803–1807, the large-scale classical compositions of the eighteenth century, in which generals formed the main or even exclusive focus of attention, were replaced by battle paintings depicting vast groups in which soldiery of all ranks, but primarily common soldiers, took pride of place. In battle scene paintings, the general now made way for the citizen soldier, and artists, responding more to the aspirations of the new century than to the classicism of the Enlightenment's aesthetic canons, sought to depict an essentially human experience and to chart the psychology of the suffering of the combatants.[1] The demise of the aristocratic culture of warfare, confirmed in pictorial art, and the emergence of the crowd, the people, and the citizen soldier, signalled the beginnings of Romanticism, a cultural movement that from its onset was bound up with war. In its literary and pictorial representations, the revolutionary and Napoleonic battle was the first romantic battle of the nineteenth century.

If culture does indeed parallel or reflect the major changes occurring within a society, the birth of a new culture of war, taken to signify the individual and collective representations of war,[2] clearly attests to a sweeping social change, a revolution that is not merely political but military, a profound transformation of the art of warfare in the West. Commenting on this period in 1911, the military historian General Jean Colin noted that 'from a military viewpoint, it was the end of a world.'[3] The revolutionary and Napoleonic wars present a set of characteristics – military, political, and social – that distinguish them from the wars of the ancien régime, and herald the great conflicts of the twentieth century and what has come to be defined as 'total war'.

One element in this transformation of military practice is the markedly more offensive nature of warfare, resulting in the increased importance of battle. Prior to 1792, the battle was not viewed as the climax of the entire war. Indeed, whenever possible, chiefs of staff actively avoided battle, so as to conserve their resources in manpower. During the revolutionary and Napoleonic wars, by contrast, the generals aimed for speedy victory through an abrupt and decisive weakening of the enemy's forces. Since battle was the way to achieve this objective, it became the surest and fastest means to annihilate the adversary and win the war. In eighteenth-century conflicts, an essential factor in the balance of power between opposing forces was the quality of manoeuvre, but in the revolutionary and Napoleonic wars this was reduced to a mere auxiliary role to serve the openly stated aim of provoking – and winning – the battle. This substitution of the end for the means, and of crude effectiveness (the outcome of the battle) for technical virtuosity (the quality of manoeuvre), reflects both the ideological nature of these wars and the new economics of warfare, since as the supply of potential soldiers became more plentiful, so the soldiers themselves became less valuable. Also, thanks to the improved mobility of weaponry (notably cannons) and of convoys (because of the increasingly common practice of living off the conquered lands) a war of fixed position was replaced by a war of movement. The increased size of armies imposed a new, more 'efficient' form of warfare, in place of the discrete, almost private, affairs of the past. The total number of battles in Europe grew exponentially over this period: whereas from the end of the Middle Ages to the French Revolution (1480–1790), they totalled 2,659, for the period 1790–1820 alone they numbered 713.[4] Battles thus became more frequent, and above all were conducted on a more massive scale. Rank-and-file troops played an increasingly important role, notably through the exercise of greater initiative (with the adoption of skirmishing tactics, particularly by the French).

An attempt to shed light on the nature of lived human experience during these wars thus necessarily begins with a study of what now emerged as the decisive point in conflict, namely battle. This chapter analyses the changes affecting the conduct of battle, how the actors in the field, the military, reacted to these changes, and how the experience and perception of battle were conveyed in their writings.

I. The changing face of battle

War in this period became more intensive on several levels. Intensification was first of all quantitative: 'massive' battles became the defining characteristic of war.

This contrasted sharply with what had gone before. Eighteenth-century armies, composed of professional soldiers, some of them French, others foreign, were relatively small. An army could put only limited numbers of men on to the battlefield. Frederick the Great deployed no more than 50,000 men in any of his battles, with the sole exceptions of Hohenfriedenberg (77,000) and Prague (64,000). Napoleon commanded forces twice this size, on average. In seven of his battles Napoleon assembled over 100,000 men, and his army at Jena, though split, still numbered 96,000.[5] The reason for this massive increase in combatant numbers, far exceeding those in eighteenth-century conflicts, was the presence in the French Army of *soldats-citoyens* – citizen soldiers, enlisted as volunteers or conscripts. Carl von Clausewitz, an officer in the Prussian Army during the Napoleonic wars, highlighted the difficulties this change in the social nature of war caused for the Prussian General Staff.

> Austria and Prussia put their diplomatic art of war to the test and it was quickly shown to be inadequate... A force of which no one had an inkling appeared on the scene in 1793. War had again suddenly become the business of the people, and that of a people numbering thirty millions, every one of whom regarded himself as a citizen of the state... The involvement in the war of the people, instead of a government or a merely professional army, threw into the balance the weight of an entire nation. Henceforth, the means available and the energies that could be devoted to using them no longer had any definite limits.[6]

The great expansion in French armed forces was quickly matched by a rise in Allied (anti-French European coalition) troop numbers. Thus 130,000 Austrians opposed the French at Wagram, 78,000 at Ratisbon, and 74,000 at Eckmühl; Blücher commanded 100,000 men at Craonne and 128,000 at La Rothière in 1814;[7] and Kutuzov led 120,000 men at Borodino. This development had inevitable consequences for the physiology of battle. Battles became more massive in scale. They were fought with vast numbers of men, exceeding 100,000 for the most important battles and in exceptional cases 300,000 (320,000 at Wagram in 1809, 420,000 at Leipzig in 1813).[8] The trend to mass armies did not escape the attention of military men in the field, like Chevallier, who was struck by the sheer human scale of battles such as Wagram where 'over half a million men and over twelve hundred cannon vomit death unceasingly over every post.'[9]

The trend to mass armies was reinforced by changes in combat tactics. Central to the ancien régime battle was the tactic of line fighting, the carefully ordered confrontation that followed the precepts of the Age of Enlightenment. Not so the battle of the revolutionary and Napoleonic wars, when the classical formation of the long thin line, usually only three men deep, was increasingly replaced by a compact, dense column formation and by frontal attack, the so-called shock tactic. This change was particularly visible after the battle of Wattignies, which for John Lynn marks a turning point in the art of war.[10]

This represented a complete break from the practices of ancien régime army commanders, who refused to employ the tactics of offensive shock, partly in order to avoid excessive human losses and partly from respect for a certain aesthetics of battle. From the Revolution onwards, the plentiful supply of potential soldiers and their lack of experience in the art of war (notably the positioning skills vital for effective line formation), plus the political and ideological war aims that gave primacy to obtaining the enemy's surrender and thus a rapid and decisive weakening of his forces, together turned the political and military authorities away from the formal and elegant art of battle, in favour of the brute force, speed, and efficiency of shock tactics. For Saint Just, this change in the physiology of battle, now conducted on a massive scale and openly offensive, was better suited to the new French spirit engendered by the Revolution: 'At a time of innovation, everything that is not new is pernicious', he declared on 10 October 1793, 'Because the French nation is borne along in this war by the strongest and most generous of passions, a love of liberty, a hatred of tyrants and oppression, while its enemies are mercenary slaves, passionless automatons, the French armies' system of war must be shock action.'[11]

The transformation in combat tactics was accompanied by a change in weaponry. No civilized country in the eighteenth century would have armed its soldiers with a weapon judged as primitive or uncivilized as the bayonet, use of which was left to countries considered backward by the standards of western civilization, notably Russia. After 1792, however, side arms, the bayonet particularly, reappeared on the battlefield on the French side. Two reasons can be advanced to explain the widespread use of this most simple of weapons. The first is ideological. Often presented as the military equivalent of the civilian's pike (the symbol and preferred arm of the sans-culotte),[12] the bayonet was, in the eyes of political leaders, public opinion, and volunteer soldiers, the weapon of the true fighter and patriot, in that it required the courage to engage the enemy directly in close, practically hand-to-hand combat.

It was also the *arme populaire*, the weapon of the people, and thus of the true revolutionary. On 6 September 1793, Collot d'Herbois (a member of the Committee of Public Safety) declared:

> Is it not the bayonet... that confirms the superiority of the French over the slaves of tyrants? By making them wait for guns are you not cooling the spiritual energy and fervour that is carrying 30,000 men to the frontiers? Let us arm our soldiers with pikes, and recall the words of a Spartan to his son. "My sword is indeed short" said the son, to which the republican replied: "Then, my son, you will step forward another pace." So we too will make another step forward, the better to crush the enemies of Liberty![13]

Collot d'Herbois was followed by the members of the Committee of Public Safety, who wrote on 2 February 1794: 'General rules are: act always as a mass and on the offensive, always keep the troops on alert, and on every occasion deliver combat with bayonets.' The reasons for this choice of tactics were given on 21 August:

> By spreading the troops out along a large frontier, it is obvious that we are weak everywhere and that the enemy, by concentrating his forces on a single point and making a surprise attack, will be able to open a breach whenever he feels like attacking... [So we must] strike with the speed of lightning and the force of the thunderbolt.[14]

In the early stages of the Revolution, the political authorities' well-publicized preference for combat with side arms was also explained by less ideological and more practical considerations. The under-development of the arms industry resulted in a shortage of firearms, and the young volunteers and conscript soldiers lacked training and experience in the handling of weapons compared with the professional armies of the ancien régime. Despite increases in rates of fire and in output of arms and ammunition, the French Army continued to use the bayonet up to 1815. In their diaries, letters, and memoirs, several soldiers refer to bayonet charges, often made while singing patriotic songs like the 'Marseillaise', intended to bolster the courage of the French and unnerve and terrify the enemy.[15]

The trend to battles on a massive scale was also associated with an increase in the average length of combat. Wars in the past were wars of attrition, involving armies in long marches and counter-marches to find a suitable battlefield. Once the command had established that the location was also acceptable to the enemy, it launched the assault. Often the fighting did not last long. Until the end of the eighteenth century, the length and scale of battles were limited by a difficulty that was both technical and economic, namely the restricted range of artillery, which precluded killing from a distance. For the same reason, officers seldom gave orders to pursue the fleeing enemy, since the technical conditions prevailing at the time made this too hazardous. To intensify the battle and improve the capacity to pursue and annihilate the enemy, major technological and logistic changes had to come about: an increase in the accuracy, speed, and range of cannon fire (to reach more distant targets); a greater mobility of artillery and its supply vehicles; plus a substantial increase in output from the war industries, especially of iron. All these innovations occurred at the very end of the eighteenth century, and helped to modify the art of warfare and the conduct of battle in the revolutionary and Napoleonic wars.[16]

The transition over this period from a war of position to a war of movement was associated with a change of tempo in military campaigns.[17] Composed largely of mercenaries for whom soldiering was a career, ancien régime armies were accustomed to a pattern of lengthy wars punctuated by a relatively small number of short encounters with the enemy and pitched battle engagements. From the Revolution onwards, however, the French Army was composed mainly of citizen soldiers (although it still contained some professional soldiers, including mercenaries); what this army desired was the decisive combat that would end the war and allow its men to return to their homes.[18]

For these two reasons, one technological, the other socio-political, the average length of battles tended to increase, especially when, as was often the case, they ended with the pursuit of a retreating enemy. For Hubert Camon, this is one of the key points of the Napoleonic theory of battle as part of a wider strategy, where the role of the battle was to decide the outcome of the campaign. The aim was not simply to win the battle but, by means of an encircling or outflanking manoeuvre, to cut off the enemy's retreat.[19]

The result was that fighting and then pursuing the enemy often extended over several days, subjecting the troops to an increased burden of fatigue and tension. The major battles generally lasted between 1 and 3 days, typically from morning till evening and possibly resuming the next morning.

In addition to large-scale battles, war included a multitude of smaller battles lasting several days, weeks, and on occasions over a month, with a break of a few days in the middle. Pierre Valleron, a young volunteer soldier who had enlisted in the National Guard battalions in 1792 aged 16 and moved to an infantry regiment in 1793, wrote to his parents on 29 August 1794 from the Army of the Rhine: 'I am keeping well despite the hardships of war, for we are still in action. In the last one and a half months we have pushed the enemy back ten leagues. The attack began on 25 messidor [13 July].'[20] The situation was the same in later years. François-Joseph Jacquin, a young conscript of 1798 from the Bresse region and grenadier in the 37th Demi-Brigade of the line, noted in his diary on 3 June 1799, during a campaign in the Tyrol: 'We encountered the enemy at Clauten and a combat was joined that lasted nearly two successive days from morning to evening.'[21]

The revolutionary and Napoleonic wars did not consist solely of great battles between vast armies. They also included conflicts fought over smaller areas and with fewer combatants, and in forms that could be either traditional (city sieges) or more novel (guerrilla warfare). Indeed, one of the main problems for the French chiefs of staff at this time was how to deal with guerrilla attacks that were increasing in number, scale, and violence.

Nor was the trend to more massive battles invariably associated with an increase in battlefield area. Total war may have been born in this period, but it retained certain characteristics of ancien régime war and had yet to acquire its full modern form. The front might be longer and in particular deeper – through use of the column formation – but the weapons employed remained limited in range. This meant that battles had to be fought at relatively close quarters and on battlefields of restricted area, except for a few great battles fought in wide, open country. Narcisse Faucheur noted the difference in this respect between two great battles he took part in, Lützen and Bautzen, in Germany in 1813:

> In the course of 18th and 19th May [at Bautzen] we saw the Imperial Guard and the rest of our troops arrive. I had never seen so many armed men assembled in such a small area, because the battle of Lützen was fought on a plain so wide it was impossible to see what was happening in the distance, whereas at Bautzen, from the position occupied by our brigade we could take in both the French and the enemy armies at a single glance.[22]

In battles like Lützen, fought over a wide area, all experience and perception of the battle was unavoidably partial, incomplete. More surprisingly, however, the same was also true on smaller battlefields. The smoke from cannons and muskets combined with the dust raised by the combatants and their horses to create a dense smoke screen – what Gunther Rothenberg calls 'the fog of battle'[23] – that severely reduced the troops' visibility. The 'fog of battle' that impaired his visibility and obscured the enemy ranks into which he fired blindly, was cited by François Vigo-Roussillon to mitigate any feelings of guilt that he might have killed a man during his first action (the combat of the Col Noir, in Italy, on 15 March 1793): 'There was firing at short-range from both sides, I saw none of those near me fall and I fired many musket shots into the enemy's smoke though know nothing of their effect.'[24] François-Joseph Jacquin observed the same phenomenon. He noted in his *carnet de route*, on 25 September 1799, at the battle of Ditten: 'We fired at them [the Austrians] in their camp for nearly half an hour. You could barely see forty paces in front of you, there was a thick fog.'[25]

In these conditions, the individual soldier's experience and perception of battle was unavoidably partial and limited. Except for Napoleon and a handful of high-ranking officers and their aides-de-camp who were continually moving round the battlefield to monitor the advance of the opposing forces and to issue or pass on orders, the troops engaged in active fighting, whether officers, NCOs, or ordinary soldiers, had only a restricted range of vision. What they knew of the battle was as a result limited to a small area immediately surrounding themselves and their battalion.

II. Battle experience and individual identity

Among soldiers, battle was widely conceived, perceived, and presented as a test or examination in which each man's physical and, in particular, moral strengths and weaknesses were revealed. It was a moment of truth, when the soldier or officer directly exposed to danger or death showed his true character. In this sense, battle hastened the forming or forging of each man's identity.

One of the main character traits revealed during a conflict is courage or its opposite, cowardice. In time of war, a man's ability to measure up to this supreme quality defined his human and military worth. The figure of the warrior, along with the values of strength, bravery, glory, and heroism that he represented, was openly idealized. Paul Gerbod has identified the period after the Franco-Prussian war as that when a 'heroic ethic' developed in France, a state of mind rooted in the defeat and that fostered acceptance for going to war in 1914.[26] But heroism has been valued and sought after in other periods in French history, and notably during the revolutionary and Napoleonic wars, when the incarnation of this supreme value by the soldier went together with a democratization of the warrior ideal of ancient Greece. The widespread yearning for heroism and glory, particularly among younger men, comes across in the accounts by soldiers and officers, some of whom do not hesitate to use the word 'hero', even using it to describe themselves.

The soldier who knew how to face enemy fire, confronted danger without flinching, bore his wounds and died with dignity, attained the rank of an honourable man or even, if he was also the author of some daring action or outstanding feat, the status of hero. Descriptions of combatants who had displayed exemplary courage or, on the contrary, a shameful and often despised cowardice, fill the pages of accounts by soldiers. But if knowing how to fight valiantly was a precondition for earning admiration and glory, so too was knowing how to die with courage and dignity. Accounts of battles are frequently punctuated by descriptions of heroic deaths in the form of a personal sacrifice. Thus Fricasse notes in his campaign diary for 8 messidor Year II, on the evening of the siege of Charleroi:

> In the midst of the most acute pain, none of those who lost their lives in the siege gave any sign of complaint. Their expressions were calm and tranquil and their last words were *Vive la République!* To see our warriors on their deathbed is to grasp the difference between free men and slaves. The lackeys of kings die cursing the cruel ambition of their masters. The defender of liberty blesses the blow that struck him; he knows that his blood is flowing only for freedom, glory and to succour his fatherland.[27]

This heroic and sacrificial dimension is the individual expression of higher, collectively held ideological convictions. Many descriptions of courageous deaths, particularly in the contemporary war writings of volunteers, are accompanied by impassioned political and patriotic declarations that combine personal bravura and political convictions.[28] In the final moments, individual and collective identities are as one. The sacrificial character confers a collective dimension on the singularly individual phenomenon of death. Each soldier killed on the field of battle dies a hero, having given his life for a higher cause. The individual act that would have remained anonymous in a different context is here transformed into part of something larger. This collective, almost mystical dimension of death in combat, which bestowed a halo of glory on the victim, helps explain why soldiers enlisted voluntarily and why volunteers accepted the possibility of their own death. An illustration of this is the declaration by the volunteer soldier François-Xavier Joliclerc, in which he contrasts the glory and utility of death in war with an anonymous death serving no purpose and bringing no glory:

> I am at my post, I am where I should be, and all decent men should rush to assist the fatherland in danger. Were I to perish, you should rejoice. What finer sacrifice is there than to sacrifice oneself for one's country? Can one sacrifice oneself for anything more glorious, more right and more just? No. Would you rather see me die miserable, in my bed, at Froidefontaine, or doing some job of work in the wood or the quarry or on some building?[29]

But the study of attitudes towards danger, of courage and fear, runs up against the same difficulty that affects the study of the experience of killing: what is left unsaid. Just as soldiers find it easier to talk about the deaths inflicted by other combatants rather than by themselves, so they scarcely ever mention their own cowardly actions or feelings, preferring to point the finger at other soldiers or officers who were guilty on this count. Thus Claude Simon, a young Parisian born in 1773 who enlisted as a simple volunteer soldier in 1791 and the following year was promoted to lieutenant in the grenadiers of Walsh's regiment, wrote on 28 March 1793, with a disarming false modesty:

> Terror had taken hold of the *national volunteers*; nothing could stop them, for with his own hands M. de l'Egalité blew out the brains of one of their own officers who, when eight leagues from the field of battle, carried on running away without looking back, in the belief that the enemy was still on his tail. You may perhaps ask me if I didn't do the same. I can swear on my honour that fear never crossed my mind for a single instant. Having seen something of war, I have observed that it is always the most stubborn who wins. That is why I always stay calm... I can even say with confidence that during this unfortunate retreat, where we always formed the rear guard and where a huge number of men were killed, I earned the esteem of my grenadiers and of the other companies that are with us, thanks to my steadfastness and a certain daring that they like to call bravery.[30]

This is far from being an isolated example. Distinguishing between façade and reality in accounts of these men's battle experience, notably as regards their feelings of fear or cowardice, is a delicate and at times impossible exercise.

The difficulty is compounded by the extreme diversity of individual perceptions of combat. There is no single experience of battle; rather, multiple and different experiences. Defining a single, monolithic culture of war that all troops are assumed to share is problematic. The notion of a 'culture of war' that has recently been proposed by a number of historians is perhaps best understood as a loosely defined and inclusive concept, as a framework of experience rather than an identical collective conception of military realities.

A few common elements do nevertheless stand out from the diversity of accounts of battle experiences. One of the most salient is the impression of contingency, chance, luck, or destiny. In war more than at other times, men are prone to feelings of fragility and vulnerability, of being at the mercy of higher forces, and above all of being bound to life by an extremely tenuous and uncertain thread. The dominant theme in contemporary military accounts is not so much the fear of death as the tangible impression of its daily presence, of being on intimate terms with it. When death became such a familiar companion, soldiers got used to the possible imminence of their own demise. In a letter to his uncle dated 25 September 1793, written from hospital in Amiens after being wounded in a battle between Menin and Courtrai on 15 September, Joliclerc, who enlisted in the 7th volunteer battalion of the Jura in 1791, describes in simple yet touching and poignant words the gradual coming to terms with the idea of his own death.

> Since we have been in this army [the Armée du Nord], I have already been in four battles. We utterly defeated the English and the Dutch. We destroyed over twenty thousand of their men and captured a large quantity of artillery and camp equipment. It's at times like this, when you get up, or when it's morning (because we are not in houses or tents, always under the open sky, come rain or shine), that you can indeed say, 'I may well not see the evening'. There are already twelve fewer of us than when we arrived here. Some are dead and the others crippled. The company is getting smaller.[31]

By the daily first-hand contact it afforded with the random nature of existence and death, battle resembled a metaphysical experience for many of these soldiers, though it was not one they were given to theorizing about. A few expressed something akin to a sense of invincibility, attributed variously to military prowess, exceptional ingenuity, or impregnable armour. But most of those who evoke the death of comrades, reveal beliefs in interchangeability and chance, or a bewilderment about their own survival that in turn created anxiety about the future. All felt more or less 'like a bird on the branch', an expression several soldiers used to convey the fragility of their existence in the war.[32] As the years went by and the list of battles he had taken part in got longer, Joliclerc referred more and more to what he saw as his inevitable misfortune. On 30 May 1794, he wrote,

> I am expecting death each day. I have already escaped it so many times that my turn will come in the end. I have already seen so many brave comrades die at my side (men who were certainly more worthy than me) that I think it will be without fear that I shall pass into the other world. In this country [the Vendée] where we are surrounded by danger and you cannot take a step without feeling the bullets whistling around your ears, woe betide him who gets hit. I am quite ready [to die].[33]

The fear of death is generally omitted from contemporary writings. Letter-writers practised self-censorship, as much to protect their own state of mind as to shield their families. It appears more frequently and more openly in accounts put together some years after the events by men who now have the status of survivors and are no longer afraid of dying in combat. In his memoirs compiled between 1865 and 1869, Narcisse Faucheur evokes the retrospective fear of death under enemy fire, and expands upon the random character of death or survival in war. He had been proposed for promotion to the rank of sergeant-major, but in the end the captain passed him over for another soldier, Dehorter. The latter was named sergeant-major on 19 May and on the next day received a serious wound to the top of the skull while fighting in the regulatory position of sergeant-major, a position that Faucheur would have occupied had he been appointed instead. 'As I was a few centimetres taller than Dehorter, I would probably have been killed outright if I had been in the same place as my comrade, and I probably would have been in that place, since he was wounded at his regulatory battle rank.' And he concluded, 'Everything in life comes down to chance, especially in war.'[34] It is instructive to compare this extract with another passage from Faucheur's memoirs, in which he relates his state of mind during the war, immediately before or after a battle, and that involves blotting out the self-same fear of death that he evoked in his memoirs 60 years later, in conditions of complete safety. In this particular instance, therefore, the version of the facts varies depending on whether it is made during or after the war. In the immediate aftermath of the battle of

Bautzen, he wanted most of all to forget everything that evoked death and danger. 'At that moment I needed companions who would not easily allow themselves be discouraged by the wretched scene before our eyes and who would communicate to me their satisfaction at coming through such a great battle safe and sound, for the spectacle I had just witnessed made a most painful impression on me.'[35]

On occasions, however, the discretion and fortitude that soldiers displayed in letters to their nearest and dearest, and their efforts to forget about death, break down under the stress and anxiety produced by a string of bloody conflicts. The letter-writer would then give way to his fears, as did the young *requis* or conscript soldier from the Auvergne, Gilbert Moulier, aged 21, who took part in the war in the Vendée, one of the hardest and most violent campaigns. On 6 August 1793, on the eve of leaving for action against the enemy, he confided to his father: 'We plan to leave at first light for Luçon... where the enemy is encamped. I firmly believe that I shall never see home again but have sacrificed my life....'[36] The same fear of death appears in a few other letters by soldiers and officers. But these common points are exceptions, and diversity is the defining characteristic of accounts by soldiers concerning the experience and perception of battle. The differences and varied viewpoints can be traced to a number of factors, including the soldier's age and previous battle experience, the army he belonged to, his degree of exposure to danger and position in the army (advanced guard or rearguard), and whether he had already been wounded in combat.

When studying individuals' experience of war, consideration must also be given to the type of sources used. The expression of this private perception can vary widely according to the nature and date of the writing in which it is found. Writing after the event, in a memoir or journal penned several years after the war, the soldier may tend to embellish the facts and present himself as a brave fighter, particularly when, as was generally the case, this is what an audience or readership eager for evidence of France's former greatness was looking for in these accounts. How the personal experience of battle is presented can also vary according to its intended audience. In many cases the description of the dangers of the war and even of the feelings the soldier or officer experienced (such as fear, exhilaration, desire to kill, revulsion) is deliberately adapted to the letter's recipient – not by distorting the truth, but by giving a more or less complete account, by perhaps leaving certain things unsaid, in letters to close family members.

Attitudes among soldiers towards combat in battle were ambivalent. Some dreaded it, others longed for it. The most enthusiastic and impassioned were often the young soldiers and officers. Filled with youthful illusions, they thirsted for action and glory, eager to experience the reality of battle and undergo their baptism of fire, particularly when they had the additional spur of political zeal (this applied particularly to the volunteers of 1793, 1794, and 1795) or military ambition, encouraged by prospects of promotion on merit (especially among the young NCOs and officers trained at the military schools under the Consulate and Empire). In contrast, a desire to stay out of the fighting is occasionally observed among soldiers and officers of an older generation.[37]

The somewhat naive statements of impatience prior to combat and of joy at the signal for battle to start are particularly common in letters written in the course of the war, without the detachment and experience brought by the passing of time. Julien Martin, a 28-year-old volunteer soldier in the 1st battalion of the Creuse, wrote to his cousin on 29 September 1793 from Thonne le Thil, where he was serving with the Army of the Ardennes. 'For two or three days the talk is that the army will be leaving and moving in the direction of Valenciennes. That would please us greatly, for we shall be wholeheartedly glad to fight our enemy, there being no finer sight than war.'[38] Young Bravy Soulbost, a 19-year-old volunteer soldier from the Auvergne, was even more explicit in a letter written to his father, on 3 February 1793, from Metz. 'There is nothing new to tell you at present. Since leaving Paris we have still not seen action. But we are hoping that this summer we shall set about the enemy and I shall do my utmost to send you the ear of an *uhlan* in an envelope.'[39] For his part, Antoine Jabouille, an enlisted volunteer and lieutenant in the 34th gendarmerie division of the Armée du Nord, admitted to regretting his temporary posting as pay and quartermaster in October 1793, on the grounds that, shut up in the treasury away from the fighting, he no longer had 'the pleasure of seeing the enemy'.[40] And François Lavaux, a sergeant in the 103rd Line Regiment, notes in his memoirs, on the subject of a battle against the Austrians in 1799, that 'Fighting was a pleasure to me. It was like playing prisoner's base, when you can gain or give ground, especially when you don't get hurt.'[41]

Several years after the end of hostilities, Clausewitz demonstrated the close link forged between war and politics in this period. Yet we should not see the enthusiasm of young soldiers for battle as limited to the periods of the *levées* of volunteers and the sans-culotte ideal. In the army, the end of the Revolution and the coming to power of Napoleon, or later the replacement of the Republic by the Empire, did not cause military fervour or enrolments to slump, nor did it push veterans of the revolutionary wars to leave in droves.[42] From 1804, the fading republican ideal began to be replaced by other, equally powerful motivations: patriotism, the quest for individual and collective (national) glory, the sense of belonging to a military community (one that was all the stronger for being increasingly distinct from the civilian world). Perhaps most important of all was the charisma of a leader who was both statesman and supreme commander, Napoleon. He figures in almost all accounts by soldiers from the post-Consulate period, whether contemporary accounts (letters, campaign diaries) or memoirs written years afterwards. The growth of the Napoleonic legend ensured for the Emperor an even larger place in memoirs, especially those compiled after his ashes were returned to France or during the Second Empire. The political patriotism of the volunteers of the Year II was grounded in society – since the volunteers were the extension of the nation – and was slightly abstract in character. The patriotism of the Napoleonic *grognards* that replaced it was more corporatist in nature, based on a military community with its own leader, that was more concrete, personified and embodied by a single man. The revolutionary authorities had sought to sustain or revive the troops' republican zeal by sending out deputies-on-mission to the armies (where they were seldom popular). In contrast, Napoleon, after 1799, was careful to be seen on the battlefield as much as possible, where, according to accounts by his soldiers, his presence stimulated and galvanized the ranks. This would seem to demonstrate the important role of the leader's person and charisma in the conduct of war and in the awakening of national feeling. For this to happen, however, the leader must lead his soldiers to victory. After 1812–1813, when the tide began to turn, the Napoleonic mystique suffered a decline and criticism from within the army became more vociferous.

When studying the state of mind and attitude towards battle among soldiers over the entire period from 1792 to 1815, no sharp distinction can be drawn, between the patriots of Year II and the conscripts of the Napoleonic period. Freshly graduated officers from the military schools so valued by Napoleon, soldiers who enlisted voluntarily, together with large numbers of veterans of the revolutionary wars and young conscripts – all showed the same enthusiasm and ardour in combat as the troops of the Republic. Like many other eyewitnesses, Dominique Larrey noted the fervour of the troops on the eve of Austerlitz.

> As the proclamation announcing the next day's battle was included in the order of the day, every soldier knew of the emperor's decision, and showed the joy he felt at being about to pit himself against the

> enemy; a loud display of enthusiasm erupted when His Majesty rode along the lines of his army.[43]

Such was the diversity of men's experience and perception that the same attitude could have very different causes. The joy that soldiers felt and expressed at the news of the start of battle could be explained in several ways. It might reflect the enthusiasm and eagerness of the novice soldier, or the ambition and satisfaction of the professional soldier eager to prove himself and apply his theoretical training,[44] or the exhilaration of the republican volunteer animated by his political beliefs and patriotism, or the less worthy exhilaration of the seasoned soldier looking for powerful sensations (including that of killing), or indeed the far more peaceable desire for the final battle that would bring an end to the fighting and a return to homes and civilian lives.[45] Impatience for battle did not necessarily betray an enthusiasm for war.

The expectations attached to combat could also reflect a soldier's search for a social purpose. This was especially the case for the volunteer, seeking to prove to his family, and to himself, that his enlistment had a meaning and that his presence in the army was useful to his country. A good instance of this comes from Claude Combes, a 22-year-old volunteer from the Auvergne, in a letter written at Nice (with the Army of Italy) to his godfather, a merchant at Riom, on 24 May 1795.

> Each day we expect to measure up to the Piedmontese; they are encamped at a short distance from us; their bivouac can be seen from our advanced posts... We are all waiting impatiently for the time when we can be of use to our country by shedding our blood for its prosperity and for the downfall of its enemies.[46]

The motivations and reasons – or lack of them – for joining the army and going off to war also had a powerful effect on the way soldiers perceived difficulties and dangers. Soldiers found these easier to accept when going to the war was a personal choice, a deliberate action that might be prompted by political idealism (for the volunteers in the early years of the Revolution), or a liking for the profession and career of soldier, or other reasons such as curiosity and a desire to travel, a craving for action, adventure or glory. The situation was altogether different for men who had been forcibly conscripted into the army, whose accounts often give a very different view of the experience of battle. Conscription was indeed quite often resented and even sometimes resisted (through desertion).[47]

The letters of volunteer soldiers and officers are often sprinkled with fervent patriotic and republican declarations,[48] which also justify the writers in their own and their families' eyes and legitimate their decision to serve. The young volunteer soldier François Mireur wrote, on 28 August 1792,

> Remind my mother, who must be extremely worried about me, of the noble principle that I belong to our country before I belong to her; I will fly into her arms as soon as the war is over, if I have the luck to come through it. If I do not, let her recall the following motto, which should be permanently etched on the heart of every mother: *"It is a fine and becoming thing to die for one's country"*.[49]

Conscript soldiers, on the other hand, more often give vent to disillusionment and bitterness in their letters. One such, Piot, requisitioned under the law of 24 February 1793 and enrolled as a *chasseur* or light infantryman in the 7th battalion of the Army of the Bas-Rhin, judged harshly the decision by his father, a master slate-worker at Riom, to enrol in the army in return for a sum of money.

> So my poor father has given himself into the slavery of the soldier's state... He must have been tired of living to do what he did, or else he did not love his wife and children to leave them as he has... How fortunate the soldier's lot must be for my father to have wanted it. But he will regret it and it will be too late, because I regret it and see clearly that it is too late, and he will do the same, but it will be too late.[50]

But although battle is synonymous with danger, not all soldiers dreaded and avoided it. Some were like Narcisse Faucheur, who, though a conscript, admitted to looking upon a battle with 'sang-froid and... even a certain pleasure'.[51] Others even admitted finding battle too short, 'over too soon'.[52] In his memoirs, François Vigo-Roussillon indicates that when he reached the battlefield of Friedland, on 14 June 1807, he and the other grenadiers of his regiment were last to arrive because they were bringing up the rear of the army. Hearing the cannonade from far off they were afraid of 'seeing the battle end without [them]'.[53]

Differences in perceptions of battle also depended on the reality and degree of danger involved, the level of exposure to the enemy's fire. Soldiers in some combat arms were more exposed to danger than those in others, and experience of battle differed accordingly. Gunners, for instance, had a reputation for great bravery. Many soldiers in other arms singled out the gunners for their courageous – or foolhardy – behaviour, staying at their posts until death – 'stuck to their pieces as to their mistresses'[54] – and never leaving the field of battle before the end. In some battles there were 'hundreds killed at their guns'.[55]

By contrast, some other categories of soldiers enjoyed relative safety. They were usually treated with a degree of contempt by soldiers taking an active part in combat, contempt sometimes expressed by calling into question their masculinity, their virility. One young conscript, in a letter to his mother dated 29 May 1793, asked her to reassure the mother of another soldier from the same locality, whose incompetence was keeping him safe.

> You can tell the mother of Robert not to worry about her son, for he is with the regiment's master tailor and the women of the regiment... Like this he is at no risk from musket or cannon balls, for that makes a poor soldier; all his comrades complain about him.[56]

The perception of battle from a position of safety is entirely different. An indication of this comes from Claude Simon, in a letter written to a friend from the camp of Bienne on 17 September 1792. 'I have just come away from the *combat* (or to be truthful, from watching it). This sort of entertainment is, I believe, the finest thing in the world (especially when one is safe up a mountain and can watch others fighting on a plain).'[57] Even when not exposed to danger, however, many men were painfully marked by their first combat experience, by the din, the shock, the smell of blood and the sight of bodies. Unlike Claude Simon, few had an aesthetic vision of battle. Indeed, being away from the action, and thus able to give free rein to one's thoughts and feelings, could heighten the sensations of fear, disgust, and shock. Dominique Larrey, surgeon major to the hospitals with the Army of the Rhine, describes the painful impression made on him by his first close involvement in a large-scale combat, when accompanying the vanguard of the army to Oberuchel, near Königstein, in winter 1792.

> The combat, which I witnessed so closely, made a deep impression upon me at first. But the thoughts troubling me were soon dispelled by the inner pleasure I felt at the idea of the immense service that my new institution ['flying' hospitals] had just rendered to the wounded. Ever since that time I have looked calmly upon any combat or battle at which I have been present.[58]

A number of key themes do therefore emerge from soldiers' writings – the confrontation with death and the eventuality of one's own death, the subjective and incomplete perception of events, the overall impression of chaos. Yet generalization remains difficult on account of the great diversity that characterizes individual battle experience. Such differences originate partly in independent external factors (battle size and type, country, outcome or result, date). But the essential factor is the personality of the individual, who is simultaneously subject and object, actor and victim, in the conflict. Age, physical and mental strength – or weakness – and the prop to morale that comes from strongly held beliefs, values, and ideals, all make for diversity in how the same event is understood by a range of different individuals.

III. Modern war: site of mass mortality

Modern war produces casualties on a mass scale, plunging combatants into a universe of death and dying. And nowhere is this more true than on the battlefield, 'the field of battle and slaughter' as one soldier described it.[59]

Soldiers saw men going down, from their own side or from the enemy's. After witnessing their agonies, they might well remain for several hours on the field of battle. On occasions soldiers lived, slept, and ate surrounded by corpses. Battlefields were rarely cleared once the fighting was over, and it was not unusual for bodies to be left exposed to the elements and wild animals instead of being taken away for burial. Yet it was here that soldiers frequently had to camp for up to several days.[60] One member of the Imperial Guard observed in 1813 that it was 'often dreadful after a battle, when the only thing to tie your horse up to might be a dead body'.[61]

As well as the threat to health from the contamination of air and water from decomposing bodies, being surrounded by the dead had the effect of gradually turning the soldiers' world into one where the dead body was no longer subject to a taboo and excluded from the company of the living, but became a component of everyday life. As a soldier in the Russian campaign commented, 'Everything around us is dead.'[62]

Such close proximity to the dead produced contrasting forms of behaviour, revealing the effect of shock as well as instincts of survival and self-preservation. Initially, the sight of corpses usually gave rise to feelings of revulsion and distress. But later, whether from an instinct of survival or the effect of shock, soldiers came to regard the situation as unremarkable. Rendered anonymous by death, corpses were no longer treated with even a modicum of respect. They were plundered for anything of use that could be found on them (clothes, shoes, food, or money) or even employed as pieces of furniture (in place of benches and tables). Jean-Marc Bussy, a Swiss light infantryman, describes a night spent on the battlefield of Burgos, following Soult's victory in November 1808: 'I am on guard duty on the battlefield, with lieutenant Jayet. We are using the dead as benches, around our fire.'[63] A few years later, during the retreat from Russia, Belgian brigadier Scheltens also mentions this commonplace practice, noting that, in the evening, in the bivouac, 'so as not to sit in the snow melted by the fire, we used seats formed of corpses stiff and blackened from the cold.'[64]

Repeated exposure to danger and death was not without psychological consequences. Modern medical research has shown that the longest soldiers can expect to maintain their psychological balance in war conditions is a few months.[65] The effects of combat trauma, often though not always accurately termed *vent du boulet* or shell shock, have been studied almost exclusively in relation to the two world wars of the twentieth century. The attention of researchers in this field focused originally on the Second World War, before shifting to the 1914–1918 War.[66] It was shown, for instance, that one-tenth of Americans mobilized between 1942 and 1945 had to spend time in hospital for psychiatric reasons. The intensity of post-combat trauma caused by exposure to danger, death, and the stress of battle increases with the length of exposure. An increase in the length of battles is thus an aggravating factor. During the Second World War, among US soldiers who had taken part in a campaign of 35 days of continuous fighting, 98 per cent suffered from psychiatric disorders.[67]

But the twentieth century did not invent combat trauma, and soldiers in earlier wars were not spared the effects of shell shock. A striking example comes from Adrien Bourgogne, who had enlisted in the corps of *vélites*[68] when aged 20 in 1805, and was a sergeant of the foot grenadiers. During the retreat from Russia, he and a friend, Picart, wandered away from the main group for a few days, in the course of which they came upon a French soldier who had been taken prisoner by the Russians and then abandoned in the snowy and icy wastes, without food or clothes. The soldier's physical condition was appalling. He was horribly thin, his nose was frozen 'and almost gone', his ears were covered in sores, all the fingers of his right hand except the thumb were frozen and gone, and he was unable to speak or eat for 'he could not move apart his teeth which chattered horribly.' Bourgogne and Picart at first tried to warm and feed him, and then witnessed his brief agony followed by his death. 'We saw him... shudder, turn pale, and crumple up, without any word or cry passing his lips. Picart made to raise him up; but he was already a mere corpse. The whole scene lasted less than ten minutes.'[69] While Adrien Bourgogne quickly recovered from the incident, he noted that it had marked his friend deeply. At first he thought that it had merely weakened his comrade's morale,[70] but he soon realized that its effects were more serious and that Picart had suffered a traumatic shock.

> Poor Picart... was no longer the same. It had affected his character, and indeed at times he told me that he had a great pain in the head, that it was not the result of the wound from the Cossack's pistol shot but a thing he could not explain to me... He told me he would not be surprised if they came at any moment and hunted us down like wolves.[71]

The psychological trauma or shell shock induced by war can also have the effect of making violence and death appear unremarkable and of numbing individuals' response to them. Many soldiers, like Robert Guillemard,[72] refer to this phenomenon in their writings. Octave Levavasseur observed it during the campaign of 1807 and the battles of Eylau and Friedland:

> The feeling of indifference had spread to the entire army, down to the last soldier. The sight of the battlefields and the endless spectacle of the dead and wounded... eventually render the soldier callous and inhuman. There was the soldier who heard one of his comrades crying out in agony and said to him roughly, 'Be quiet, will you!' Another one, tearing the shoes off a dying man, stroked his face mockingly and said 'Time to die now, my friend.' I am afraid to say that this frame of mind and contempt for death helped to secure victory.[73]

In wartime soldiers see men die or may die themselves, but their role is not limited to that of spectator or victim: they may also be required to take life. A study of personal battle experience thus needs to examine the issue of interpersonal violence and perceptions of the act of killing. Historians disagree over the extent of interpersonal violence during the First World War.[74] Some, notably Joanna Bourke, whose book on the subject compares the First World War, the Second World War, and the Vietnam War, have emphasized the importance of direct confrontation and face-to-face killing.[75] Others, however, have pointed out that technical developments and in particular the expanded role of artillery had the effect of limiting direct interpersonal violence in the First World War.[76] Death was now inflicted at long range, against enemies whose features were indistinguishable, making them anonymous, impersonal figures. The question does not really arise in these terms for the revolutionary and Napoleonic wars. Much of the battlefield violence over this 20-year period was of course an anonymous violence, as in many other wars. But use of artillery was not as widespread as it became later, and there were still ample opportunities for using the full range of side arms, from swords to bayonets. In the large battles it was rare for fighting with cannons and muskets fired over large distances to last until the engagement was over. Typically they ended in gigantic pitched battles that brought French and enemy soldiers into close proximity.[77] In these conditions, the act of killing, far from being unreal or abstract, was a concrete reality.

Yet despite this, the act of killing seldom if ever appears in soldiers' writings. This may reflect guilt feelings, trauma after the event, shame at violating a major taboo of a civilization still marked by Christian values despite the Revolution's dechristianizing drive, fear of being misunderstood by a civilian audience – whatever the reason, the combatants never refer to their active role in this interpersonal violence. For the revolutionary and Napoleonic wars, there is no text comparable to *J'ai tué*, the short eyewitness account that Blaise Cendras wrote in early 1918.[78] The legalized murder practiced in the specific context of war instead undergoes a process of collective repression. The same response is observed in many conflicts and is part of a common culture of war that accepts victimization while rejecting active responsibility. The anthropologist Evelyne Desbois has noted an identical phenomenon for the First World War and draws attention to the literary form taken by this repression or denial. She shows that in accounts by soldiers the substantive *tué* (the man who is killed) occurs far more often than the verb conjugated in its direct form.[79] An idea of combatant experience and private perception of one-to-one fighting has to be gleaned from the isolated confidences and impressions, not always clearly or explicitly stated, that crop up in letters, diaries, and memoirs.

Chevallier, a former member of the Imperial Guard and a volunteer soldier during the Revolution, touches on the subject in his memoirs. In his account, what made the act of killing possible was the exhilaration of battle mixed with patriotism and a desire to avenge the comrades or compatriots who had fallen at his side.

> We made a strong charge, knocking and cutting down everything in our way... The Neapolitans gave up the fight, threw down their weapons and retreated to Capua where we pursued them... We *killed*... a number of them... I will now attempt to describe the first impression produced by a battlefield... Appearing for the first time on a field of slaughter it is hard to say what I felt on seeing my comrades fall and men and horses going down. The many wounded returning from the fighting, disfigured, carried, haggard, dishevelled, covered in blood and dust, the cries of the dying, the fury of the combatants – all this caused an indefinable turmoil in my senses. Facing the enemy's artillery batteries spewing terror and death into our ranks, I was seized by a trembling, was it dread or fear? I was about to faint... But we hurled ourselves against the enemy... And then the dread left me... French blood was flowing in my veins... I was still shaking but now it was from rage... I wanted to mow them all down, avenge my brothers, and I spurred my horse into the midst of the enemy... I parried all the blows made against me, but my own were terrible, my hand was guided by anger and rage.[80]

In his memoirs Bourgogne relates with equal openness his killing of a Russian at point-blank range in the battle of Krasnoë in 1813.

> We fought furiously, man-to-man. The slaughter was appalling, we were split up, each man was fighting on his own... A Russian soldier stopped me at two paces from the end of his musket barrel and fired. It was probably only the fuse that ignited, for if the charge had gone off it would have been over for me. Realizing that I was unwounded I moved back a few steps from my adversary who, believing me badly wounded, was calmly reloading his weapon. Roustant... had seen my danger and ran over to me. Taking me in his arms he said... 'Be sure not to miss him!' That was exactly what I intended. Had my gun misfired (as often happened, because of the snow) I would have gone after him with my bayonet. He didn't have time to reload before I had put a shot clear through him. Though mortally wounded he did not fall immediately; he staggered backwards unsteadily and, giving me a threatening look and without letting go of his weapon, he fell onto the horse of the officer.[81]

These accounts manage to remain relatively detached and reserved. Neither author describes his feelings and sensations at the thought of having killed a man, and in the scene related above, Bourgogne emphasizes the self-defensive character of his action: it was not killing for conquest or extermination, but killing to stay alive. These two accounts, among the few to evoke one-to-one combat involving the author in person, actually tell us little about the individual experience of taking human life; they cannot be used to map the sensations – disgust or exhilaration, guilty trauma or proud satisfaction – experienced during and after the act, nor to explain these men's tacit acceptance of the violence of warfare. Among the sources used for this study one account alone goes some way towards supplying an explanation on this point. Reflecting on the practice of combat and the confrontation with death, Octave Levavasseur explains the acceptance and even enthusiasm of many soldiers by pointing to a feeling of exhilaration that transcends notions of good and evil and moral values, and is instead related to patriotism and particularly to glory and to the battlefield context itself. As he admitted:

> The destruction of a man is always harrowing for those who witness it, even for those responsible... the dead man becomes the focus for countless thoughts of sadness, despair, regret. But this idea slowly fades, and when instead of one individual there are one hundred or one thousand, the soul becomes steadily less sensitive, as if a sort of callus had formed over it. And before long the soul is actually elated and uplifted in the presence of these great catastrophes, which become identified uniquely with glory, power, and majesty. At Memmingen [1805], our soldiers were so eager to fight that the enemy was charged and routed without being able to offer any resistance.[82]

IV. The enemy: perception, representation, and treatment

A depiction of the enemy as the embodiment of evil, an intense hatred of the adversary coupled with a desire for extermination and annihilation, are characteristics of total war. Over and above the violence inherent to combat, this implacable hatred of the enemy, often fuelled by ideology and propaganda, was reflected in aggressiveness that persisted beyond the conflict itself, in violence towards enemy soldiers who were disarmed, wounded, or taken prisoner. The First World War was long considered to be the first instance of total war, especially as regards the level of combatant violence. On one side stood the wars of the nineteenth century, from the revolutionary and Napoleonic wars to the American Civil War and the Franco-Prussian War – wars fought 'according to rules', characterized by a self-imposed limit on levels of violence and in particular by a treatment of the defeated enemy in accordance with codes of honour and humanity. On the other side were the two great world conflicts of the twentieth century, characterized by an end to this self-imposed restraint on violence, an intense hatred of the enemy, and a 'brutalization' of behaviour, to take the concept of George Mosse and apply it not to the aftermath of war but to the conflict itself.[83] Stéphane Audoin-Rouzeau notes a sharp contrast in this respect between the Franco-Prussian War of 1870–1871 and the First World War.

> The tradition of a self-imposed limit on wartime violence collapsed abruptly and definitively in 1914–1918. Where city sieges once followed a strict ceremonial order, right down to the forms of surrender, now cities were bombed until they were totally destroyed. Where captured officers were once treated with genuine consideration – to the point of being prisoners on parole, like those defeated at Sedan in 1870 and allowed to return to their homes for the rest of the campaign – they now suffered the common lot of the internment camps. That a limit had been crossed is even clearer in the treatment of the wounded. Gone now was the cease-fire for the stretcher-bearers and for recovery of the survivors, that traditionally followed the end of fighting... The wounded were fired upon, as too of course were their would-be rescuers. As for prisoners, it was not unknown for them to be dispatched, whether wounded or not.[84]

Somewhat provocatively, David Bell recently pushed back the birth of total war in the West to the French revolutionary and Napoleonic wars. His thesis rests primarily on the idea of a radical increase in wartime violence both between combatants and towards civilian populations. In this he is following an earlier intuition of Jean-Paul Bertaud, who in 1979 wrote that 'the manner of waging war had already been transformed for a first time in late 1792–early 1793... War was to become a war of terror: exterminating the enemy would hasten the coming of peace.' Bertaud notes that from 1793 onwards the French soldiers gave up trying to convince their adversaries of the legitimacy of their cause and of the advantages of the Revolution. Having lost all hope of rallying the enemy to their republican ideal, their attitude changed: messianic proselytizing was replaced by the aim not just of securing victory but of crushing and destroying the enemy. 'Since it wished to remain enslaved to the despots, it must be shown no mercy.'[85] In this the military was complying with the orders coming from its political masters. On 2 February 1794, the members of the Committee of Public Safety required that they not merely be victorious and win the battle but 'pursue the enemy until he is utterly destroyed'.[86]

But the argument for a major change in the art of warfare dating from 1793–1794, shown especially in the treatment of the enemy, cannot be accepted without qualification. While levels of violence were indeed higher than in the past – in certain campaigns in particular (the Egyptian campaign; the Vendean, Calabrian, and Spanish wars; the Russian campaign; and the 1813 German campaign) – it would nonetheless be wrong to generalize these instances of a 'brutalization' of conduct and fighting to the revolutionary and Napoleonic wars as a whole and conclude that the traditional self-limitation of violence was abandoned.

The radical increase in violence among combatants, as displayed by French soldiers in particular, seems to have been primarily a response to the danger they faced in a new kind of war – guerrilla warfare – and to the involvement of the civilian population in the conflict. Thus the change is observed mainly in the campaigns marked by extremely violent guerrilla activity. In other campaigns, by contrast, the French army's treatment of wounded or captured enemy officers and soldiers followed the same practices as in the wars of the previous century, and the troops continued to respect the same code of honour and basic notion of humanity and solidarity between soldiers.

To judge the attitudes of French soldiers towards the enemy we need to study the forms of treatment meted out to disarmed, wounded, or captured enemy fighters. What characterizes a 'total' or 'terrorist' war, to use the expression employed by Bertaud, is an ambition to exterminate, to annihilate the enemy, civilian as well as military. To this end, they were to be shown no mercy: no prisoners should be taken, and enemy wounded should either be killed where they lay or left without medical care. But while it is true that this corresponded to a number of orders issued by the political and military hierarchy, accounts written by men present on the ground make it clear that such extreme measures were hardly ever applied in reality.

Most soldiers in their accounts refer to French doctors and surgeons attending the enemy wounded, and to the decent treatment given to those taken prisoner in the fighting. Sergeant Fricasse, who had enlisted as a volunteer, noted in his journal in Vendémiaire Year III (1794), just after the siege of Maastricht, that

> The battle was bloody for both sides, and went on from morning till evening... In the evening, when the firing had ceased, we pulled back

> a little and spent the night in the plain by the river. We saw them [the Austrians] building large fires... from which we concluded that they were going to turn tail. That was it all right: around midnight they broke camp... In the morning, at day break, we moved through the centre of their positions, and found them full of arms, legs and whole bodies, that they had left without burying. A number of wounded wretches were crying for mercy and we carried them straight to the ambulance with our own people.[87]

This view is confirmed by numerous other accounts from the revolutionary and Napoleonic wars. In their own letters, journals and memoirs, the doctors and surgeons describe tending any wounded soldier or officer brought to them, regardless of nationality or the side they were on.[88]

Fricasse later gives another example of respect for a code of honour in war. This time it concerns the consideration shown towards the Prussian, Austrian, and Dutch soldiers after their surrender, while being evacuated from the city of Maastricht, on 17 Brumaire Year III, at the end of a siege lasting 44 days. The imperial garrison came out of the city between 10 and 11 in the morning, through the German Gate, with French soldiers lining their route, and Fricasse notes, 'They marched out with the honours of war, drums beating, guns loaded, and flags flying. When almost at the end of the column they lay down their arms in front of us; the cavalry and infantry kept their sabres.'[89]

On the whole, therefore, the French military displayed a reasonably humane attitude towards its adversaries, although some individual soldiers, notably those who had witnessed the ravages of war in France, would have liked to see them receive harsher treatment. On 22 October 1792, after going through the town of Verdun which had been devastated by the Prussians, Louis-Joseph Bricard, a gunner from the Saint-Merry section in Paris, was critical of the French officers' leniency towards the enemy.

> Despite the slow march of their columns, many [Prussian] soldiers fell behind. None of them were taken prisoner of war, and it was clear that there was an indulgence that we could not understand. An army that had just been ravaging our country and had fallen into our hands was protected by our generals.[90]

In fact, this was not evidence of a conspiracy or treason, or of a reprehensible leniency on the part of the French high command, merely an act of humanity towards an enemy seriously weakened by disease, in this case an epidemic of diarrhoea.

The situation was of course very different in those campaigns where the soldiers faced hatred and attacks from an entire population (including civilians), and had to contend with a new form of war, guerrilla activity, that they found hard to control and viewed as the work of traitors. In the Vendée, in Calabria, Spain, Russia, and in Germany in 1813, the enemy was no longer designated or treated as an honourable adversary worthy of respect, but as a savage beast to be slaughtered. Language itself underwent a change. The emotive term 'extermination', encouraging the use of the notion of genocide that some historians[91] have applied to the Vendée war (incorrectly, as Jean-Clément Martin has shown[92]), was employed by soldiers in a few instances, attesting perhaps to the use of this concept in the official propaganda they received from their leaders. Here is François Bravy Benard, a 24-year-old soldier in the 57th infantry regiment of the Armée de l'Ouest, writing to his brother, a master baker at Pionsat (in Auvergne).

> We are in the Vendée to exterminate this crowd of brigands who have gathered here. Many of them enrol the peasants by force, and tell them they will not die from a musket or cannon shot. They tell them plenty of other lies; well, let them get a hundred paces from me when I have my musket, and we'll see about not dying.'[93]

This was entirely consistent with the instructions issued by the general leading the Armée de l'Ouest, Turreau. 'Every means will be employed to track down the rebels [the Vendeans]; all will be put to the bayonet, and the villages, farms, woods, heath, broom and anything else that can be burned will be consigned to the flames.'[94]

The excesses committed by soldiers and officers during the Vendean war took place in a framework of legality and in response to official orders, and it seems likely that demonization of the enemy, at times reflected in an overtly stated goal of extermination, was instrumentalized by the military and civilian authorities for political ends. Certain officers were eager to demonstrate their zeal in the matter to their superiors. In a report to Turreau dated 23 January 1794 Boucret wrote, 'The country will be cleansed by fire and by sword. Not a single brigand shall escape me. This morning I had fourteen women and girls shot.'[95]

Yet while many soldiers and officers acknowledge the barbarity of the treatment inflicted on the Vendeans in this war, at no point do they express the slightest sense of personal guilt. It is in open, frank terms that Joliclerc relates his experience of the cruelty practised in the Vendée war.

> We are going to set off in fourteen columns to ravage the departments of Deux-Sèvres and Vendée. We shall go in with iron and fire, a rifle in one hand and a torch in the other. Men and women, all will be put to the sword. All must perish, all except little children. These departments must serve as an example to others that might wish to rise in rebellion. We have already scorched seven leagues of the country.

Joliclerc nonetheless ended the same letter with words that display a completely clear conscience. 'I am wonderfully well . . . I get plenty to drink, and I spend my pay on food. I think that is what keeps me well. I have got used to drinking wine and I have to have it.'[96] A few months later, on 2 April 1794, while still serving in the Armée de l'Ouest, he confided to his mother, 'If I told you the cruelties being committed by both sides in the Vendée it would make your hair stand on end.'[97] What Joliclerc writes here contains three elements that help to explain how men can commit such acts and at the same time feel no guilt: first, the irresponsibility – in the literal sense – that comes from obeying orders ('All must . . .'); second, the cruelty the Vendeans show towards French soldiers ('by both sides'); and lastly, particular to this case, the representation of the enemy – instrumentalized in official discourse and assimilated by the soldiers – whereby the Vendean personifies evil and the forces hostile to the progress of liberty and democracy. This being so, slaughtering or even exterminating the Vendeans is equivalent to saving the nation, the Revolution, and the *patrie* or fatherland, that 'glorious cause that should inspire the whole world'[98]. Anyone who did not understand the underlying reason for the actions of the soldiers in the Vendée could only be a traitor, someone who 'did not feel himself a Frenchman when facing the enemy'.[99]

The Vendée was not the only theatre of excesses against the enemy during these wars. Most soldiers who participated in the Peninsular War have comparable scenes of violence and cruelty to relate.[100] In his memoirs, Belgian conscript Henri Scheltens, who joined the Imperial Guard in 1806 after a period spent in the Boulogne camp, evokes the atrocities committed against the enemy, both military and civilian. 'Misery renders men cruel, yes, very cruel! I saw things in Spain that I would never dare write down. No one would believe them, and yet it would be the truth. Prisoners were hardly ever taken.'[101] Numerous accounts from the Spanish War also refer to the widespread practice on both sides (French and Anglo-Spanish) of not taking prisoners. In the battle of Medellin, after the Spanish forces massacred the French prisoners of war under the eyes of the French forces, the latter responded by mercilessly killing every Spanish soldier that fell into their hands, including those who laid down their arms, surrendered and asked to be spared.[102]

Even in the most bitterly fought campaigns, however, hatred and demonization of the enemy were not universally shared or expressed by French soldiers. Some retained a more humane culture of war and continued to view the enemy, even insurgents and guerrilla fighters, as fair and honourable opponents. In a letter to his parents of 9 Ventôse Year III (27 February 1795), written just after the announcement that peace was imminent, François Dugarel, who had enlisted as a volunteer in the 1st battalion of Puy-de-Dôme in 1793 and was a sergeant in the 4th battalion of the Armée de l'Ouest, refers to the *Chouan* or Vendean rebels in highly conciliatory terms as 'former misguided brothers' from the 'former rebel lands'. He closes with a statement full of optimism: 'So my dear father, the war that cost the Republic so much blood finished with fraternal embraces. Dear father, please let all your republican friends know of this. We hope that the aristocrats will now keep their heads low and that the Republic will triumph. *Vive la République*!'[103]

But if the enemy was certainly not always demonized, he was – and this perhaps contrasted with wars in previous centuries – perceived as being fundamentally other, as alien to the body politic. Indeed, the enemy frequently served as the motor force, the federating element, for national union, a role encouraged in some cases by a political instrumentalization based on propaganda. In the early years of the revolutionary wars, it was common for French soldiers to designate an enemy who had many forms (and many nationalities) by unspecific and all-embracing terms, 'enemies of liberty', 'tyrants' (for leaders and sovereigns), or by terms with more national and patriotic connotations, like 'enemy of the fatherland' or 'enemy of the nation'.

French national identity was constructed negatively through the identification of a common enemy, a 'national' enemy, an enemy of the Nation. First established during the revolutionary and Napoleonic wars, this relationship between the identification of the enemy in time of war and the construction of national identity was a striking innovation, and it was to last throughout the nineteenth and twentieth centuries. In a comparative study of the dialectic between representation of the enemy and construction of national identity in France and Germany, Michael

Jeismann identifies three main periods between the revolutionary and Napoleonic wars and the First World War, though he admits that there were significant continuities between them, with the memory of 1815 fuelling the ideology of 1870, in particular. First, there were the years from 1792 to 1815, defined for him (as regards war aims) by the triad of 'Liberty, Enemy, and Fatherland'; second, 1870, when the notion of liberty disappeared; and lastly 1914–1918, when all that remained was the Enemy.[104] There is no doubting that from the revolutionary and Napoleonic wars onwards, the enemy was defined and perceived as a crucial challenge, unambiguously foreign and threatening, or that how the enemy was represented by civilians and soldiers contributed, by reaction, to delineate and construct national identity.

The continuation of practices indicating empathy or even solidarity within a supranational community of soldierhood ('fraternization' between enemy soldiers or officers[105]), which is observed in later conflicts too (the First and Second World Wars), are mere epiphenomena and cannot obscure the profound change that affected the nature of war and above all attitudes towards the enemy, during the revolutionary and Napoleonic wars. The aristocratic culture of warfare that was the norm in the ancien régime, coexisted with a dominant supranational aristocratic model in other spheres (notably travel, with the fashion for the Grand Tour, for example) and established a community of manners, thought, and even of language (through the widespread use of French by European elites in the eighteenth century) that transcended political and military divisions. From the time of the French Revolution, the emergence of more democratic politics, the rise of national and patriotic sentiment, and the arrival in the military sphere of the citizen soldier forced the replacement of this supranational aristocratic culture by a new model. The social divisions within the army (between soldiers from different social backgrounds) did not vanish, but, contrary to the situation under ancien régime, they now counted for less than political and national divisions. The enemy might be defined secondarily as an individual from a particular social group; first and foremost he was the adversary of the nation, the danger without. Thus defined the enemy contributed to creating a stronger and clearer sense of national identity among soldiers, an identity usually invested with a strong political content, particularly during the Revolution, when it was associated with defence of a territory *and* of republican political values. The duality in the sense of national identity characteristic of many soldiers in this period is expressed particularly well in a letter that Bravy Soulbost wrote to his father shortly after joining the army.

> I have enlisted in Paris in the volunteers and am ready to leave to fight the *enemies* of the fatherland. I was born a Frenchman and I wish to share both danger and glory with the French people... In a word, in head and heart I am devoting myself to the defence of *the fatherland*, and my motto is Live *free* or die.[106]

These few short lines, similar to those found in many letters by soldiers and officers, state with perfect clarity, using the same words and concepts, the three themes identified by Michael Jeismann: enemy, liberty, and fatherland.

V. Conclusion

The French revolutionary and Napoleonic wars are rightly seen as marking the advent of the modern battle, both in the representation and culture of war and in the reality of the fighting. This is confirmed by the personal experience of soldiers in all combat arms and from all countries. Battles now increased both in frequency and in intensity; they were fought on a more massive scale and had a more decisive role in the course of the war. This 20-year period witnessed a profound change in the physiology of battle itself. Several factors operated together – social, as armies became larger through the arrival in the military arena of the citizen soldier; political, due to the ideological nature of the conflict on both sides; and technological and tactical. The result was a new framework for military experience. The change in the art of warfare was as yet incomplete, however. From the point of view of the battle and its related characteristics (the representation and treatment of the enemy), war was not yet fully total or modern and continued to exhibit elements from the eighteenth century's culture of war. Total war was indeed born in this period, but for the time being was still in its early stages. The anonymity of what is termed 'modern' battle was not a feature of the revolutionary and Napoleonic wars: the charge, offensive shock, hand-to-hand and close combat – all still played a large role. Technological developments, notably in artillery, were of course important, but there is no ignoring the widespread use of the bayonet right through until 1815. Lastly, when analysed at the micro-level of individuals, the change in the art of war comes up against the indeterminacy of individual perception and behaviour, the sheer variety of experience that confounds macro-level generalizations about military strategies and tactics.

2
The War at Sea

The navy and the maritime war during the revolutionary and Napoleonic wars, though the subject of numerous excellent studies by Anglo-Saxon scholars,[1] still occupy the position of poor relation to the army and land operations in the French historiography of this period. The naval war – less glorious for France and apparently of secondary importance – is often neglected by French historians of the revolutionary and Napoleonic wars. Works on the subject include former naval officer Auguste Thomazi's now dated study of Napoleon's sailors,[2] plus the more recent works by Jean Meyer and Martine Acerra on the French Navy during the Revolution,[3] William Cormack's on the impact of the new revolutionary ideology in the ranks of the navy and the latter's involvement in the political conflicts of 1789–1794,[4] Michèle Battesti's on the battle of Trafalgar and Napoleon's naval strategy,[5] and Pierre Lévêque's social study of the naval officer corps.[6] But these studies are exceptions, and fail to focus on the human experience of war among sailors.

Yet naval combat was an integral part of these wars and of the military and economic strategy of Napoleon and the Allies, with major implications for economy and society in the large ports and in French coastal communities. The topic is all the more interesting in that, as for land warfare, this was a period of far-reaching changes for maritime warfare. It, too, assumed more massive proportions, requiring more men (thus adding to recruitment problems) and more ships – and in particular a faster replacement of vessels – and culminating more often in naval battles of unprecedented intensity and violence (exemplified by the bloody battles of Aboukir and Trafalgar). It was also characterized by a blurring of divisions: between the civilian and military worlds, between naval warfare and economic warfare, between the national navy and the privateers of the Republic and later of the Empire. The naval warfare of this period was also defined by its global or worldwide dimension: at any given time it was fought out simultaneously across practically every sea and ocean, from the English Channel to the Red Sea, and from the Atlantic Ocean to the Indian Ocean. One of the key naval battlegrounds, though, as Piers Mackesy has shown,[7] was the Mediterranean, especially between 1803 and 1810. This was where the decisive battles of Aboukir and Trafalgar were fought. The Mediterranean was also the confined theatre in which France and Britain struggled to dominate the seas and control the trade routes, notably through conquest of strategic points like Corsica, Malta, and the Ionian Islands. Unlike the land war, the war at sea, except for privateering, was not associated with success for the French side. Despite his insular origins and his genuine interest in maritime issues, Napoleon did not excel as a naval strategist. Where 1805 saw striking victories for French land forces, for the French Navy it was dominated by the fiasco of Trafalgar (21 October), which led to near total destruction of the French fleet (18 vessels destroyed, the remaining 13 badly damaged). While the victories of the Austrian campaign, such as Elchingen, were the subject of numerous official accounts in the French press, the authorities actively tried to suppress news of Trafalgar. It could not be kept hidden, however, and before long was public knowledge. In his memoirs, Bourrienne describes how he found out about the battle while serving as plenipotentiary minister in Hamburg:

> The Emperor learned the disastrous news of the combat at Trafalgar while in Vienna, the news being known only through public rumour and the foreign papers, banned in France at that time. So intent was he on consigning the disaster to oblivion that until the Restoration no public news-sheet was allowed to report it throughout the jurisdiction of the Empire. The details were no secret at Hamburg, where the trading community was the first to be informed, and I learned them from the report of my agents before receiving official confirmation in a dispatch from the Minister of External Relations, then in Vienna [. . .]. Not since the famous Armada had a naval battle stained the sea with more blood.[8]

The news of the resounding defeat also spread in France, with catastrophic consequences. The population's morale was undermined, causing a crisis of confidence and, stoked up by false rumours from speculators and mischief-makers, triggering a financial and stock-market crisis in early November 1805. The major 'stock-market revolution'[9] began in the Paris market whence it reverberated out to all the major cities with commercial relations with the capital of the Empire. It generated a wave of panic: 'the bank was besieged by people wanting the repayment of bank notes that quickly changed hands and lost more than 50/1,000.... For a while notes drawn on Paris were trading at 22% below face value.'[10] On 7 November, Joseph Bonaparte wrote to Napoleon: 'For the last two days public opinion has been troubled [...]. The 1000 franc note was trading today for up to 60 francs. As many as two thousand people were queuing at the bank, and there is much discontented talk, even some incidents.'[11] Businesses failures multiplied, that of Récamier being particularly spectacular. Discontent was increasing and social disorder was in the air.[12] In an attempt to halt the panic and the banking crisis, the authorities took emergency measures. A decree was hurriedly introduced whereby holders of sight notes were called to the bank's pay desk in the order of numbers issued to them by their district town hall.

The maritime war thus had a large impact on the situation in France, particularly on economic activity, while also making a deep impression on public opinion. Napoleon may have wanted this less glorious side of military operations to be hidden from view, but the historian cannot be expected to ignore it. A study of the war at sea is necessary to understand the true nature of the revolutionary and Napoleonic wars and their relationship with civilian society.

I. The French Navy in the revolutionary and Napoleonic wars

After Britain's entry into the war in 1793, France was fighting a war at sea against a coalition containing most of the great maritime powers of north-western Europe.

The disastrous Seven Years' War had seemed to put a definitive end to French dominance of the high seas. Even before the conflict was over, however, an ambitious policy to restore and reorganize the French Navy was initiated by the Duc de Choiseul, who became minister of the navy and war in 1761. Choiseul's role in this process and the exact origins of the eighteenth-century revival in the French Navy are debated by historians,[13] but all agree that towards the end of the ancien régime the French Navy compared favourably with the British Navy and even played an essential role in the American War of Independence.[14] By the end of the ancien régime, however, the French Navy was suffering from an acute shortage of public funds. The efforts to restore French naval power were undermined by the combination of the monarchy's fragile finances and a lack of investment.[15] An already insecure position was made worse by the start of the revolutionary troubles, since to financial difficulties were now added problems of command and crews. A large proportion of the ancien régime naval officer corps – most of whom were nobles – either emigrated or were executed during the Revolution, while the system of naval conscription steadily became less effective.

Difficulties in manning and servicing the war fleet put it at a disadvantage compared to France's enemies. France won dazzling successes in the continental land war (at least up until the Spanish War), but in the war at sea she was quickly dominated by Britain. There was a clear realization of this among contemporaries, like Maximilien Sébastien Foy who pointed to the contrast between war on land and sea in the balance of Anglo-French forces. 'England threw against France her land and sea forces [...]. After being regenerated during the American war, our navy was disorganized by the Revolution. With our fleets lacking officers and manned with undisciplined or untried sailors we could not match the superiority of this race of Tritons, who had united almost all the maritime forces of Europe under its flag. Our vessels were captured or destroyed, either singly or in fleets', though he added that 'The early military expeditions by the English succeeded only where they depended on the navy.'[16]

For General Foy, Britain's superiority and France's inferiority in the field of naval warfare were due principally to the composition of the fleets, to their manpower resources. It is certainly the case that recruiting sailors was frequently problematic during these wars, more so even than recruiting soldiers for the army. Under the system of naval conscription that had been introduced by Colbert and reformed by Marshal de Castries, recruitment to the naval fleet depended on the prosperity of the commercial fleet. The French Navy had no full-time crews. Instead, at the end of each war, the sailors were paid off and found employment either in the merchant marine or, failing this, in the royal arsenals. When a new war broke out, they were required to return to military service.

Naval recruitment was not a problem in the first 2 years of the revolutionary wars. The *levée des 300,000*, the law of February 1793 that raised 300,000 additional soldiers, was a national measure and applied equally to the army and the navy. By putting an end to compulsory service for sailors only, a practice inherited from the ancien régime and widely perceived to be unjust, the law restored a balance between army and navy and improved the latter's image. As a result, the requisitioning of sailors in 1793 and 1794 met with little opposition and desertions were few. But it soon became clear that requisition was not enough. The total number of sailors at the start of the revolutionary wars was not particularly high – roughly 60,000 in 1794 – and was whittled down by the French naval defeats and, more importantly, by the ravages of disease both on board the ships, through scurvy, and in the ports, where sanitary conditions were appalling.

Under the ancien régime, recruitment of sailors was traditionally both coastal and local, with each port recruiting from its own geographical area, its own 'district'. However, due to limited numbers and in particular the shortage of professional seamen – a chronic problem for the French Navy at this time – it soon became necessary to look further afield and recruit from other port regions. In Nivôse of Year VII, the Brest fleet was short of 8000 seamen and naval officers, forcing the port commander to turn to other ports for a contribution. Thus it was that Le Havre, Cherbourg, Nantes, Bordeaux, and Rochefort were drained of their manpower to supply the needs of Brest. The controller of shipping at Nantes claimed to have reached the limits for this part of the war effort in Thermidor Year VII. He informed the Minister of the 'spent supply of sailors in the arrondissement of Nantes on account of the crews we have provided and in particular the large number of seamen we have sent to Brest in the last five months'.[17] At Rochefort, a number of ships – a frigate, the *Volontaire*, two corvettes, the *Vénus* and the *Diligente*, and eight gunboats – had to be taken out of service to provide 300 seamen for Brest.[18] Some of these geographical transfers offended feelings of regional identity and produced discontent among the sailors. When the crews of the corvettes stationed at Bordeaux were cut to three-quarters strength and the men sent to Brest in 50-strong brigades escorted by line soldiers, the commissioner noted that 'sailors from the Midi have long shown a dislike for the northern provinces.'[19]

Problems over recruitment were exacerbated by political considerations. Several of the coastal departments that formed the traditional recruiting grounds for the navy were affected by counter-revolutionary unrest in this period. The Revolution, the war, and conscription were opposed by a majority of the people in Brittany, which looked set to become a northern Vendée in 1793, as well as in the Vendée itself and in the departments of Provence. In his memoirs written in 1820, Narcisse Boutilier de Saint André, who was 12 years old when war broke out in his native Vendée, relates his experience as a civilian, based on his childhood recollections and on conversations with older family members.

In 1793 he witnessed the open hostility of the population in the Vendée to the raising of troops:

> The Vendéan has always been deeply attached to the soil of his birthplace and would have found it extremely hard to go off to serve a government for which he felt only hatred and contempt. When people learned of the raising of troops they became restive and tempers rose, and from November 1792 troubles broke out at Bressuire.... As the Vendean war made a deep impression on me at an early age... I have decided to give some details of the events that for four years had such a direct influence on my existence... exposing me and my brothers and sisters to the greatest dangers ever faced by children of our age.... The main driving force of the uprising was the special levy of all males between twenty and forty... The same result can be expected whenever the government wishes to take all the annual age groups at the same time. For this reason I have always viewed the invention of conscription by Bonaparte as most adroit, since by raising only one annual group at a time, those unaffected have no reason to resist the law. So I firmly believe that the levy of 300,000 men caused the war in the Vendée, and if my personal experience were not enough to make me certain of this, the views expressed by one of my relatives would have done so...[20]

The Vendée was of course an extreme case, but the Revolution and conscription met strong opposition from a majority of inhabitants in other French coastal regions, such as the Léon in Brittany, and in parts of Provence, particularly around Toulon. The coastal location of these centres of counter-revolutionary unrest was especially worrying from the viewpoint of naval recruitment.

As a further measure to make up the crews, the naval authorities then requisitioned all the seafarers – captains, fishermen, merchant seamen – in a locality. But numbers were limited and it was scarcely possible to requisition a locality's entire merchant seagoing population without risking disruption of the economy and supply system. Other solutions had to be found.

The naval authorities sought to form crews with sailors or seamen (requisitioned from the merchant fleet or from members of the arsenal workforces with seagoing experience). But once these possibilities were exhausted the authorities had no choice but to incorporate troops who had no seagoing experience – soldiers from the army. In doing so, however, they ran up against two major problems: competition from the army and the geographical pattern of recruitment.

For the army, the largest contingents of both volunteer and conscript soldiers between Year III and Year V were supplied by departments in the frontier regions of northern and eastern France, in decreasing order: Nord Pas-de-Calais, Bas-Rhin, Haut-Rhin, Moselle, and Isère.[21] The army also contained large numbers of Parisians. However, none of these departments were in regions that traditionally supplied recruits for the navy, and men from here served mainly in the army. Consequently, the popular acceptance of war and conscription in these departments, though important for recruitment to the army, had no influence on naval recruitment. A small number of men from inland departments did, of course, choose the navy in preference to the army because they were attracted to sea voyaging. One such was Chevallier, a young man from Versailles, who eventually enlisted in the army after failing to get into the navy. At several points in his memoirs he refers to his dreams of life as a sailor:

> When I was barely twelve I already wanted to serve in the navy. My father took me to Paris where I stayed eight days with a relative who worked in the Ministry of the Marine and who, using various excuses, avoided presenting me to the minister. Tired with this lack of success, I returned to Versailles and put off my maritime service ... As I grew up, my love of travel grew too, and then an opportunity arose ... Representatives ... who had come to pay tribute to the Republic got permission from the French government to form and take away a group of assorted craftsmen. I succeeded in joining this group as an armourer, and a few days later we left for Brest. I already pictured myself on the high seas, discovering a new America or at the very least some unknown islands. But fate decided otherwise; only a few workers were embarked and all the rest were dismissed. We were summoned back to Versailles and had to obey ... Still gripped by the idea of serving France and going around the world, I at last found an opportunity: Cide, Fauvel, myself and Fourquois (who had already been to America) went to the Ministry to enlist in the navy.[22]

This plan also failed and Chevallier eventually finished up a soldier, in the Imperial Guard.

But cases like this are fairly exceptional in our sources. A life at sea was not a common ambition at this time. For this reason the authorities often had to use force to complete the crews, by requisitioning soldiers and putting them in the navy.

The French Navy had used soldiers to complete its crews during the ancien régime. What was new in the revolutionary period was that soldiers often outnumbered sailors on ships. For example, in 1795, the vessel the *Ca ira* counted 496 soldiers for 187 seamen. Such a situation had serious consequences for naval combat. During the battle of Cap Noli (13 March 1795), the *Ca ira,* on account of its largely incompetent crew containing too few sailors, hampered the fleet by its clumsy manoeuvring, eventually becoming separated from the other vessels and ending up in a dire state (unmasted, with 12 feet of water in the hull, and more than 500 crewmen killed or wounded) and forced to surrender.[23]

The naval high command was aware of the problems caused by the shortage of experienced mariners. The recently appointed commander of arms at Brest, Morard de Galle, complained in Nivôse of Year VII about the difficulty of forming crews when the numbers conscripted into the navy were so low, with matters made worse by the lack of seasoned sailors among them. 'It pains me to see the tiny numbers arriving, while most of those taken on board are in truth worse than poor sailors, particularly those sent from Paris.'[24] For men who were not seafarers at heart, the sea itself produced as much apprehension as fighting the enemy did; in bad weather, action of any kind became problematic. In 1795, frigates from Toulon surrendered without having fired a single cannon shot, for the simple reason that all the gunners were seasick.[25]

The verdict of General Foy that France's revolutionary navy was formed of 'undisciplined and untried sailors' was not without justification. In addition to the difficulties caused by the shortage of experienced seamen, the naval authorities also faced the problem of poor discipline among crew members, especially those conscripted by force or 'pressed' into naval service. Men in this category were typically incompetent, lacking in seamanship, motivation, and physical courage, and averse to discipline and taking orders. This could have serious consequences for the fighting of naval battles. When the squadron from Brest comprising three ships of the line and five frigates and commanded by an experienced and skilled officer, Morand de Galle – a noble who rallied to the Revolution and served under Suffren in the American War of Independence – left Brest in March 1793, a collision between the ships caused extensive material damage (unmasting several ships) without a single British vessel being encountered. The subsequent report by Morand de Galle refers to widespread indiscipline. A mere squall, not a gale, unnerved the crews. The terrified sailors refused to come up on deck and carry out the required manoeuvres. On the flagship, only 30 men followed orders and came on deck. On another ship none of the men would carry out the manoeuvre ordered by the captain (who died doing it himself).[26] This example illustrates the extent of the difficulties the high command encountered with untried and reluctant mariners who lacked knowledge and experience of nautical matters.

Another reason why a life at sea attracted few candidates lay in the harsh conditions for sailors at this time. The shortage of money had implications for logistics and provisioning. Naval magazines frequently fell empty, and the victuals issued to sailors were commonly of deplorable quality.[27] More serious still was the irregular and often infrequent intervals at which sailors were paid. At Rochefort, in Vendémiaire of Year VIII, there were 'men-of-war whose crews were owed for eight or nine months'.[28] An identical situation prevailed at Lorient – where the crews of the *Argonaute* and the frigates *Cocarde* and *Sémillante* were owed 18 months' pay – and at Nantes.[29]

Officers fared no better. At Rochefort, in Year VIII, they had not received their pay for over 4 months and were in extremely straightened economic circumstances.[30] In the Mediterranean, several officers at Toulon were reduced to selling their 'linen and jewels' to make up for the lateness of pay and to cover basic needs.[31] Things were no better under the Consulate. Pierre-Edouard Plucket, born into a seafaring family in Dunkirk on 12 October 1759, served in the French Navy as a lieutenant commander in charge of privateers operating in the Channel. In his memoirs he notes that 'The government under the Directory and Consulate showed an equal lack of concern about pay . . . I and all my fellow officers on the corvette *Jalouse* went for over a year without receiving a penny towards our pay or our table money. The crew members were no better off,' and adds that this state of affairs had regrettable consequences for recruitment: 'Large numbers of fine, brave officers were so demoralized that they were forced to resign so as to seek the means of making a living; and the best sailors deserted to sail under a neutral flag as soon as a good opportunity arose.'[32]

Grievances sometimes erupted into rebellion. The port director of Brest expressed concern in Thermidor of Year V because the port's population was 'clamouring loudly for pay, refusing salt meat and calling for tobacco'.[33] On other occasions, sailors who had not received their pay refused to work and mutinied, as happened at Brest in Messidor of Year V (on the *Formidable*). The risk of desertion is frequently mentioned in the reports from the military authorities, like that from the controller of shipping at Nantes, who was reluctant to allow two schooners to leave, explaining that 'desertion would be high in a port where there is no means of stopping it.'[34] The risk was real, since desertion was an endemic problem, much larger in scale than in the army, and one from which no port was immune. The ships berthed at Toulon in Germinal of Year VII required crews of 2,947 men, of whom 976 were missing.[35] At Lorient, the port commander noted on 1 Prairial of Year VII that 'desertion remained as great as ever in Captain Villemadrin's division' and that 'although everyone was confined to ship, the men managed to get away by jumping into the sea.'[36] At Brest, in Ventôse of Year VIII, 1100 men were missing, and each day brought more desertions (100 men in 5 days at the end of Ventôse, 208 in the 10 days between 10 and 20 Frimaire).[37] The main reason for the steady stream of deserters was delay in the sailors getting their pay. In these conditions, sailors were tempted to join the crews of corsairs or privateers. Privateering was expanding rapidly at this time thanks to the lucrative rewards from prize warfare, so that seamen were in strong demand. At Rochefort, Admiral Martin estimated that 1270 men, many of them experienced elite sailors, deserted in Pluviôse of Year VII to join the corsairs at Bordeaux.[38] At the same time, the port commander of Brest was also unable to stem the movement, and acknowledged that 'In spite of all the measures taken to stop desertion, it continues still and will probably continue to do so as long as there are corsairs operating in the vicinity of the naval ports.'[39] The Mediterranean ports, too, were affected. Sailors at Ancona left to join the corsairs by jumping into the sea under cover of night.[40]

Outside agents, such as privateers, merchants, shipowners, growers, and planters, might also encourage the decision to desert, by promising a position and an income for the sailor who deserted. Thus it was that young Guillaume-Marie Angenard from Saint-Malo, who joined the national navy as a 14-year-old cabin boy on the three-master *Bon Ménage* in 1790, deserted 2 years later in response to the urging of a planter in Mauritius:

> On 10 June 1792, I deserted from the ship on the advice of M. Faucheur, of Saint-Servan, who at that time was an indigo-manufacturer at La Ville-Baguer. I was taken to a dwelling at La Poudre d'Or belonging to M. Gentil. There I was supposed to learn the trade of indigo-maker... I was... well treated by this colonial proprietor who looked on me as one of his children. He often told me that he wanted to set me on the path to fortune.[41]

The situation of the navy improved little during the Consulate and Empire. Recruiting sailors remained as difficult as ever and there was a serious shortage of manpower. The shortcomings of the revolutionary years persisted. Ships' crews contained too large a proportion of soldiers, although some officers, taking their cue from Napoleon, refused to see this as a drawback. Thus Admiral Jurien de la Gravière replied to critics of this expedient policy by claiming that the military identity was stronger than membership of the seafaring community: 'It is said that the soldier does not have sea legs; but perhaps the merchant seaman does not have a military heart. On which side is the disadvantage greater?' But lack of experience and seamanship represented a genuine handicap and even Jurien de la Gravière had to recognize that incorporating soldiers into the crews was merely an expedient, not a principle.[42]

The system of impressment was introduced in all the ports, with visible consequences. Men who had been conscripted by force would use any means to desert. In 1807, at Toulon, 900 sailors were judged for desertion, 700 of them in their absence. In Brittany, special troop units (*colonnes mobiles*) were set up to root out sailors who had deserted.[43]

The effect of impressment was to fill the ships with heterogeneous collections of social misfits, vagabonds, family outcasts, underage adolescents (foundlings and abandoned children were requisitioned from age 12) plus an assortment of jailbirds, thieves, and petty criminals, noted for their brutality and dishonesty – all of which put an obstacle to the cohesion of the group and the development of a military identity. On the basis of his personal experience in the Egyptian expedition and in the Napoleonic wars as a whole, Chevallier claimed that: 'By and large, sailors are brutish, filthy and foul-mouthed.'[44]

The territorial conquests made under the Directory, Consulate, and Empire made it possible to complete crews by conscripting foreign sailors. Following the annexation of Holland, Dutch vessels were incorporated into the French Navy complete with their own crews. Other annexed states received the same treatment and were required to supply France with sailors. These included inhabitants of the German North Sea ports (Hamburg and Bremen), Poles, and Sardinians and Dalmatians in the Mediterranean. In addition to conscripts, some annexed countries also contributed volunteer sailors. Thus in 1807, after being forced to hand over its fleet to the British, Denmark offered its sailors to France. A number of French vessels operated with Danish commanders and officers and with mixed crews – three-quarters Danish, one-quarter French – until 1813, when the Danish government recalled its sailors. However, enrolling large numbers of foreign conscripts in the navy also brought problems. Sailors who had been compelled to serve thought only of running away. Napoleon responded by passing a law banning naval impressment and conscription, and stipulating that foreign sailors should serve on French ships only of their own free will. Despite this, the large foreign presence continued to make some navy officers uneasy. Aboard the *Polonais*, in Troude's division, where Dutch outnumbered French, the captain feared a nationalist mutiny to seize control and make off with the vessel.

The supply of naval officers was also problematic. The outbreak of the Revolution caused far greater disruption to the high command of the Royal French Navy than to that of the army, since many naval officers were nobles and royalists. Large numbers joined the emigration, thereby depleting the navy's professional cadres.[45] To fill the gaps in the officer corps, the naval authorities were quickly forced to use the captains of the merchant fleet, not all of whom had the skills needed for military operations. Pierre Lévêque notes that in 1811, 44 per cent of officers in the French war fleet were former merchant navy officers who had entered military service after 1792 to replace officers who had emigrated.[46]

Napoleon was keen for these men from merchant navy backgrounds to receive an adequate military training, and in 1810 he set up two naval schools to train future naval officers. The schools were established on two vessels – *Tourville* and *Dusquesne*, one at Brest, the other at Toulon – and each had an annual intake of 150 students from 1811.[47] But while this innovation represented a considerable improvement and a step towards creating a professional navy, it came too late for the effects to be felt during the wars.

If sailors were in short supply, so too were ships. Once Britain entered the war in 1793, France was fighting a maritime war against a coalition of the principal naval powers of north-western Europe. The contributions of Britain's allies reinforced the superiority of her own fleet. In 1793, the Royal Navy possessed 85 warships – not counting the vessels of 50 and 64 guns, which were officially reserved for convoy defence but which, besides defending British maritime trade played an important role in the conquest of the French colonies – against 61 for the French Republic. The addition of the sizeable Spanish and Dutch fleets to these 85 ships gave an overwhelming superiority to the maritime coalition. In 1795, however, the situation was reversed as a result of the French Army's conquests in Italy and Holland and the peace treaty with Spain. At this point, thanks to the Spanish and Dutch contributions and the annexation of the Venetian fleet, and despite the losses incurred between 1793 and 1795, the French actually had numerical superiority over the British in terms of ships.

But while production of warships in the arsenals was maintained in the early stages of the Revolution, in 1795 it fell to a much lower level from which it never recovered. The sharp reduction in naval expenditure had two causes: first, the chronic deficit of the French Navy inherited from the ancien régime (400 million francs of debt for the navy alone in 1789, a sum almost equal to the entire taxation revenues of France[48]); second and more importantly, the priority now given to funding for the army. The reduction had dramatic consequences. As of 1795, the French Navy suffered from chronic shortages of everything: manpower and ships; material and facilities for repairs, dry-docking and refitting; food to feed its sailors; and money to pay their wages. Its ships became increasingly outdated and poorly maintained, and many were not in a fit state to face the enemy or even to put to sea in safety. Pierre-Edouard Plucket noted in his memoirs: 'The navy was neglected terribly under the Directory and Consulate, especially the government warships in the northern ports, so that on many occasions the captains were unable to obtain even small amounts of tar and paint to keep the ships seaworthy...'[49] Up to 1795, with naval construction running at high levels, France managed, albeit with difficulty, to maintain an annual balance between shipping losses (through naval battles or shipwreck) and the production of new ships. The size of the fleet remained stable and, with around 80 warships and 80 frigates, comparable to the enemy's. Following the battle of Aboukir in 1798, however, the rate at which shipping losses were replaced by new vessels fell sharply.

When the peace of Amiens ended in 1802, France possessed 60 vessels, half as many as the British (120). Napoleon wrote to Decrès on 21 April 1804:

> We must have a navy, and we will not be reputed to have one until we have a hundred vessels. Kindly draw up a report for next week giving me the exact situation of our navy, of shipbuilding, of what we need to build and in which ports, and with the cost per month.

Napoleon now launched a vast and ambitious shipbuilding programme. All the ports were concerned, beginning with the military ports (Dunkirk, Brest, Lorient, Rochefort, and Toulon), followed by the commercial ports (Le Havre and Nantes), whose dry dock facilities were available now that orders from shipowners had dwindled almost to nothing. The Empire was a period of intense activity in the ports of Toulon and Rochefort.[50]

Napoleon also intended to draw on the resources of his foreign conquests. Following the annexation of Liguria, he sent Navy engineer Pierre-Alexandre-Laurent Forfait to Genoa as commander-in-chief of the port with the task of encouraging shipbuilding and setting up an arsenal at La Spezia. With control of the entire Adriatic littoral, Napoleon spent several million francs annually over subsequent years on setting up and operating a fleet based in the Adriatic. The naval dockyards of Venice were used to build the ships that would operate in these waters, ships such as the *Rivoli*, with 74 guns, which, when launched in 1810, was the largest ship ever built there. Slipway facilities were also installed in the neighbouring port of Trieste, while Ragusa was organized as the supply port for the Franco-Italian fleet Napoleon planned to create in the Adriatic.

Napoleon was no less attentive to the Atlantic and Mediterranean ports of the Iberian Peninsula. In this region the aim was to challenge the ascendancy of the British. Thus when Junot left for Portugal, Napoleon had naval officers secretly assigned to him with the mission of seizing the port of Lisbonand some vessels.

Further to the north, along the Channel coast, interest centred on the Dutch and Belgian ports. Once France had annexed Holland, the ports of Rotterdam and in particular Amsterdam were organized to function as arsenals for the French Navy. On 24 Pluviôse of Year III (12 February 1795), Plucket received orders from Vice-Admiral Villaret-Joyeuse to follow Rear-Admiral Vanstabel to Flessingue with 40 captains and assorted officers for the purpose of readying the Dutch warships and vessels and bringing them back to France.[51]

Particular places were also of strategic importance. Texel harbour at the entrance to the port of Amsterdam was specially reorganized to provide the base for an expedition against Britain. Following the annexation of Belgium, the mouth of the River Scheldt that the Dutch had kept closed to navigation for over 200 years (to advantage Amsterdam) was reopened to serve French interests. The Antwerp arsenal was officially set up by a decree of 21 July 1803, which fixed the positions of the docks, workshops, and magazines, marked the course of a canal to the Meuse and Rhine, and set out the order and timetable of the work. At this time Napoleon wrote to Decrès:

> Assemble three thousand workers at Antwerp. Goods from the North, wood and iron, everything reaches Antwerp easily. The war is no

> obstacle to shipbuilding at Antwerp. If we were at war for three years, twenty-five vessels would need to be built there. This is impossible anywhere else.

The port of Antwerp quickly emerged as one of the main shipbuilding sites for the new fleet in Napoleon's Europe, and before long also acquired an outport that functioned as a naval port, Flessingue, granted to France by the new king of Holland, Louis Bonaparte. Ships were built in the port of Antwerp, then launched and sent to Flessingue for fitting out with cannons and other equipment. In 1807, eight vessels launched at Antwerp went down the Scheldt to Flessingue to be coppered and fitted out. They formed the core of a fleet intended for a future cross-Channel expedition, justifying Napoleon's comment that Antwerp was 'a pistol aimed at the heart of England'.

After Trafalgar, in 1807, the number of French vessels fell to 35 (a total of 29 ships having been lost in the battles of Aboukir, Trafalgar, and Saint Domingue). But Napoleon's decision to build, or rebuild, the French Navy as an instrument of warfare bore fruit. By 1810, with the naval shipyards working to capacity and despite the loss of the Cadiz fleet and the fire-boat attack off the Ile d'Aix, France possessed 55 vessels, with a further 25 nearing completion in the shipyards. Three years later, in 1813, the number of vessels in service had risen to 71, with 42 under construction. Between 1809 and 1814 the French Navy totalled on average over 60 ships of the line, some 40 frigates, plus 800–900 lighter craft, and operated out of ports from Hamburg to Bayonne and from Sète to Ragusa. Addressing the General Council of Industry and Manufacture (*Conseil général des Fabriques et Manufactures*) on 24 March 1811, Napoleon proclaimed:

> I am the successor of Charlemagne. It is a continuation of the empire he founded. Where Louis XIV had Brest alone, I have all of Europe's coastlines! In four years I shall have a navy ... I can build twenty-five vessels a year. When my squadrons have had three or four years at sea, we will be able to confront the English. I know that I may lose three or four squadrons, but we are courageous and always ready for action, and in less than ten years we shall succeed. I shall subjugate England ...[52]

For this is what was at stake: challenge Britain for maritime supremacy and dominance over the oceans, chase the British out of the Mediterranean and gain control of the trade routes.

II. Dominance over the oceans, control of the trade routes: the war in the Mediterranean

The Mediterranean had a central place in the war at sea in this period. By their number and intensity, the combats that occurred there – naval battles but also port sieges – made it one of the main battle grounds and a strategic zone. It was in the Mediterranean that the struggle between the British and the French for mastery of the seas was most fiercely contested.

When war broke out in 1793, Britain had a single naval base in the Mediterranean, the rock and harbour of Gibraltar (the island of Minorca had been returned to Spain in 1783 under the Treaty of Versailles). France, on the other hand, had several ports along its Mediterranean coast. The most important in naval terms was Toulon, a deep-water port with a spacious harbour, which was close to the training harbours of Villefranche and Hyères. Also valuable was Corsica, acquired in 1768, which supplied high quality timber (*Larico pine*) for the arsenal of Toulon. By 1793, France and Britain were waging naval war in the Mediterranean. British, Spanish, and Neapolitan squadrons occupied the port of Toulon between 27 August and 19 December 1793. When the allies finally evacuated the harbour they left behind 14 vessels, 3 frigates, and 2 corvettes, but had inflicted heavy losses on the French Mediterranean fleet (10 vessels and 3 frigates) and had destroyed the general magazine of the French arsenal and a large proportion of their supplies. After leaving the port of Toulon, the fleets of the maritime coalition maintained a strong presence in the Mediterranean, keeping a tight control over the French coastline that was intended to disrupt commerce and create a climate of insecurity. An initial line of advanced bases extended from Barcelona to Leghorn, via Minorca, Majorca, and Corsica (the latter was allied to the British between 1793 and 1795, thus enabling them to use the Gulf of Saint Florent, directly opposite the French coast). Supporting these advanced bases was a second line of rear bases (Gibraltar, Sardinia, Sicily, and Naples).

The threat from the British in the Mediterranean subsequently receded temporarily, thanks to the French conquests on land and the reversal of alliances. By the treaties of Bâle (1795) and San Ildefonse, Spain and Naples came out of the war. Spain was now allied with France, bringing a good quality fleet and strategic naval bases (on the Spanish coast and islands). The conquest of the Italian regions, and Venice in particular, further strengthened the French system of defence in the Mediterranean, by the addition of the Venetian fleet and important strategic bases in the Ionian Islands and Corfu. As commander-in-chief of the Army of Italy, Napoleon had strategic as well as personal reasons for wishing to see the British driven from his native island. As he confided to Gentili: 'Restoring Corsica to the Republic will provide resources for our navy and also be a source of recruitment for our light infantry...Driving the English out of the Mediterranean is most important for the success of our military operations in Italy.'[53] The reconquest of Corsica for the Republic in 1796 – organized by Napoleon during the Italian campaign – drove the British from the island for good, and did indeed supply France with plentiful reserves of soldiers and sailors, since Corsicans volunteered in large numbers for service in the army or navy.

The capture of Malta in 1798 by the expeditionary force en route for Egypt, added a few more ships (including galleys, four ships of the line, and several frigates) to set against earlier losses, plus some new recruits. Referring in his memoirs to the surrender by the Order of the Knights of Malta and the subsequent conquest of Malta by the French, François Vigo-Roussillon noted:

> General Bonaparte declared the Order of Malta abolished in the name of the French Republic. The Grand Master Ferdinand de Hompesh and most of the knights received pensions from France. Those who wanted to serve in the army were incorporated in a newly formed Maltese legion recruited from the order's troops. This legion later took the name of "Nautical Legion", when the fleet sailors who made it to land after the naval battle of Aboukir were incorporated into it. In this way the army received nearly four thousand extra men.[54]

In 1796–1798, when Britain had withdrawn from the Mediterranean and fallen back to Gibraltar, France was able to establish a large logistics network centred on the naval base at Toulon and comprising several arsenals and naval shipyards (Toulon, Venice, Corfu, Genoa, Leghorn). But the French Navy failed to exploit this advantage and at Aboukir would be crushed by a British Navy that was itself weakened. Jean Meyer attributes this outcome to two causes: the organization of the Egyptian expedition, and the collapse of French logistics due to the sharp reduction in spending on the naval war effort after 1795.[55]

Under the Consulate and Empire, the Mediterranean held an increasingly central place in Napoleon's military and naval strategy. In 1803 he established control over the Papal States and, contravening the Treaty of Florence, ordered General Gouvion Saint-Cyr to invade the Kingdom of the Two Sicilies. French forces reoccupied the strategic ports of Taranto,

Otranto, and Brindisi. The French troops stationed in the Kingdom of Naples lived off the country through taxes levied on the population, thus easing the burden on the French treasury. Napoleon continued to pursue his 'Mediterranean policy' in subsequent years. In 1804, following annexation of Venice and the Ionian Islands, he sent spies to the Greek and Albanian coasts to prepare the way for invasion and annexation of the region, an action that caused a rift between himself and Tsar Alexander.[56] Napoleon's ambitions in the Mediterranean, particularly the threat they posed to Russian interests in the eastern Mediterranean, helped to bring Russia under British influence and eventually into the Third Coalition.[57] After 1805, the British regained control of large parts of the Mediterranean and the Adriatic. They established their base in Sicily, and supported anti-French guerrilla activity in Calabria. Corfu provided them with a footing in the Adriatic, whence attacks could be launched against the French in the Illyrian provinces.

The Mediterranean was a strategic zone over which the French and British waged a bitter struggle. In some instances the civilian populations had to organize their own coastal defences, as happened to the inhabitants of Centuri, in Cap-Corse, in June 1810. The minister of police, Savary, recounted to the Emperor how the inhabitants of this tiny municipality had conducted themselves:

> On 9 June, an English frigate tried to capture a French schooner off Centuri. Led by two mayors, the inhabitants forced the frigate to withdraw. The frigate made renewed attacks on 13 and 17 June, which the inhabitants resisted with equal success. The schooner got away and made it into the port of Macinajo, under the battery of La Coscia. The Prefect of Golo who reported this incident notes that the military authorities had not had the foresight to place under observation the point where the landing occurred. The battery position was captured; one gunner was killed, another wounded, four taken prisoner along with a sergeant, a corporal and a soldier. The enemy at once seized the schooner and the mortar. The tocsin was rung at Tomin and Rogliano; the lack of weapons caused a slight delay. First to arrive were the inhabitants of Tomino, led by their mayor. After aiming the Macinajo battery's guns on to that of La Coscia occupied by the enemy, they marched off to recapture this station. The inhabitants of Rogliano joined them. The enemy spiked the guns, set fire to the building, and after a small combat re-embarked under the battery. It then withdrew with the schooner and the mortar. The fire was put out and the guns repaired. The prefect notes that the inhabitants

> had shown zeal and deserved to be issued with weapons to defend the coast.[58]

The Mediterranean is a crossroads of cultures and civilizations. French soldiers serving here acquired an awareness of what it was that bound them together as members of the same nation, or indeed of the same civilization. From encounters with populations with quite different religions, customs, and behaviour, a sense of European identity began to form. The Mediterranean thus became the geographical incarnation of a frontier between civilizations. This notion of a frontier crops up in accounts by several soldiers. They wanted to establish something like a dividing line between two worlds, Europe and Africa, or Europe and Asia. Some of them considered Spain, or at least its southern regions, to be already outside of the European zone. In his memoirs, Octave Levavasseur recalls his arrival in Spain in August 1808:

> From that point on everything I saw interested me. In the countries I had been through previously, the civilization of the inhabitants appeared to differ little from French civilization. Since Germany touches our frontier it must have borrowed some of our customs, and vice-versa. The mores and practices of people in Europe extend by degrees as far as Warsaw, though they are modified by climate, religion, and laws. As for Spain, nothing there is like what is seen elsewhere. At four leagues from Bayonne you would think you were a thousand leagues from France.[59]

In some cases the frontier is not geographical but ethnic, and runs inside a European society. Sébastien Blaze, a pharmacist who took part in the Spanish War between 1808 and 1814, clearly felt Spain to be a European country, including its southernmost provinces like Andalousia, 'the most beautiful province of Spain and perhaps of Europe',[60] a sort of end point to the European landmass facing the 'coasts of Africa'.[61] But Blaze identified one category of population that, in his view, were not Europeans but already Arabs: 'The gipsies (*gitans*) are the pariahs of Spain, and because they always intermarry they keep their almost black colour. It is a remnant of their Moorish blood, which has been little altered because of the infrequent mixing of races.'[62]

For others, finally, the frontier was not on land but at sea. If Corsica and the Italian islands were obviously European, Malta was considered a halfway house – in the words of Martin, an engineer on the Egyptian expedition – 'between Sicily and Barbary',[63] an intermediary between the two cultures, as it had been since the sixteenth century.[64] The descriptions of the island combine European and African elements. As Joseph-Marie Moiret put it, 'the character of the Maltese people let us know that we were no longer in the centre of Europe and of civilization.'[65]

III. The return of the privateers

The revolutionary and Napoleonic wars were the heyday of commerce-raiding corsairs or privateers. At the start of the Revolution, the British were able to ruin French maritime commerce thanks to their mastery of the seas. In retaliation the Convention envisaged – as had Louis XIV's ministers – a destruction of British maritime commerce by a war based not on naval squadrons, in which France was at a disadvantage, but on corsairs that would disrupt her trade. After war broke out between Britain and France, the deputies of the Convention voted a decree that re-established prize warfare by corsairs. To attract candidates the decree stipulated that the 'corsairs of the Republic' would share out all the proceeds, in contrast to the practice under the ancien régime, when the crews of the king's corsairs received a one-third share. Drawn by the prospect of material gain, the prestige of illustrious predecessors, patriotism, and a taste for adventure, thousands of privateers began operating against enemy shipping after 1793. Their activity was global in scale and affected practically every ocean and sea, though the main ones were the Atlantic, the Channel, the Mediterranean, the East Indian and the Red seas, and the Indian Ocean.

Privateers were not pirates. The privateer operated in a legal framework and his activity was an integral part of the war at sea, unlike the pirate who was an outlaw. The privateer required an official authorization – the 'letters of marque' issued to French corsairs – and was not authorized to attack the shipping of nations with which his country had concluded non-aggression agreements. While attacking or boarding their target, privateers were supposed to fly the national flag, rather than the black flag of pirates, although as a ruse to facilitate capture a false flag (usually British) was often flown prior to interception. Privateers captured the cargo a ship was carrying and took the crew and any passengers prisoner (although they might decide to let them go, possibly in return for payment). As a rule, however, and unlike pirates, they did not destroy the vessel or kill the passengers. All countries practised prize warfare at this time, and proof of the activity's legal status is that states levied taxes on the profits from the sale of captured cargoes.

Some insight into the motivations of the men who became the 'corsairs of the Republic' can be gained from the memoirs a few of them have left. Predictably, these show that they were motivated chiefly by a taste for seafaring and adventure, a desire for rapid personal enrichment, and an admiration for the legend and exploits of famous corsairs from the past (like Duguay-Trouin and Jean Bart) or of their own day (notably Nicolas Surcouf from Saint-Malo). The decision to become a privateer also depended closely on the men's background, since they invariably came from the regions of ports that were centres of privateering (principally Saint-Malo and Dunkirk) and often from families that had supplied privateers in earlier wars. But although ideology, politics, or patriotism were not the main forces driving the men who became corsairs, these preoccupations were not completely absent. Once war had broken out, commerce raiding was not motivated solely by individual economic interest; often it also reflected these men's wish to be of use to their country in their particular field of activity. Pierre-Edouard Plucket, a sailor who later became a privateer, had already served as cabin boy on a privateer during the American War of Independence.[66] In his memoirs, he recounts his thoughts and reactions when the Convention re-established privateering:

> It was in February 1793, a year when glory and crimes merged dreadfully. I was having supper in Nantes, at the home of my broker, Monsieur Laporte, when the drum suddenly began to sound in the streets amidst the hubbub from an immense crowd. Monsieur Laporte sent his maid servant to get the news, who came back directly to tell us that war had been declared with England. Monsieur Laporte had served on a Dunkirk corsair, as writer, during the American war. He said to me: 'Captain Plucket, we must commission a corsair. A number of suitable ships are available and are certainly going to be laid up, being used for the slave trade. They are excellent sailors.' I greeted this proposal with enthusiasm.... I was keen to have my revenge for the prison at Gosport, Liverpool and Traley. Nothing else was needed to fuel my patriotism and my hatred for the freebooters of Europe... The deal was struck. We bought one of the ships and took possession as soon as her cargo had been landed... We each took a 10,000 *livres* share in the fitting out operation. The other shares were swiftly subscribed. I made all possible haste with the fitting out. We rebaptized the slaver as a corsair by naming it the *Sans-Culotte Nantais*.[67]

Several thousand kilometres from Nantes, in the Indian Ocean, Guillaume-Marie Angenard, a young seaman from Saint-Malo, learned from the crew of a merchant schooner that war had broken out between France and 'all the European powers' and that prize warfare was again to be authorized. Like their counterparts in Nantes, the corsairs of Mauritius set about commissioning ships. Angenard was a seaman on a slave ship, but he now joined a corsair belonging to shipowners from his home port of Saint-Malo. In his memoirs he records his feelings at this time:

> Before long a number of corsairs were being fitted out, and in each neighbourhood of the city registers were opened in which anyone could enter his name and the rank he thought he was fit to hold on a corsair. My mind was filled with new ideas and all my thoughts turned towards this kind of seafaring. I had often read the life of the famous Duguay-Trouin, who came from my hometown of Saint-Malo; my head was so filled with memories of this hero's great deeds that I was afire with the urge to find myself in similar situations. Although my younger brother, who was in the colony at the time, advised me against it, I could even say forbade me, I went and entered my name in the register for *Le Cerf*, a fine corsair, along with a request to be put on the crew list as an unpaid volunteer [who would be remunerated only with a share of the prize money].[68]

The decree of the Convention also triggered a scramble into privateering in the French West Indies. On 14 March 1793, General Rochambeau addressed a declaration to the military commanders of the Windward Islands or *Iles sous le Vent* (Martinique and Guadeloupe) announcing the reintroduction of privateering and officially asking them to prepare for war. Two days later, Guadeloupe was declared to be in a state of danger. British privateers, operating from their base in Dominica, opened hostilities by disrupting coastal trade between the islands' ports.[69] In 1794, the war between French and British privateers raged in the West Indies. In his memoirs, corvette captain, Jean-François Landolphe, a native of Auxerre who had enlisted in the French Navy in 1766, noted the importance of French privateers in the war between French and British in the West Indies (where there were few actual warships):

> The commandant [Victor Hugues] swiftly commissioned a number of small corsairs, commanded by captains from the coastal waters who knew all the approaches to the French and British islands in the region. The privateers captured numerous merchant ships daily,

> inflicting great losses on Britain's trade while adding to that of Guadeloupe.[70]

To prey upon merchant shipping, the privateer had to obtain an authorization from the Ministry of the Navy in the form of a 'letter of marque' that gave him a registration number. Plucket, for example, obtained a letter of marque with the number 1.[71] The vessels used for privateering were paid for by the privateers themselves or in partnership with the merchants and shipowners of their port, though financial help sometimes came from the government or from political clubs. The corsairs had a free hand in forming their crew. Prize warfare and naval warfare were in some cases even more closely linked. During preparations for the expedition to Ireland in the Year VII, the 'corsairs of the Republic' had to serve as auxiliaries to the navy: 'the commissioning of corsairs at this time was on condition that they be commanded by an officer of the national navy, and that they transport troops to the coast of Ireland.'[72]

All such vessels were equipped with cannons for intercepting and capturing merchantmen, and for combating enemy warships. Most were of low tonnage and carried small crews. The *Sans-Culotte Nantais* on which Plucket served was equipped with 12 cannons and had a 20-strong crew.[73] But some of the privateers paid for by major private shipowners were much larger. Cruising in the Indian Ocean and the entrance to the Java Sea (the Sunda Strait was well known to corsairs), the *Cerf* carried 30 cannons and was manned by a 300-strong crew that included 150 musketeers.[74]

If the French Navy could not get the upper hand over the Royal Navy, French privateers achieved great success and played an important role in the war against Britain. The capture of British merchant shipping by French privateers inflicted significant damage on the enemy. For this reason, the government took a close interest in their activity. Indeed, during Truguet's time as minister the government-sponsored corsair frigates were actually organized into divisions so as to make them more effective and improve their chances against men-of-war. Combats were frequent, and the volumes of shipping captured were large. In his memoirs, Pierre-Edouard Plucket, privateering out of Dunkirk, gives a list of the prizes 'taken during one hundred and fifty-one days of cruising, minus seven port calls, in Holland and at Bergen in Norway, and twenty-five days of lying to on account of bad weather, in 1793, Years IV, V and VII of the French Republic… [during which he] joined and sustained five combats against battleships two or three times more heavily armed and… received four wounds'. During his time on four successive ships – the *Sans-Culotte Nantais*, the *Patriote de Brest*, the government corvette *Jalouse*, and the corsair *Résolue de Brest* – he captured 48 ships, sank or burned a further 19, drove 4 onto the coast, and boarded 59 neutral ships. The final total for Plucket's privateering activity was impressive: in all he had captured 8302 tons of shipping and 54 cannons, and taken 511 prisoners.[75]

Corsairs could also act as intelligence gatherers. The police report for Tuesday 5 June 1810 from Savary, the minister of police, to the Emperor explained how

> Monsieur Depaux, born at Le Havre, who was long a corsair captain, supplied important information about the Scheldt expedition. He observed from the start the progress the enemy was making. He counted in the shipyards the ships the enemy was building and the men he was recruiting. He continued to live at Middelbourg solely to examine what was happening there and to transmit potentially valuable information. After the English left, he went back to Ostend. The commissioner-general points out that Monsieur Depaux wishes to obtain the sea captain's certificate. This favour would reward his zeal and the services he has rendered.[76]

On privateers commissioned not by the government but by shipowners or merchants, the captains could either transport the prize on the privateer itself (when they released the ship) or, after noting in detail its composition and value, have it conveyed to the home port. Once the prizes reached port they were sold and the proceeds divided between the shipowner, the captain, and the crew, plus the share taken by the government. A captain always received more than other crew members, and in some cases the amount was agreed beforehand between him and the shipowner. In August 1812, when the Saint-Malo shipowners Thomazeaux and Amiel asked Angenard to take command of a three-master, the *Miquelonnaise*, he fixed his share of the profits in advance:

> They said that by accepting I would do them a great service and could define my conditions of service myself, which they agreed to in advance. This is what I asked for and obtained: I was to be free to leave the ship when I thought fit, I was to have 12 per cent for me and for my 11-year old son, 1.2 per cent of the net sale proceeds and a further 1.2 per cent of the gross proceeds from the sale of any prize

> I landed, assuming I had the good fortune to do this. The shipowners agreed to all these conditions and I was entered on the crew list as lieutenant and commanding officer.[77]

The government always took a share of the proceeds from prizes, and the 1793 decree providing for prizes to be shared out in full between crew members was far from being universally applied. In general, crews received around one-third of the value of captured cargoes. Angenard gives details of the payments for some of the prizes taken during his command of the three-master *Miquelonnaise* in the Channel in autumn 1812. In the 25 days it was at sea or 'cruising' it captured three merchantmen, a three-master coming from Jamaica (*Commerce*) with a cargo of two-thirds rum; a ship from Fernamboue (*Alfred*) carrying 1400 bales of cotton, 200 bottles of Madeira wine, 58 elephant's teeth, plus dried skins, dyewood, and 10,000 *piastres*; and lastly a sloop out of Guernsey (*Alerte*) with a cargo of sugar for Gibraltar. Angenard consigned his prizes to warehouses at Quimper belonging to an associate of the Saint-Malo shipowners, Fougeral, who organized their sale. The amounts thus raised were 430,000 francs for the *Commerce*, 2,600,000 francs for the *Alfred*, and 200,000 francs for the sloop. In each case, more than half went to the government. After payment of taxes, the shipowner was left with roughly 1,700,000 francs, and with 1,300,000 francs after payment of miscellaneous costs. Of this profit, one-third was shared between the 130 crewmembers. As for Angenard, his share of the prize money plus gratuities from the shipowners netted him roughly 34,000 francs.[78]

Terms were much less favourable for the 'corsairs of the Republic' operating on ships paid for in part by the government. All Plucket had to show for 10 years of privateering between 1793 and 1803 was a small annuity calculated on an estimated value of his ship of 30,000 francs (the government paid compensation for requisitioned ships), while for his share of the prizes taken he received securities worth barely 10,000 francs, a sum he considered so paltry that he turned it down and requested that it instead be paid to the civilian hospital of Dunkirk. His sense of disillusionment comes over strongly in his memoirs. Commenting on the decree passed by the Convention in 1793 to re-establish commerce raiding and its provision that prizes taken by the ships of the Republic be distributed in full (against one-third under the ancien régime) to the officers and crews of the capturing corsairs, he notes that it 'was truly a delusion. No doubt the *sans-culotte* Cincinnatus had far more important things to do than guarantee the future for the families of sailors who with their blood had defended the interests and glory of the French flag. That is why the commanders of government ships were not only never paid their emoluments but like me were awarded absolutely nothing for the prizes they captured.'[79] The peace concluded by the Treaty of Amiens put a stop to commerce raiding, and with his career as a corsair over Plucket decided to retire. He went to Napoleon to ask to be paid the sums he was due for his shipping prizes:

> Bonaparte replied... that as regards the prizes, the final accounts were not yet closed and all he could do was ask me to be patient. For five months I repeated my request, and every time I attended one of the meetings my wife urged me to accept what I was offered, until finally, wearied by it all, I decided to ask the First Consul to pay me what the government owed me for taking my ship. The figures used to calculate the payment were so cleverly arranged that, in return for an estimated value of thirty thousand francs, the Consulate's arithmeticians put me down for a pension worth two hundred and seventeen francs in the register of five-per cent consolidated stock, not to mention the six years of interest I was cheated out of, since the pension was paid only from 1 Vendémiaire of Year XII... I was also awarded, on account, for the estimated value of my shares in the prizes, ten thousand francs in securities, with a cash value of barely two hundred francs. I refused to accept this and suggested that it be donated to the civilian hospital of Dunkirk... If I had ever had any strong liking for republican governments, swindles like this would certainly have put me off forever.[80]

When prizes were small, however, and especially when corsairs were operating in distant waters far from France and the French authorities, there was a tendency for captains and crews to pilfer and take a share of what had been captured without informing the government or the shipowner. While cruising on the three-master the *Cerf* in Malaysian waters in 1793, Guillaume-Marie Angenard took part in the capture of six large proas (multihull sailing vessels) carrying cargoes from Europe and China. Angenard was among the crew members who went in boats to board the proas and ferry their cargo back to the privateer, in the course of which, he admits, he stole a small part of the booty for himself, like the other seamen: 'I did what I saw others doing. I pocketed various gold objects and a nice little pearl necklace that I sold in Mauritius.'[81]

IV. Conclusion

The maritime war of the revolutionary and Napoleonic era – less glorious and less successful for France than the war on land – had direct and far-reaching implications for French society and made a deep impression on public opinion. The war on land was spectacular in scale and extent, encompassing practically the whole of continental Europe, from southern Spain to the Russian steppes and from Italy to the Baltic. But the maritime war was a truly world war in the literal sense of the term: it extended over several seas and oceans and posed a threat to long-established trading relations in an increasingly integrated or 'global' world economic system, most notably in the colonial and Mediterranean markets.

War at sea, like war on land, moved closer to being 'total' in this period. Naval combat reached new levels of intensity and violence, a trend reinforced by the new practice of refusing surrender and taking the enemy in pursuit. Secondly, it required quantities and concentrations of men, ships, and materials on a massive scale. Finally, the war at sea now involved civilians, either through choice, as corsairs, or involuntarily, through exposure to the effects of the war on maritime trade. For a small number of privateers and speculators, the war at sea was an opportunity to amass large fortunes, but for the majority of civilians it was synonymous with hardship, crisis, and in some cases financial ruin.

In continental Europe, at least until the war in Spain, Napoleon accumulated a string of military successes. But he failed to defeat Britain at sea, despite committing to a vigorous policy of naval reconstruction. Furthermore, the indirect method conceived to destroy British foreign trade, by pitting land power against sea power in an economic blockade made possible by French domination over most of continental Europe and its resources, merely added to the economic difficulties of French ports and merchants. The study of the war at sea thus supplies a necessary corrective to the picture of the wars and conquests on land, by showing the weaknesses that characterized French military organization from the very start of the wars.

3
The Body in War

The changes in the art of war during this period – marked by increases in the number of battles and combatants, in the scale of these battles, and in their duration and geographical range (into the world beyond Europe) – were all elements in the transition from the old style of limited warfare to modern total war. One consequence of these changes was a huge increase in the numbers of sick and wounded, and hence in the pressure that was placed upon the army's medical services and medical personnel.

Any study of war needs to consider the history of the body. War, both on and off the battlefield, is above all else an experience of the human body, a physical ordeal. All attention, all interest focuses on the soldier's body – whether glorified and idealized in political and military propaganda, toughened by physical exercise, weakened by disease, injured or mutilated by wounds, rendered sublime in art and literature, examined and dissected by medical services, counted and classified by bureaucrats, inspected or standardized by military authorities, or debased and dehumanized by the enemy. The body also has a central place in the personal writings of combatants. Letters, diaries, notebooks, and memoirs all contain references to the various pressures upon the body (disease, fatigue, starvation), and to the people with a professional interest in the body – the doctors and surgeons – whether to praise their devotion and skill, or to denounce the ineptitude and corruption that characterized the administration of the army medical service.

For all this, however, the history of the body in war remains largely unwritten. Alain Corbin and Stéphane Audoin-Rouzeau have noted the wary attitude of many historians towards sensitive research topics such as the body, medicine, and violence.[1] In the last few years, military historians have shown renewed interest in the organization and functioning of military medical services and the particularities of wartime medicine. Characteristically though, the revolutionary and Napoleonic wars have been left behind in this historiographical movement which, except for physician-historian Jean-François Lemaire's thesis on the wounded of Napoleon's armies,[2] has concentrated on the wars of the Second Empire,[3] the Franco-Prussian War of 1870–1871,[4] and the principal conflicts of the twentieth century.[5]

Yet it is difficult to study the *experience* of war without addressing the topics of the body and medicine. Soldiers lived the battles and long marches 'in the flesh', and some of them would bear the physical traces of their participation in the conflict long after the war was over. This chapter is therefore devoted to the physical transformations that occurred during the conflict, to the individual and collective representations of the soldier's body (at times made to stand for the body politic as the nation), and to the development of an army medical service.

I. From the body of the soldier to the body of the nation: war and the body politic

The soldier's body was at times assimilated, consciously or unconsciously, into the body politic, the body of the nation itself. Soldiers had the representational function of embodying the nation in its revolutionary[6] and then imperial forms, a nation seeking through war to renew its vitality, youthfulness, and above all virility. To the moral qualities that bear the stamp of manliness (such as courage and prowess) were thus added visual elements. Physical criteria evoking virility and martial prowess were used to personify the state and the nation, in reaction against an ancien régime associated with decadence, degeneracy, effeminacy, and a crisis of masculine identity.

For this reason soldiers – men in the ranks as well as their commanders – had to be models of physical strength and beauty. In theory at least, recruitment and conscription only concerned young, able-bodied men of robust physical constitution. The effect of this selectivity, albeit incomplete, in the recruitment process was to drain the country of its most vigorous and strongest young men, while leaving in civilian society those whose bodies did not conform to the canons of the military ideal. A number of observers were struck by the changing profile of the 'typical' male body in France during the revolutionary and Napoleonic wars, by the visible scarcity of young men of good physical stature. Poumiès de la Sibourie, a young man from the Périgord who came to

Paris to study at the Faculty of Medicine in 1810, remarked on the large number of his fellow students who were hunchbacked, crippled, or otherwise disabled, adding that 'The same observation could be made in all classes of society. Conscription, voluntary enlistment, and the military academies have drawn off the strongest young men, leaving at home just the weak, the feeble, those unfit for military service.'[7]

After this initial selection, the process of constructing an ideal national masculine identity based on a physical valorization of the soldier's body was continued through military exercise, first in training camps, then during campaigns. The regime of marches and training had the effect of toughening and strengthening bodies. A gradual transformation took place in the physique of the young conscript or volunteer. Continual exposure to the elements, even in the bivouac, made him more tanned in complexion, more muscular, and also more resilient. Many soldiers in their writing use the image of the '*homme de fer*' (man of iron) when referring to those who had been through this regime of physical training in the field, through the school of war that educated and moulded the body. One of the most common themes in accounts of the physical transformations undergone by soldiers is that of the toughening and hardening of their bodies, principally for soldiers originating from towns and cities as opposed to those from the countryside. Men unused to hard manual labour, field work, or other bodily exertion now got their first taste of open-air life and intensive physical exercise. Many noted the coarsening and thickening effect this had on their skin – on the soft skin of the townsman's hands and feet. After the blisters and bleeding feet of the first few days, a protective covering of hard skin formed on the feet of young recruits, allowing them to put up with the heavy and ill-fitting shoes – if they had any – and daily marches.

The physical exercise imposed by the demands of war thus helped to define a new ideal for the national body politic, one associated with and embodied in the person of the soldier. His trained and toughened body evoked the Greek-warrior ideal of Antiquity and anticipated the figure of the regenerated male, healthy and athletic, used in the propaganda of both totalitarian[8] and democratic regimes (notably American democracy[9]) in the twentieth century, and that culminated in posters and other propaganda forms during the Second World War. Incarnating the nation as a whole, the heroic figure of the soldier acquired a symbolic status, and physical force and muscles – represented pictorially – are fundamental elements in this symbolic status, as Kenneth Dutton has shown.[10] This new celebration of a strong, athletic French soldier, officers and men alike, was far removed from the aesthetic norms and aristocratic culture of war that prevailed at the end of the ancien régime. In future, the soldier was expected to embody a revolutionary France newly charged with youthful vigour, virility, and strength. Another aspect of the birth of a body politic associated with national identity was that physical factors became predominant in the perception and description of the enemy, both civilians and soldiers. The enemy's body was observed, gauged, and compared with the Frenchman's, based on criteria of physical beauty, health, and the capacity to resist disease. Robust good health now mattered more than elegance, and physical attributes revealed an individual's inner character.

Accounts by French soldiers of the foreign countries they travelled through thus usually begin with a description of the inhabitants' physical appearance. A society's degree of civilization was judged by how it treated the human body: standards of hygiene and cleanliness, notions of beauty or ugliness, aesthetic sensibilities, ways of dressing, standards of reserve and immodesty, and the existence or absence of imposed rules, like wearing the veil in Egypt all assumed a new importance.

The collective representations that emerge from the accounts written by soldiers provide rich information both about their perceptions of foreigners and about the stereotypes they brought with them. In these writings, a country's economic and cultural backwardness, like the state of political despotism, is usually linked to the degeneracy of its population. Among the most harshly criticized populations are Russian Cossacks, Polish country dwellers, Italians from Calabria and lower-class Egyptians. Conversely, the peoples of western Europe who came closest to the French model in their material comfort, personal hygiene, and modes of dress – those in northern Italy and western Germany, male and particularly female town dwellers in Poland, the Dutch – are described in generally favourable terms, although the French are often held to be superior in matters of physical beauty and elegance.

By their perceptions and collective representations, these soldiers helped to delineate the contours of a national body politic, providing a base for uniting the country, for shaping its collective imagination and the patriotism that resulted. The French nation was refashioned and above all embodied in a bodily ideal defined through opposition to foreign bodies. Female representations played a key role in this process. Soldiers far from their home country sustained their morale and patriotism by elevating French womanhood to the status of an ideal that embodied female qualities of beauty, gentleness, elegance, and intelligence, and became a symbol and an object in the struggle between rival nations. More often than not, therefore, the comparison between the foreign female type and the French national ideal is to the advantage of the latter. At issue here is not reality itself, obviously irrelevant to these generalized and standardized forms based on dominant male and female types, but rather the unconscious political exploitation that accompanied the development of collective representations of womanhood.

The shift in the vision and judgement of soldiers, from a standpoint of 'anthropological' interest to one of political sociology, also appears clearly in the willingness to classify different peoples. The criteria used for classification are drawn from a variety of disciplines such as political geography, medicine, and sociology. Depending on the observer, the factors invoked to explain a state of physical inferiority, whether aesthetic or medical in form, are political (liberty or tyranny, democracy or despotism), economic (poverty or wealth), religious (belief or non-belief, type of religion), or geographical.

In the case of geography the distinctions made are of two sorts. The East–West contrast that some historians consider marks the transition to modernity in the mental cartography of Europeans in the nineteenth century had not yet completely replaced the older and more traditional North–South divide. What is novel in this field, however, is the existence of two radically different discourses on the North–South division. For some, the intellectual heirs of Montesquieu and *L'Esprit des lois*, the North still stood for progress and wealth, in comparison with a South that was poor, backward, and superstitious. For others, by contrast, the trend ran in the opposite direction, so that in future it is the nations in the south of Europe (and here France was presented as a southern country) that would embody the new values associated with a strong and healthy body. Dominique Larrey epitomized this new way of looking at the southern countries among certain elite groups, which contradicts the conventional view of late eighteenth century ideas. During the Russian campaign he noted that,

> other things being equal, the temperaments referred to as sanguine and hot are far more resistant to the action of this sedative agent [cold] than those designated by the generic term lymphatic. Thus death has been more sparing of individuals from Europe's southern countries than from the damp northern countries, like the Dutch, Hanoverians, the Prussians and other German peoples. The Russians themselves ... have lost, from this single cause, proportionally more men than the French.[11]

A few days later, in December 1812, he made his views clearer:

> I observed that, contrary to a widely held opinion, dark-haired subjects with a bilio-sanguine temperament, mostly from the southern countries of Europe, withstood the effects of this extreme cold better than fair-haired subjects of phlegmatic temperament who are mostly from the countries of the North. The former probably have a faster circulation and more energetic life forces; and their blood may well retain, even when exposed to the most intense cold, the principles of animal heat identified with its coloured component. By the same cause, their morale is stronger; their courage does not desert them; and by an intelligent concern for their self-preservation they are more adept at avoiding dangers than are the generally phlegmatic inhabitants of the cold and damp climates. Thus we saw the Dutchmen of the 3rd Regiment of Imperial Guard Grenadiers, comprising 1787 officers and men, perish almost to a man.... two years later, only 41 had returned to France... whereas the two other grenadier regiments, composed almost entirely of men born in the southern provinces of France, saved a fair number of their soldiers. Also, it is quite true that, in proportion to their number, German losses were far higher than the French.[12]

The author's argument, like the prejudices and stereotypes it reveals, is obviously wrongheaded and absurd. But it accurately conveys the reality behind the construction of a body politic, with the desire to see it embodied, in the literal sense, by the attribution of physical characteristics, and legitimized by use of supposedly impartial scientific arguments. The body of the soldier is now subsumed and becomes a key element of civilizational differences. The contrast between northern and southern Europe is embodied in two quite different physical types. The primacy accorded to the southern nations by Larrey – who came from the Pyrenees in south-west France – served to establish a geographical patriotism on a purportedly scientific basis.

The soldier's body could be defined in several ways: in comparison with or in opposition to that of the enemy, in contrast to that of civilians, or on its own terms, with no external reference. But however the body was defined, it had to uphold and embody the national identity, the body politic, and thus conform to the ideal.

This imperative is encountered in the writings of soldiers. François Vigo-Roussillon even observed a perverse effect related to the practice of recruiting generals primarily on physical criteria, namely that many ordinary soldiers came to equate physical beauty with ability. This misconception cast a shadow over Napoleon Bonaparte's arrival in Nice in Year IV:

> In the army of which he had just taken command, the initial impression of General Buonaparte was not very favourable. It was common at this time for generals to be chosen by the people's representatives. Their choice was determined more by physical qualities and outward appearance than by military ability, the value of which they were incapable of judging. So we were used to being led by handsome men and, as I said, our general wasn't much to look at. Some soldiers concluded from this that he had no military talent.[13]

Accounts penned by soldiers frequently contain descriptions praising the physique of the troops, but these must be treated with a degree of caution. The army registers show that the conscripts included many men who, but for the intense pressure to raise large troop numbers, ought to have been exempt from military service. Some were little more than children or youths, barely over 12 years of age. Their bodies were puny, and the hardships of military life aggravated the fragility of their incompletely formed bone structures and encouraged malformations.

In theory, conscription only applied to men aged over 18, raised to 20 by a *senatus consulte* issued by Napoleon in 1807 under pressure from Larrey. In practice, however, conditions were totally different. The escalating manpower requirements forced civilian and military authorities to relax the rules. An apology made to Montalivet by the prefect of the Lippe in August 1812 for failing to find any child over 12 in the poorhouses of his department gives an idea as to the application – or non-application – of the official lower age limit.

A similar slackness was observed in the medical examinations to decide conscripts' physical fitness for military service. After 1811 in particular, under the pressure of increased demands for manpower, the army accepted numbers of wounded and maimed men into its ranks. Still, feebler and less robust conscripts were only a minority, and some of the more youthful among them, once their bodies had been altered and strengthened by the army's regime of compulsory physical exercise, would go on to play their part in identifying the nation with the ideal of the militarized body.

The soldier's healthy and robust body offered a mirror in which the nation found the self-image it sought. But bodies like this were mostly to be found in the garrisons and camps, on the 'easy' campaigns, and of course in propaganda. In gruelling campaigns, like the expedition to Egypt and the Russian campaign, the situation was utterly different. Then, maintaining soldiers in a healthy and vigorous state was made difficult by the privations of military life, disease, wounds, and weight loss caused by a lack of food and water. In the section of his memoirs recounting the retreat from Moscow, Sergeant Bourgogne compares the physical appearance of regiments that had spent time in a garrison with that of regiments worn down by the long march and shortages. 'We saw a detachment of around thirty men, sappers and pontooneers. I recognized them as those we took at Orcha, where they were garrisoned. This detachment... had been with us for only four days and had not suffered. That is why they looked vigorous', he notes, and then compares them with the weakened and often disfigured bodies of the survivors from the retreat:

> The first to appear were generals, a few still on horseback but most on foot, along with a lot of other senior officers... who, after three days, had practically ceased to exist, so to speak. Those coming on foot were dragging along with difficulty, nearly all with frozen feet wrapped in rags or pieces of sheepskin, and dying of hunger.... Next came the Emperor, on foot and carrying a staff.... Then followed over thirty thousand men, almost all with frozen feet and hands, some without weapons... They would have been incapable of using them.[14]

The retreat from Moscow brought the total collapse of imperial propaganda, putting an end to the celebration of the French soldier's moral and physical virtues, to the construction of a body politic identified with the soldier's body, and to hopes of regenerating the nation by a reassertion of masculinity. There was nothing new, of course, about the sight of soldiers who were wounded, sick, crippled, disfigured, or physically weakened, but in this campaign the spectacle was on a vast scale. In the words of soldiers at the time, all that remained of the Grand Army was a pitiful hotchpotch of the 'debris' of former regiments. The accounts that filtered back to civilians in France shocked and demoralized the public. And the soldiers themselves, while concerned primarily with their own survival, were painfully affected by the disintegration of the physical ideal with which Napoleon, his army, and the men serving in it were associated. It is with true feeling that Bourgogne describes the feelings of sadness and demoralization that came over one of his companions when he saw this group of unrecognizable survivors:

> My dear Picart, who had not seen the army for a month, watched all this without saying anything. But his involuntary movements showed quite clearly what he was feeling. On several occasions he struck his rifle butt on the ground, and his fist against his chest and forehead. I saw large tears run down his cheeks and fall onto his moustache from where icicles were hanging. Then, turning to me, 'I don't know whether I am asleep or awake. I am crying at the sight of our Emperor walking, on foot, with a staff in his hand...'[15]

II. The human experience of wounds and illness in war

Unlike in some later conflicts, battle was not the principal cause of losses during the revolutionary and Napoleonic wars. As in centuries past, victims of disease still greatly outnumbered combat deaths. The Italian War of 1859 was the first war in which deaths from combat exceeded deaths from disease. Thereafter this pattern became more accentuated, so that in World War I, while disease still claimed large numbers, wartime death was overwhelmingly a violent death on the battlefield. Mortality from disease represented only one-sixth of military losses in 1914–1918.[16] There is uncertainty over the total number of deaths in the revolutionary and Napoleonic wars. Jean-Paul Bertaud puts at between 320,000 and 400,000 the number of dead for the period 1794–1797.[17] Most of these military losses occurred not on the battlefield but in the hospitals. Losses in the 2nd Battalion of the Ille-et-Vilaine in 1793 were 18.3 per cent but only 4 per cent actually died in combat. In the district of Mamers, two-thirds of the citizens killed in the war between 1794 and 1797 died in hospital from disease or as a result of their wounds. Although records were not always kept scrupulously up to date, the few extant statistics for hospital mortality show the numerical superiority of disease over wounds as cause of death. Thus fever, scabies, and venereal disease accounted for 68 per cent of deaths at the Hôpital de Béziers in September 1793.[18] The figures for the Hôpital de Nantes in 1794 are more or less identical: 30–40 per cent of wounded among all deaths, depending on the week, hence 60–70 per cent of deaths from disease.[19] The primacy of deaths from disease or as a result of wounds compared with deaths in action is confirmed by an overall estimate for the revolutionary and Napoleonic wars, for all the belligerent nations, prepared by a historian of medicine in 1922, which puts at 2.5 million the number of combatants who died in hospitals, and 150,000 the number killed in action.[20]

Battle alone was not responsible for military losses under enemy fire. Large numbers of soldiers wounded in combat would have survived had they received treatment, but help did not always reach the wounded on the battlefield in time. François Vigo-Roussillon noted in his campaign diary for 28 Germinal Year V, after the battle of Neumarck, that 'a large proportion of the wounded ... perished in the woods because they were not evacuated and treated.'[21]

Military medicine by its nature is more urgent than civilian medicine, yet all too often the wounded were left for long periods without treatment. At best they would be collected up the next day, as happened after the battle of Lutzen on 2 May 1813.[22] Some lay for hours in agony before dying from their wounds, where more prompt medical attention might have saved them.

By not going immediately to the help of men who fell on the battlefield, soldiers and medical crews were obeying orders and official directives. The orders in this respect were particularly strict during the Empire. So as to avoid dispersing the fighting troops, it was forbidden to help wounded soldiers while the fighting continued. This pitiless policy was strongly criticized by some soldiers, who pointed to its impact on the plight of the wounded. In May 1809 Jacquin noted in his campaign diary that, 'An order of the day stipulated that no soldier was allowed to quit his rank in order to help a wounded man; we were forced to leave them on the battlefield ...'[23]

But these orders could also be justified on safety grounds. When soldiers went to help the wounded under enemy fire they could not be certain of reaching the ambulances safe and sound. Chevallier records how, during the battle of Wagram,

> In one hour we lost ... a hundred and fifty men wounded and twenty-five killed. Those who were unhorsed or wounded and fled across the plain were in even greater danger. How many times did I see foot soldiers carrying a wounded officer, and the number of projectiles that ripped up the plain in all directions killed both the wounded and those carrying them.[24]

Another important cause of post-battle mortality in some campaigns was the leaving behind of the sick and wounded by an army on the move. The decision to do so would be taken because of a lack of carts or other suitable means of conveyance, but it was often also due to orders from on high. The priority that Napoleon gave to speedy troop movements meant that the local military authorities often had to leave behind – in campaign garrisons – men who were unfit to march.[25] Some soldiers did not conceal the indignation they felt about such pitilessly harsh orders. Helping the wounded was expressly forbidden while fighting raged, but also even at times when there was no fighting, so as not to slow the progress of the armies. The logic that applied was entirely and purely utilitarian. Selection of the wounded to be helped by being transported in convoys and in ambulances at the rear, or, alternatively, those to be abandoned to the care – or vengeance – of the enemy, was made on a criterion of efficacy, namely whether they could still be of use to the army, in service, once they recovered. Men whose wounds required an amputation were thus put at the bottom of the list. Octave Levavasseur witnessed one such scene after the battle of Friedland, when travelling on the road to Poland. 'I noted on many occasions that the Emperor…had no humanitarian feelings. One day, in the rear, some soldiers were carrying their wounded officer in front of him. "Will he be crippled?" he asked as he passed. "Yes, Sire", was the reply. "Right then, have the men return to their companies", he told the officers around him, so these fine soldiers were forced to deposit their wounded man on the ground and go back to their company.'[26] Wounded men abandoned in such circumstances would probably die of hunger or else be captured and possibly killed by the enemy, notably at the hands of the Cossacks during the Russian campaign.

Wounding was not the only or even the greatest danger faced by soldiers in these wars. Epidemics of disease had an enormous impact and caused heavy losses in the army's ranks. Statistics are again scarce, but according to a credible estimate made by an American historian in 1935, in the months before the battle of Leipzig in 1813 the French Army lost 105,000 dead through combat (on the battlefield or as a result of their wounds) compared with 219,000 to disease.[27] The biggest killers were the infectious diseases, of which the most virulent and lethal were the fever epidemic in Saint Domingue in 1801–1803 and the bubonic plague during the campaign in Egypt and Syria. But Europe did not escape, and soldiers in campaigns in central and eastern Europe, in particular, repeatedly fell victim to a range of infectious diseases including influenza, malaria, and typhus and typhoid fever.

Disease inspired particular fear therefore, often more so than battle and its consequences. Antoine Bravard, a young soldier enrolled in the Alpine Legion, noted in a letter of 26 September 1794, written from Dalhunden: 'Ever since I have been in this accursed country, nearly all the soldiers have been ill. Our battalion had 1,500 men, of whom only 250 are left, all the rest are in the hospitals.'[28] Similar comments can be found in nearly all soldiers' writings. Here is what Fricasse noted in his campaign diary for 22 Thermidor Year IV (8 August 1795) in the Vauban fort at Benheim:

> On account of the bad air in this fort, the whole battalion and the other two as well, fell ill; it was like a plague. As many as ten men in each company had to go to the hospital...they were smitten by a violent fever. Of the sixty men who were in our company, only two of us did not end up sick. The fever was a bad one...many died from it.[29]

In these two examples, disease is due essentially to an unhealthy climate or to bad drinking water. Lack of clean drinking water and consumption of brackish or contaminated water were responsible for many diseases, notably dysentery. During the war in Spain, Brun de Villeret observed that, 'Consumed by thirst and exhausted by fatigue, the soldiers deployed in this raging hot climate threw themselves with an unrestrainable force upon the fountains and freshwater streams that are so numerous in these regions. This led to appalling diseases, and at the end of each expedition, our hospitals were always brimming over.'[30]

The outbreak of any particularly contagious and deadly epidemic increased soldiers' fears even further. Larrey diagnosed the first case of bubonic plague in the winter of 1798 in Cairo. The epidemic then spread. During the spring campaign of 1799 in Syria, up to 15 men died daily.[31] Nearly 10,000 men (out of about 40,000 men in total) died during the Egyptian campaign, many of them of bubonic plague.[32]

This epidemic disease thus prompted reactions of terror among the military. One officer who was in Alexandria during the bubonic plague epidemic wrote, with a wry sense of humour, that after reports spread about the large number of plague deaths in Alexandria, French soldiers elsewhere in the country, hunting down Murad Bey's troops in Upper Egypt, were more frightened of catching the disease through the arrival of French troops from Alexandria than they were of enemy fire: 'They are more afraid of us', he noted, 'than of the Mamelukes.'[33] This is a view confirmed by many other soldiers. At Aboukir, in late January 1799, Louis Thurman wrote in his journal, 'We no longer meet, or if so with suspicion...When we do get together, which only happens for urgent business, we stand in a circle, several metres away from each other. Directives, orders and letters are sprinkled with vinegar and handled with wooden tongs.'[34] At Acre, in May 1799, Charles François (a volunteer soldier) writes in his diary about the 'dark terror' which overwhelms him at the sight of the spread of the epidemics of bubonic plague.[35]

This fear also extended to military doctors, so that Napoleon eventually issued a decree or order of the day in January 1799 stating 'Any health officer abandoning a first-aid station in battle or refusing to care for patients who might carry a contagious disease shall be arrested, tried by a military tribunal, and judged according to the law dealing with deserters. Whatever his station, no Frenchman shall fear death.' This order of the day was strengthened by a decree passed by Napoleon later on, denouncing surgeon Boyer, in post at Alexandria, for being 'coward enough to refuse his services to patients who had had contact with supposedly contagious cases'. The sentence was particularly harsh: 'He shall be dressed as a woman, paraded through the streets of Alexandria on a donkey with a sign on his back saying "Afraid to die, unworthy of being a Frenchman". After that, he shall be sent back to France [...] and deprived of his citizenship.'[36]

Another epidemic disease that took a heavy toll among soldiers in these wars was yellow fever, which large numbers caught during the campaign in Saint-Domingue (1801–1803). In order to reconquer the former French colony lost during the slave rebellion or Haitian Revolution led by Toussaint Louverture in 1797, and to fulfil the wishes of French settlers lobbying in Paris,[37] Napoleon decided to launch a campaign in 1801 headed by his brother-in-law, Charles Victor Emmanuel Leclerc. In addition to the hardships of combat and of the guerrilla warfare waged by Toussaint's army, the French sailors and military were faced with a lethal epidemic disease, yellow fever, transmitted by mosquitoes. The number of men claimed by this epidemic was extremely high, due to the fact that French physicians did not know how to cure it and had no real idea of its causes and sometimes of its contagious character. According to the French chief medical officer on the island, Nicolas-Pierre Gilbert, over half of the military pharmacists in post there and the majority of the military surgeons died of yellow fever during the campaign, along with numerous soldiers and officers. Death rates only increased, since soldiers admitted to the hospital at Le Cap had to share the same bed, in spite of the highly contagious nature of the yellow fever.[38] The French lost 35,000 men in all during the Caribbean campaign, both in Guadeloupe and in Saint-Domingue, most of them to yellow fever.[39] In Saint-Domingue alone, out of the 36,000 men of the whole military force of this expedition, only 3000 men were still alive in the spring of 1803,[40] and many of the losses were due to the epidemic disease. The yellow fever was all the more frightening as it was very sudden. The 14-year-old trainee sailor Christophe-Paulin de la Poix Fréminville recalls the feeling of terror that took hold of him and of the rest of the crew on board the *Intrépide* on the outbreak of this epidemic disease when they arrived in Saint-Domingue in 1801:

> Three quarters of the crew were struck. The scourge was violent. I saw sailors manning the yards, cheerful and healthy, feel suddenly hit by a violent headache, get down hastily and faint suddenly at the bottom of the mast. They started to rave in the boat on their way to the hospital. The following day, they were dead.[41]

Not only was this disease sudden, it was also lethal. The 28-year-old captain Joseph Elysée Peyre-Ferry mentioned in his memoirs the shock produced by the sight of his battalion reduced from 1400 or 1500 men on arrival in Saint-Domingue in February 1802 to 22 men in January 1803: 'Our beautiful battalion [...] has completely vanished. All those who did not die in combat fell to disease. There are still a few men left in the hospitals but they are likely to follow their mates very soon [...] It would be hard to describe the pain that I felt [...] I could not make a step to go and observe the sad and miserable remains of this superb battalion.'[42]

However, the most common disease affecting the army at this time was in fact dysentery, which, though seemingly benign and without visible after-effects, could have fatal consequences when accompanied by acute diarrhoea. The disease often resulted from drinking unclean or infected water, and the main centres for outbreaks were the countries that experienced severe droughts and water shortages – Spain, Italy, and, in the summer, eastern Europe. Although dysentery did not have the fearsome connotations of plague or typhus and left the soldier's physical appearance unscathed, it was no less dangerous. Unless they made a quick recovery or received medical attention (preferably in a hospital), men with dysentery found themselves in a similar position to wounded amputees. By severely restricting their mobility, the illness prevented them from keeping up with the advancing army. Condemned to stay in the rear, they were vulnerable to attack from partisan fighters and enemy forces, and were often unable to get enough supplies to fend for themselves by marauding.

Experience of wounds or disease was thus an integral part of the experience of war. Disease commonly inflicted heavier mortality rates than battle, and frequently had after-effects of comparable severity and permanence. Just as those wounded in battle carried the memory of it in their flesh, through disfigurement or amputation, so victims of serious illnesses were often marked physically by their ordeal. Soldiers who witnessed the ravages of disease could sustain an emotional trauma almost as powerful as 'shell shock' during battle. Some diseases produced a brutal transformation, changing victims beyond recognition, causing physical degeneration (loss of hair, loss of fingers, dramatic weight loss), and even dehumanization.

In his memoirs, Sergeant Faucheur conveys the horror of the conditions created in some German cities in 1813 by typhus (known as the 'typhus of the armies' because it was caught in the hospitals on the banks of the Elbe and then spread by wounded or sick soldiers evacuated to France). At Mainz all the public buildings had been turned into hospitals, but the doctors were still unable to halt the disease. Between November 1813 and May 1814 it claimed the lives of nearly one-third of the civilian population, and mortality among soldiers was even higher, estimated at two-thirds of the garrison. Death became an everyday spectacle. Daily – and twice a day at the peak of the epidemic – men with carts went through the city's streets to remove the bodies of soldiers that were left on the pavement by the civilians on whom they had been billeted so as to facilitate their collection and avoid contamination of the house. Faucheur, who was stationed at Mainz during the epidemic, received orders to inspect the hospitals and give whatever material help he could to the sick men from his company. The sight he beheld was as shocking as that on a battlefield, though for different reasons. Violence was done to healthy bodies on the battlefield, but bodies were also transformed by the ravages of disease. Faucheur noted:

> I was witness to a truly harrowing sight, for at every step I had before my eyes the dead and dying, and men so altered by disease as to be barely recognizable... When recovering, the rare survivors of the terrible typhus exhibited distinctive marks of the disease that had struck them down. Many had gangrene of the extremities, particularly the toes; the eyes of all were glazed over and unnaturally staring, and the facial skin was so wrinkled that the lips were drawn back, revealing the teeth; they had lost their hair, or what little remained of it appeared dead.

During these wars, disease killed hundreds of thousands of soldiers (and civilians) in the same random fashion as battle, and it engendered the same sense of arbitrariness and vulnerability. But although battle and disease were both occasions to confront death, the experience of wounding or death in combat and the experience of disease are quite different, and this difference is apparent in how soldiers describe them in their writings. The effects of disease on the body, and the emotional shock caused by the sight of desperately ill men, are unlike those associated with combat. In particular, deaths from disease were perceived as unjust and meaningless, being invested with none of the sentiments of honour, patriotism, glory, or bravura that many soldiers held dear. Faucheur's account of visiting the hospitals in Mainz concludes with an eloquent statement of the difference between death in combat and death from disease and how this affects the manner in which they are interpreted and understood.

> Since becoming a soldier I had seen many dead men, I had slept on battlefields strewn with dead bodies, amidst the wounded and the dying, but never had I felt such anguish as during this wretched inspection. Death had spared no one: doctors, nurses, hospital workers, every group had paid its tribute to the dreadful disease, and all without the smoke of glory, the noise of cannon, the smell of powder, or the inebriation of victory.[43]

In some cases disease caused temporary or permanent memory loss and an impairment of mental faculties. This was the painful experience of Louis Bégos who fell victim to Spanish fever in 1808 at Elvas:

> From the start of hostilities I went down with a fever so debilitating that my memory went completely. While I was convalescing I was like a child, I acquired curious caprices that no one dared to refuse, I became totally bald, and for a long while they despaired for my sanity and my recovery.[44]

The young Swiss officer went on to make a full recovery and suffered no lasting after-effect from his illness. But not all soldiers were so lucky. Large numbers of participants in the Egyptian expedition suffered loss of vision through outbreaks of eye disease (desert ophthalmia) and cataracts caused by the sun's rays reflecting off the sand. This loss of vision was sometimes temporary (lasting between 1 and 2 months), but it could also become permanent and definitive.[45] Many came home from the war blind. On 28 January 1799, for example, Bonaparte warns General Berthier that he had to send over 200 French soldiers back to France because they had become blind.[46]

Being wounded was a no less grim experience. To the physical suffering from the wound and the surgical operation (performed in non-existent antiseptic conditions with primitive instruments) was added fear of the possibly permanent consequences. In cases of severe combat wounds, the key question for the victim and medical services alike was whether or not it was necessary to amputate. Even when suffering great pain and with their lives in danger, soldiers usually resisted the idea of amputation, especially of the leg since that would leave them with restricted mobility. How to avoid amputation by means of alternative medical procedures was thus one of the challenges facing military medicine during the revolutionary and Napoleonic wars, as indeed in later conflicts. Amputation was not the automatic choice and was in fact the last resort. François Vigo-Roussillon received a bullet in the leg during the battle of San Giorgio di Mantua on 28 Fructidor Year IV, and in his campaign diary he records the relief he felt on hearing the surgeon announce 'he will not be crippled.'[47]

Dominque Larrey instances several cases of severe wounding where he successfully avoided amputation. One such was General de Sparre, wounded during the final invasion of France.

> This was one of the cases where amputation seemed appropriate, yet since the fibula and muscles of the rear part of the limb were intact, I conceived the hope of saving his leg. I first lay open the wound; I removed the largest bone splinters, and reduced the wound to the simplest possible state. Then I applied a bone-setting device, and had the general transported to Paris, which he reached without suffering any setback; nor did any occur in the course of the illness, and he was guided towards a particularly successful recovery since today he can walk without crutches.[48]

Amputation was avoidable when the wound was not too severe and above all when infection had not had time to spread into the rest of the limb or into the rest of the body. Prompt surgery was thus indispensable, used in conjunction with specific techniques and instruments, notably a bone-setting device.[49]

All too often, though, amputation was judged necessary and did have to be performed, in some cases against the wishes of the patient. It was widely practised by surgeons in the war, some of whom – Larrey foremost among them – had understood the importance of swift amputation in military medicine to save lives. Statistics on this matter are rare, but as an example, in the battle of Craonne on 7 February 1814, the French had 1000–1200 wounded, a quarter of them seriously, and of the latter, 90 (roughly 10 per cent of the total wounded and around 40 per cent of the most severely wounded) had to have one or more limbs amputated.[50]

Once it was found necessary to amputate, the main question was how much of the uninjured limb to remove. So that the wounded man could recover a more or less normal life, and in particular be able to walk using a wooden leg, surgeons sought to cut the limb as close as possible to the wound and ideally below the knee. But this was not always possible, despite demands from patients. Thus Dominique Larrey cites the case of General de la Ferière, whose foot was shot away by a cannon ball in 1814:

> The wounded man recognized, as did several surgeon-majors present at the ambulance, the need for immediate amputation, and he told me of his desire that it be done on the lower leg. I refused to comply with his views, since I knew from experience...that this amputation was seldom successful and offered no real advantage over that practiced at the location recommended by all the experts, and I had drawn a line slightly higher. So I chose the latter...General de la Ferière is fully recovered, though the dislocation and movement of these two bone fragments cause him discomfort and pain when in motion.[51]

III. Healing mars: medical services and military medicine

The new art of warfare that developed in this period – with its emphasis on offensive shock, massive battles, and quick victory – produced an exponential increase in military casualties compared with wars of earlier times. Yet save for a small number of technical improvements, mainly the work of a few determined and skilful physicians and surgeons whose names have gone down in history, neither the organization of army medical services nor the practice of military medicine underwent any far-reaching change. Many hospitals were poorly run and suffered from appalling standards of hygiene, medicines and dressings were lacking, and doctors and nurses were too few in number and not always properly trained.

After being wounded in the retreat from Louvain in March 1793, Claude Simon described in a letter to a friend the failings he had observed in the functioning of the military hospitals:

> Perhaps you are thinking that on reaching Mons, after a twenty-four hour march, in a cart that finished off the job of breaking my head

> and body, they would have dressed my wounds and cared for me. Well not a bit of it, my friend! I could find no surgeon to dress my wounds, nor any bed to sleep in; I was told I would have to go on as far as Valenciennes. On the point of giving up the ghost, I begged and pleaded and was eventually given an awful mattress on the floor and a little hot water that they called soup. Barely ten minutes after they laid me on my mattress the order came to evacuate and I was taken and unceremoniously thrown into a wagon used for carrying the army's bread. Along with 11 wretched officers, all crippled or wounded, there I was off again, wounds still not bandaged, thrown about in that cursed wagon as no hanged man ever was, enduring agonies for the twelve hours of the wretched journey from Mons to Valenciennes, where at the third hospital they condescended to take me in. Even then I could see myself being sent off to Peronne. But compassion – and my money – won over the hearts of the nurses charged with transporting the wounded, and they quickly set me up with a bed that I have not left since getting here on the 25th.[52]

The increase in combatant numbers was not matched by a proportionate rise in the number of physicians, surgeons, and nurses.

By the end of the ancien régime, French military hospitals that had been subject to major and positive reforms under Louis XIV were in a state of indescribable chaos. Attempts to modernize the military medical service in 1772 and 1788 had dismantled the old structure but failed to put anything in its place. In 1790, the National Assembly reorganized it provisionally, and in 1792 France had about 4000 physicians, surgeons, and assistants. During the first 18 months of the war, however, this total was sharply reduced, when some 600 doctors were lost in or as a result of battle. To make up for these losses, the National Assembly passed a series of laws aimed at attracting new recruits. Medical officers were given greater autonomy, in particular freeing them from the direct supervision of field commanders (a supervision that was subsequently re-established). These measures, combined with the patriotic and republican enthusiasm and a desire for more medical experience, attracted many young medical students to enrol as volunteers. By January 1793, the French armies had some 2750 physicians and surgeons. But the effect of this measure was shortly nullified by the decree of August 1793 that put all men between the ages of 18 and 40, including physicians, surgeons, medical students, and pharmacists, on the reserve list, and hence liable for active military service.

Extending conscription for the line army to men with a medical training exacerbated the shortage of medical personnel in the armies. Understaffing reached critical levels with dangerous consequences for delivery of care. At the hospital of Pezenas in Year II, the ratio was 1 nurse for 50 patients, and this was a far from isolated case, as was observed by numerous soldiers who had had to stay in a hospital at one point or another of their time in the army. François Vigo-Roussillon, conveyed to the hospital of Mantua with a serious leg wound after the battle of San Giorgio di Mantua on 28 Fructidor Year IV, was lucky enough to be treated immediately by a surgeon. But he noted that many other soldiers were less fortunate and that 'there were, alas, so many wounded that many perished because their wounds were not dressed.'[53] Besides making it impossible to treat all patients, lack of medical personnel also had disastrous consequences for enforcing the rules of hygiene.

The situation improved little thereafter. The founding text organizing the army medical service was the decree of 18 Vendémiaire Year X (10 October 1801). It provided for a loose structure with fixed medical categories (members of the medical council, teachers, hospital physicians, physicians of the Imperial Guard, available physicians, army surgeons, surgeons of the Imperial Guard, surgeons of the gendarmerie, hospital surgeons, hospital pharmacists, pharmacists of the Imperial Guard), but the size of the categories could vary with the number of regiments in the army and depending on the campaign. In 1801, when the decree was issued, the medical corps (excluding the subaltern categories of health officers and nurses) comprised a total of 843 health professionals including 40 physicians, 650 surgeons, and 125 pharmacists. These figures changed over time, but the entire period down to 1815 was characterized by a numerical shortfall of medical personnel relative to needs, combatant numbers, number of battles, and the factors encouraging the outbreak of epidemics. For example, from 489 in 1801, the number of army surgeons was down to 351 in 1806 (several having been killed in the great battles like Austerlitz). By 1812, numbers had risen considerably (113 physicians, 824 surgeons, and 360 pharmacists) but were still less than was needed to receive and attend to the sick and wounded in the disastrous Russian campaign just about to begin. One year later, after the retreat from Moscow, the number had fallen sharply again due to losses through death, being wounded, or taken prisoner. Of 1300 physicians, surgeons, and pharmacists with the armies in early 1812, fewer than 600 (275 surgeons, 34 physicians, 280 pharmacists) were left by 1813. To remedy this situation, a decree establishing renewal of medical personnel by conscription was issued in early 1813. To recruit a total of 120 physicians, slightly more than 400 surgeons and 400 trained assistants, the prefect in each department was required to recruit one physician, four surgeons, and three attendants (circulars of April and May 1813). In practice, however, this directive proved impossible to apply. If recruiting medical assistants from the hospitals and faculties of medicine was relatively easy, finding fully trained and proficient physicians and surgeons, necessarily older than the assistants given their long studies, who were prepared to leave everything to join the army, was much harder. Many of those designated by a prefect proved recalcitrant, not hesitating to resort to desertion, and it must be remembered that the news reaching France of the retreat from Moscow did nothing to encourage candidates for the military life.[54]

Besides shortages of manpower, another common problem, especially at the lower levels of the medical hierarchy (health officers and nurses), was deficient knowledge and training. Many of the doctors and surgeons who volunteered for the army were advanced in years, or else they were incompetent and, spurned by civilian patients in France, forced to seek an alternative source of income in the army medical service. Doctors with established practices were less than enthusiastic at the prospect of abandoning their patients for an unknown length of time and going to lead a nomadic and dangerous life. Attracting trained, qualified, and competent personnel was made more difficult by the dismally low standing of the army medical services, a cause of bitter complaint from doctors and especially surgeons all through the revolutionary and Napoleonic wars. They suffered from the negative image and from the prejudice against medicine and mistrust of doctors shared by Napoleon and many officers at this period. Poorly paid, kept on the sidelines, denied status within the military organization and the prestige that went with it (promotion, rank, epaulettes), the medical officers were, to use the words of the pharmacist Blaze, in the lowest class, the fourth class of the army, which commanded neither glory nor wealth:

> Health officers, physicians, pharmacists, surgeons,... are the luckless members of this last class. Health officers frequently share the same dangers as soldiers while getting none of their glory. They are held in the same contempt as non-combatants while having none of their advantages... On several occasions the General Inspectors of the Medical Service have put forward a project to improve the standing of this corps – so respectable yet so little respected – but their efforts have produced no result... In 1814, it was proposed to

> change their uniform and award them epaulettes. Sadly, this project was rejected. I say sadly, because they would have been far more satisfied with this concession than with increased pay. The right to wear epaulettes would have given them the esteem they are denied and to which they attach great importance.... Ask [a marshal of France] if he thinks health officers should wear epaulettes. He will reply in the negative, and will even add that such people are of no use to an army, and, if he is in good health, will send them all to the devil.[55]

In the lower ranks, the health officers and assistants generally had only a superficial medical training, lasting barely 1 or 2 years. During the Revolution, military medicine attracted many young students, for whom the campaign hospitals offered a more useful and effective training than the civilian faculties of medicine that were completely disorganized by the revolutionary turmoil. These young students, short on practical experience, viewed a spell in the army as a school, as a means of acquiring the necessary experience that on their return would allow them to set up as doctors or surgeons in French towns. Far from having a professional training, they expected to learn on the job, and so it was working with apprentices who had only a limited knowledge of medicine that the doctors and nurses had to treat complex wounds and diseases. In later years, when civilian medical training had been reorganized, health officers and medical assistants no longer gave training as their reason for choosing the army. The main reason now was the desire to avoid military conscription that was becoming more pressing and less selective in its demands and thus, for many young men, increasingly hard to avoid. In addition, the cost of replacement, whereby a man designated for service by ballot could pay someone else to serve in his stead, rose sharply (from 3000 francs in 1807 to 5000 in 1813). The army medical service became a favoured choice for many middle-class families with enough money to send their son to a medical school. Shortly after entering medical school, a student could anticipate the conscription call-up by enrolling as a health officer or orderly, reasoning that, if going off to war was unavoidable, it was preferable to do so in what appeared less dangerous conditions, with the non-combatants.

To perform its work, the army medical staff relied on nurses for help with such tasks as transporting the wounded to the ambulances and the hospital, and caring for them once they had been admitted and had received attention from doctors and surgeons. But the medical service was not allowed to deplete the ranks of the combat forces, so doctors and surgeons could select their nurses only from among renegades (soldiers rejected because of acts of cowardice, such as attempted desertion), prisoners, or service soldiers (invariably disowned by combatant troops). Soldiers who had spent time in hospital tended to be highly critical of these nurses, judging them to be incompetent or dishonest. In May 1809, after the battle of Essling, Jacquin noted in his campaign diary:

> There were battalions of nurses who followed the army's movements to attend to the wounded. Some of these nurses, it was noted, were thoroughly bad specimens, most being only interested in robbing the dead and even the wounded, taking their money if they had any. The wounded men were not much better treated at the ambulance and in the hospitals. Surgeons were often seen to bleed wounded men who were to be amputated, while others after being amputated and transported to hospitals nearly all died just as they thought they were cured.[56]

Under-strength, sometimes poorly trained and inexperienced, and with inadequate support staff, army doctors and surgeons had to contend with the additional difficulty of being administered by non-combatant military authorities, the war commissioners. Soldiers despised the commissioners without exception for their incompetence, their absenteeism (particularly during battles), and above all for their corruption. Accusations of malpractice, including illegal transactions such as sales of food and medicines, were commonplace; often they were justified and on several occasions fraudulent acts by commissioners were proved. And while the war commissioners attracted deep hostility from officers and men alike, most army doctors and surgeons were well-liked and widely respected figures. Kerkhove, a Dutch doctor serving in the French Army, noted that

> it was mainly the war commissioners, employees in food stores and hospitals that the soldiers wouldn't tolerate in their bivouacs. They insulted them continually and chased them away pitilessly. Perhaps they were right to do so, for most of these employees deserved their indignation. But if, in this dreadful situation, soldiers displayed their resentment towards the people who had given them reason for complaint, they were generally well-disposed and on occasions indeed grateful towards the doctors and surgeons, even though at this dire time they had little hope of benefiting from the healing arts. They

> frequently said: the doctors have always taken an interest in us, they have only been good to us.[57]

This impression is confirmed by a study of soldiers' writings.[58]

In addition to problems of personnel and administrative control, one of the biggest difficulties facing physicians and surgeons was lack of resources. Shortage of medical supplies was endemic throughout these wars but was particularly acute during the Napoleonic period, a fact that some historians have attributed to Napoleon's distrust of medicine. Medical supplies were heavy and slowed the movement of convoys, and perhaps for this reason were not always available in sufficient quantities. Some were even lacking completely. A case in point was quinine, at this time the best remedy against fever, but which could not be imported into France and hence was unavailable.[59]

Army medical personnel also had to contend with a shortage of dressings and bandages. This was particularly worrying because of the disastrous implications for hygiene. It was not unusual for the same linen or lint to be used on several different soldiers in succession, and although the most conscientious physicians and surgeons washed them – or saw to it that they were washed – in reality these basic rules of hygiene and asepsis were by no means always respected. The urgency of the treatment and the sheer number of wounded requiring it meant that the washing of linen was necessarily perfunctory and rapid. When even supplies of used linen ran out, the medical personnel had to rely on ingenuity and improvisation and replace them with whatever materials came to hand, such as straw, wood, and paper. Belgian grenadier Henri Scheltens referred to these alternative practices during the Russian campaign, specifically after the battle of Valoutina: 'It was here that I saw the wounded being bandaged with hay and with paper from the old archives of Smolensk.'[60] Once again, dressings and bandages that fell far short of ideal norms for 'sterilization' easily became appalling vectors of infection.

The penury of medicaments, linen, and medical instruments had several causes: poor planning by government, insufficient funding and purchasing, slow and insecure transportation, all of which were made worse by the incompetence and corruption of hospital administrators.

Delivering care was also complicated by the endemic shortage of provisions and in some cases of drinking water. Soldiers who were physically weakened by hunger or dehydration were much less resistant to external aggressions in the form of disease or wounds. Large numbers perished not on the battlefield but in hospital as a consequence of '*fatigues*' – the generic term denoting the combined effect of lack of sleep and food and the resulting physical fatigue. Chevallier had observed the effects of this when soldiers were cut off without provisions on Lobau Island for three days after the battle of Essling in 1809: 'Of the wounded men, more than half died due to shortages in everything. We lost over 10,000 on the battlefield, and at least half of the nearly 20,000 wounded.'[61]

Another recurring problem for military medicine at this time was overcrowding in hospitals. Field hospitals could not cope with the sick and wounded in such large numbers. A lack of planning by government was once again to blame. The hospitals were designed for patient numbers not significantly higher than in the ancien régime whereas much larger facilities were required given the changed methods of warfare, with the emphasis on offense and battle, and the massive growth in combatant numbers. In the hospitals of the Armée du Nord and the Armée du Rhin, all places were filled when patients exceeded 13 per cent of serving troops. This was particularly disturbing given that during a general offensive the number of soldiers admitted to the hospital quickly climbed to 20 per cent and even 30 per cent of total troop numbers. In May–June 1794, hospital admissions accounted for roughly 29 per cent of the 85th Regiment serving with the Armée du Nord and 32 per cent of the Armée d'Italie.[62]

Cramped buildings and shortages of beds and stretchers forced doctors to park 100s of sick and wounded men next to each other in the corridors, thus encouraging the spread of infection. Tissot and Petetin, health officers and inspectors of the military hospitals at Besançon, noted in Year II that

> the corridors were full of sick men, most of them lying on the bare boards. Human contagion has long been widespread in the military hospitals of Besançon and in all those of the 6th military division that we visited. Its cause is the shocking disproportionality between the size of the wards and the number of sick men in them. We view these hospitals as arsenals of contagious miasmas more harmful to the human species than all the murderous instruments of war.[63]

For these reasons, therefore, the hospital appeared as the antechamber of death. Soldiers were well aware of this and rightly dreaded going into hospital. The general view on this subject was that a soldier who went into hospital for even a minor illness or slight wound had little chance of coming out alive. Joliclerc wrote to his mother on 27 June 1793, from the Armée du Rhin at Wissembourg: 'Vernier and Carrez came yesterday from the hospital. They are quite better. They say that men are dying like flies there for lack of care. Detronchet died without hardly having been ill.'[64] A similar verdict was delivered by Alexis Gosse, a volunteer in the 2nd battalion of the Puy de Dome, writing to his mother on 8 October 1794, from Rupperberg: 'Our company numbered ninety, we are now only twenty-five, and every day some go to the hospital and never come back.'[65] Whenever possible, therefore, soldiers sought to avoid staying in a hospital. Some escaped, others left of their own accord to stay in a civilian house, while others asked to be sent to their home. Bassinet, a volunteer soldier, wrote to his father from the Hospital of Toulouse, on 11 April 1794, asking him to send a certificate from the municipality of Pionsat with which he could obtain sick leave, as laid down by the law that said that any man who could not be cured in a hospital was allowed to return to his family to be tended. He gave the reason for his request: 'I have been at the Hospital of Toulouse since New Year's Day... [and] I shall remain ill as long as I stay in the hospital.'[66]

So in spite of the better training and the dedication and commitment of large numbers of doctors, and despite the discoveries and technical refinements in military medicine, treatment for soldiers was often unsuitable and ineffective, and battle-related mortality remained extremely high.

IV. Conclusion

For the men taking part in it, war was not an abstract representation but a concrete reality, an experience they lived in their flesh. In this period of their lives their bodies had particularly heavy demands placed upon them. Subject to all the vicissitudes of war, they could be modelled and reshaped, toughened and hardened, but they could also be worn down or mutilated. Battle was the climax of the war, yet it was by no means the greatest agent of destruction. Many soldiers died from wounds exacerbated by poor treatment or as a result of shortages and poor hygiene. The main cause of death in these wars, however, was not combat or even the consequences of combat – death from an infected wound, for example – but disease. The deadliest and most contagious epidemics, beginning with the bubonic plague during the Egyptian expedition, left a deep impression on contemporaries, but other diseases that might appear milder, foremost among them dysentery, could be big killers as well. Soldiers for whom this was the reality of everyday life came to fear disease and wounding more than death in combat: the latter was more glorious, quicker, and above all final. That last point was important, for what terrified soldiers just as much as shot and cannons was the physical degeneration caused by disease or serious wounding, with its potential long-term consequences, and the prospect of hardship on returning to civilian life (after losing an arm or leg or becoming blind). In its own way, the experience of being sick or wounded was no less a testing ordeal than that of battle. Indeed, in the eyes of many men, a move to hospital was tantamount to a death sentence. The defects and shortcomings of the army medical service were obstacles to effective treatment, while overcrowding, together with frequently appalling standards of cleanliness made hospitals the centres for transmission of epidemics. The sick or wounded soldier could expect little help from this quarter. The reality in the field, of bodies scarred, afflicted, and weakened by war, was at odds with the image that the Nation wanted to see and that the authorities wanted to supply – an idealized image of a soldier's body that was strong, vigorous, regenerated; a soldier's body that could become the body politic (incarnating in ideal form the collective representation of the Nation). This ideal image of the soldier's body, often akin to a propaganda image, was elaborated through comparison and in opposition to that of the enemy, civilian or military. In time, however, as the war dragged on, this image began to disintegrate, before finally collapsing during the retreat from Russia. In collective representations and combatants' accounts, the soldier's body as it really was, suffering and broken – literally so in the case of mutilated bodies – now replaced an ideal of the body politic nourished by the republican and nationalist propaganda so much in evidence at the start of the war.

4
Troop Morale and Military Unity

Napoleon claimed that 'In war, three-quarters of victory is down to morale, only one quarter to the balance of military forces.' Indeed, success in a military undertaking does not depend solely on the number and skill of the soldiers, the brilliance of the strategists, or the quality of technical performance. Something extra is needed, something intangible, invisible, contingent, volatile: that something is good troop morale. The role of combatant morale and opinion has been extensively studied for the Great War, often in relation to the various devices employed to buttress morale. Among these were recreational pursuits, notably sport, which as John Fuller has shown,[1] linked the soldier to civilian life, to his pre-war life; another element of communication with civilians was letter-writing, which played a capital role for morale and opinion among soldiers;[2] morale was also supported with material 'props', most notably alcohol;[3] military training regimes also contributed;[4] while the *journaux de tranchées* or military press,[5] besides entertaining and informing combatants, helped to create a sense of group membership, a professional military identity. The issue of combatant morale is also an important subject of study during the revolutionary and Napoleonic wars. The young conscript or volunteer soldiers who now left their homes, regions, or country for the first time, to fight in far-off conflicts, were prone to forms of severe psychological suffering that medical diagnosis recognized as genuine illnesses. One was *ennui*, a state of profound lassitude, which could develop into nostalgia or neurasthenia or the acute homesickness known as *mal du pays*. Often mentioned by soldiers in their private writings, the impact and symptoms of *mal du pays*, which have been studied by Marcel Reinhard[6] and Alan Forrest,[7] could be damaging for the conduct of the war, with large-scale desertion and the need to repatriate acute cases. It was traumatic, too, for the individual soldier, and led to instances of self-mutilation and even suicide. Morale was thus an essential element of a soldier's life and experience in the revolutionary and Napoleonic wars.

Like the body, or perhaps even more so, the mind or *esprit* of the soldier, his mental condition, was continually put to the test during these wars. Besides its physical attributes, the quality and effectiveness of an army is measured by its moral values, its state of mind, and its attitude towards the war. The relations between mind and body play a large and complex role in the ups and downs of troop morale. From a negative standpoint, worsening living conditions and the manifold physical pressures upon the body (hunger, thirst, disease, and wounds) clearly had the effect of weakening and demoralizing troops. Yet it is also true that *physical* hardships and suffering were frequently perceived and experienced through the *mental* or *psychological* prism formed by the collective state of mind and individual morale. In an army animated by an optimistic, positive outlook, shortages and sufferings meet with acceptance or even comprehension, but where troop morale is low they arouse widespread discontent and fierce criticism. Besides recreational pursuits and the other 'props' to morale, one of the most effective elements for limiting and fighting against loss of motivation among soldiers is the cohesion and unity of the group in which they live and fight on a daily basis.

Morale, motivation, state of mind, and public opinion – these impermanent and intangible elements, highly subjective and volatile indicators of an army's spirit, its mental well-being, are thus integral to a study of individual and collective experience of the revolutionary and Napoleonic wars. Following on from analysis of the war's impact on the bodies of soldiers, this chapter will study the interaction between war and the state of mind and morale of combatants.

I. Troop morale: the historical and theoretical debate

A study of tenacity and motivation among officers and especially among rank-and-file soldiers is indispensable for understanding the nature and variety of the experience of war. In essence this comes down to asking a question whose apparent simplicity belies its immense complexity: what was it that enabled men to 'keep going'? How were they able to accept and endure the difficulties, dangers, and horrors, and the inhumanity? What was the basis of the troops' 'morale', of their tenacity and motivation?

Two major sociological theories, both with ramifications in historical inquiry, are in competition in this field. One argues the thesis of the 'primary group', the other proposes the theory of 'legitimate demand'. For the former, the main driving force behind a soldier's acceptance of war and, more importantly, his will to fight, is the social group at the centre of his everyday life, and the capacity of this group to satisfy his material and psychological needs. In return, the group commands his loyalty, independently of any higher political or ideological cause. This school of thought derived from the analysis conducted by American sociologists and historians in 1947–1949 on troop morale in the German Wehrmacht and the US Army during the closing stages of the Second World War.[8] Janowitz and Shils contended that 'Where conditions were such as to allow primary group life to function smoothly, and where the primary group developed a high degree of cohesion, morale was high and resistance effective or at least very determined, regardless in the main of the political attitudes of the soldiers.'[9]

Unchallenged up to the 1960s, the theory of primary group cohesion then came under attack. The theory was weakened by the collapse in morale, will to fight, and combat performance that affected American troops during the Vietnam War, where it was further undermined by the policy of rotation and high troop turnover levels this implied, which forced a serious re-examination of the initial premise.

The result was a reappraisal of the role of ideology and the birth of what became known as the 'legitimate demand' school of thought. This viewed the soldier's will to fight as based on an underlying conviction, albeit not necessarily articulated or conscious, that the war aims are worthwhile and just, and that the means used by the military hierarchy to attain them are valid. In this approach, therefore, the primary group is less important. Indeed, in situations where the group cannot function satisfactorily (due to a high replacement rate or troop turnover, for example) the individual group members may nonetheless retain high levels of combat motivation if they believe in the socio-political system (political regime or government) to which they belong, in the need to defend it or its values, and in the legitimacy of the commander and of his methods.[10]

In recent years, this sociological theory positing the conscious integration by men and officers of a war's fairness and legitimacy has found a historiographical equivalent in the theory of 'consent' formulated by historians of the Great War. This theory, associated notably with Stéphane Audoin-Rouzeau and Annette Becker[11] and with François

Cochet,[12] has generated considerable interest and has at times been hotly debated.[13]

The difference between the two schools and the two interpretations is not purely formal. It encapsulates a conceptual contrast between two approaches to analysing the nature of the experience of war. The primary group theory, which in non-academic language might be described as that of comradeship or buddy relations,[14] makes the group the prime motor of individual attitudes and analyses the experience of war as a collective rather than an individual experience. It places human factors – the personal relations and shared professional identity of soldiers – above the political factors, individual ethical and political considerations, and national identity that form the base for the 'legitimate demand' theory.

The two theories, however, are not necessarily antithetical or mutually incompatible and may even be complementary. A number of historians, including Charles Moskos,[15] S. L. A. Marshall,[16] and John Fuller[17] have sought to combine the two theories, affirming that 'The ideological and primary-group explanations are not contradictory. Rather, an understanding of the soldier's combat motivations requires a simultaneous appreciation of the role of small groups and underlying value commitments as they are shaped by the immediate combat situation'[18] and that 'combat motivation arises out of the linkages between individual self-concern, primary-group processes, and the shared beliefs of soldiers.'[19]

In this chapter, a mixed approach combining these two theoretical models will be used to analyse the sources and evolution of troop morale during the revolutionary and Napoleonic wars.

II. The importance of the primary group and comradeship

The primary group theory has a place in any explanatory framework of troop morale and motivation. It was almost inevitable that men torn from their families, friends, regions and country – all that was familiar to them – should seek to re-form social bonds in the army, to recreate a community where they could find human warmth and a sense of belonging, in effect a substitute family.

With the generalization of conscription in France in the nineteenth century, ways had to be found to gain acceptance for the army, garrison life, and separation from civilian and family life. Camaraderie was even the subject of a theorization in the *Code-manuel du citoyen soldat* published in 1889:

> Every soldier ... separated from his parents ... seeks in comradeship the equivalent of the natural affection of which he is deprived. This affection issues from the similarity of situations, from the community of existence. The soldiers are the same age and come from the same region; they live together and do the same things; if war broke out they would face the same glorious future; and they are animated by the same desire to do their duty.[20]

But the recourse to camaraderie to make up for the absence of the biological family existed well before 1889 and emerges clearly in the writings of soldiers from the revolutionary and Napoleonic wars.

Many of these men emphasize how belonging to a small group of friends was important for both material and psychological reasons. The Belgian grenadier Scheltens noted that 'Each soldier must have a companion, the one must be responsible for the other, bringing him food and caring for him if he is sick or wounded.'[21]

In material terms, camaraderie made it possible to allocate and subdivide tasks in a way that produced an effective logistical wartime organization. Each group member had his own function: for one it would be looking for food, often by marauding; for another finding somewhere to spend the night (perhaps by constructing a bivouac himself); for a third looking for firewood and cooking the food; while another might, if in an isolated location or a bivouac on the edge of the army, keep watch at night. Chevallier in his memoirs gives the following description of how groups were organized in the encampments:

> On campaign ... when a platoon of twenty men arrives in a bivouac, the brigadier orders one quarter to go looking for provisions, one quarter to go after fodder, one quarter to go for straw and planks for making huts, and the other quarter with the officers and NCOs watch the horses, cut wood, make fire, do the cooking and build the huts. Say a man comes back with a pig, sheep or fowl, the cooks take it, and the brigadiers have a hatchet for cutting it up ... When someone who has been out after provisions gets back he finds a shelter, the one who has built the shelter shares the provisions his comrades have prepared, and so everyone can live ... But if there was no order, if everyone worked for himself, while the trooper was away looking for provisions what would become of his horse, and what would he do for a shelter, and who would feed the one who was making a shelter? This, then, was our little domestic set-up during the campaign (it was the same for everyone): Captain Moysant ... Lieutenant

> Barbanègre...Chief Maréchal de Logis Brice...lastly me and our *chasseurs*, we formed a little family. Some went after provisions, others after fodder, others made huts or did the cooking. Me, I went round any magazines there were; in the day, I looked for a village to house the company and, at night, I went looking for magazines.[22]

But the primary group cannot be reduced to this utilitarian function. It also had a psychological function, in helping soldiers to overcome the difficulties and stress caused by separation and danger. Comradeship was essential not just for the motivation and morale of troops but for their very survival. Often this was reflected in a close bond of friendship formed between two soldiers who came through the same trials over several years. In his memoirs, Louis Romand relates the moral support he received from his dearest comrade or *compagnon de route* after being wounded in battle. Romand's companion not only fetched the surgeon but helped him to endure the fear and suffering: 'My comrade had always been with me and now he gave me the consolation I needed in those dire circumstances.'[23] Sergeant Bourgogne, in his memoirs, also refers to the importance of the support he received from Grangier, another soldier in his company. During the retreat from Moscow, on reaching Smolensk in November 1813 he immediately set about looking for his comrade whom he had not seen for several weeks:

> When I had rested, and despite the cold and the snow that was falling, I made ready to go looking for one of my friends, to whom I was most closely attached; we had shared a common purse and never counted who spent what. His name was Grangier. We were together for seven years. I had not seen him since Viasma, where he left early with a detachment escorting a wagon belonging to Marshal Bessières. I had been assured that he arrived two days ago and was staying in the outskirts.

In a further comment, Bourgogne reveals the mixture of moral support, friendship and self-interest present in this wartime comradeship: 'The pleasure of seeing him again, plus the hope of having a few provisions that he had probably managed to obtain before our arrival, and also of sharing his accommodation, meant that I did not hesitate to go looking for him directly.'[24]

Understanding the primary group is not always as straightforward as some of the supporters of this theory maintain. War is an essentially shifting, unstable, and dangerous world, and membership of the primary group may change in response to military reorganization, transfers, disease, wounds, and deaths. François Lavaux, a young peasant from Champagne, became eligible for conscription in 1798 and enrolled as a soldier in the 103rd Line Regiment, going on to be promoted corporal in 1812 and sergeant in 1813. In a letter of 27 Prairial Year VIII written from Bâle, where he was imprisoned, he asked his father to inform his comrades' families of their deaths (thus showing the role of a shared regional identity in their camaraderie):

> I have to inform you of the sad news of the death of several comrades. In fact, of our band, I am the only one left. I cannot tell you of it without tears. My comrade Degual died in January at the hospital in Klankfourt. Please be so good as to let his people know... At the same time, tell Pierre Prat, of Esnom, that his son is dead too, with a comrade... They also died at Klankfourt, a part of the Empire, at the same time as Antoine Degand, from Broingt-les-Fossés, all from the same illness, caused by drinking too much bad water in the summer and being kept confined.[25]

Of the initial 'primary group', he was the only one left alive.

In other cases, the composition of the group changed as a result of transfers, new postings, or discharges. Thus, 2 years after joining the army, Henri Scheltens had to change 'campaign comrade', because his first one, François Paradis, was promoted to another regiment.[26]

Comradeship was not the only basis of the primary group: a group based on family ties was also possible. This was the case when soldiers had other family members in their regiment – a father, one or several brothers or cousins, or a wife and possibly the children that they took with them when leaving for the war. There was also the case of those who formed a family within the army itself, by marrying a civilian in army employment (usually a cook) or a foreign civilian from the locality where they were staying. In his memoirs Adrien Bourgogne recounts his 'lightning' marriage to a soldier's widow who was following the army convoy in the retreat from Moscow, and explains it by reasons that were both psychological (need for mutual moral support in adversity) and material (mutual help). Having entrusted his bag to a carrier, Labbé, Bourgogne found himself in an awkward position when the carrier was captured by the Cossacks and taken to a nearby village. Wishing to recover his bag and its contents, he had begun looking for carrier and bag when he came upon a woman he had noticed earlier, in Smolensk:

> I asked her who she was with and she replied that she was with no one, that the day after her husband was killed she was with the group I had seen her with, that she was fending for herself but that if I wanted to give her my protection, she would look after me and I would do her a great service. I immediately agreed to what she asked me for, without thinking of the figure I would cut arriving at the regiment with my 'wife'. Still walking, she asked me where my bag was; I told her the story of how I had lost it. She replied that I need not worry, that she was well provided for... The cry went up of *To arms!* and I heard the call to arms. I told my wife to follow me... Back at the company the sergeant-major asked me if I had any news of Labbé and my bag. I told him no and that it was pointless thinking about it, but that in its place I had found a wife: 'A wife!' he replied, 'What for? Not to wash your linen, because you haven't any now!' – She is going to give me some! – 'Oh! That's different, and what about food?' – She will do the same as me.[27]

The union was short-lived, however, since when he went back to the spot where he left her during this conversation, he found it empty: his 'wife' had been swept up by the stream of thousands of men from other army units. Bourgogne began looking for her – 'on account of the linen she had promised me and that I urgently needed to change' – but in vain, and he found himself 'bereft of her, as of my bag'.[28]

The primary group could extend beyond human beings. Many soldiers took a domestic animal (other than their horse) with them, moved by the need for a presence, affection, and company in a world of chaos, danger, and horror. In some cases this animal – usually a dog, though there were exceptions, goats for example – even became adopted by the whole company, a kind of mascot. If it was then killed, by a cannon ball or in some other way, its death produced genuine sadness among its two-legged companions.

But while the primary group existed in various forms and sizes, it nonetheless usually conformed to the general pattern of a community based on male comradeship, which served as a substitute for the biological family. A study of the experience of war needs to analyse how social bonds were created in the army, especially the main foundational elements that bound primary groups together. Much of what concerns the formation of these small groups of soldiers lies beyond the historian's understanding, being by nature contingent, intangible, and highly subjective, since comradeship depends ultimately on agreement or disagreement between the individuals involved. Certain factors, however, do tend to facilitate life in a community and the organization of identity-defining groups. In time of war, cut off from their family and far from home, soldiers naturally tend to seek the bonds of a shared identity.

III. Political ideology, patriotism: the role of values in troop morale

An analysis of how soldiers react to and participate in war reveals three main elements. The first is ideology and thus acceptance of a war perceived as just and legitimate. The second is self-concern or self-interest, based on expectations of promotion and military careers, the lure of plunder, and opportunities to visit foreign lands. Lastly, there is reticence or even refusal, albeit possibly attenuated by the bonds of comradeship and group solidarity. Broadly speaking, and allowing for the inevitable exceptions to any such rule, the division between the first and third attitude corresponds to that between volunteers for enlistment in the army and those requisitioned or conscripted by force. Even a few conscript soldiers, however, were prepared to recognize the rightness of the cause they were fighting for and to participate willingly in the war effort, though this was not the case of all of them.

To study the attitude of patriotic acceptance we need to analyse the state of mind of soldiers at the outbreak of war in 1792–1793. This is not easily described. Volunteer soldiers may have been wildly enthusiastic, but the *levée en masse* and conscription also encountered resistance, and strategies were developed to circumvent these measures and avoid taking part in the war. Nevertheless, the predominant feeling after the proclamation of *la patrie en danger* was definitely one of patriotism and acceptance of the war, a position all the more understandable given the widespread belief that the war would not last long. In 1792, the volunteer soldier Maurin wrote to his friend Dessalles, 'We cannot believe that this war will be long.'[29] On 27 December 1793, Joliclerc wrote to his mother: 'Toulon has been recaptured. Here is some good news that will surely bring us peace.'[30] So strong was the belief in a short war that on 25 August 1795, minister Servan suggested to the National Assembly that grenadiers and other elite company national guards should serve in the army for 1 month only.[31]

The relationship between the army, war, and patriotism is an essential characteristic of the construction of French national identity, one not universally observed in other countries. During the Great War, British troops were often struck by the strength of patriotic feeling among the French troops, by the fact that Frenchmen looked on France not as an abstraction but as the incarnation of a living, almost flesh and blood, reality. On this point they noted the sharp contrast with their own conception of the nation.

> The French . . . had their own distinctive ways. We once lay near them off Houthulst Forest, and when the French came out they would be met a mile or so back by the band and the Marseillaise and the sacred Tricolour and all that. They'd sing too, and very patriotic it sounded. Once one of our younger officers copied the idea, and we were to sing; and then about a minute later we were to stop singing. We had not got the thing right, it seemed; we had no word about the Fatherland or Glory or the Fun of Dying for the War Office. We all sang with extremely improper variations to the tune of 'We Want to Go Home'.[32]

This patriotic dimension to the commitment of French soldiers to war first took shape in the revolutionary wars with the declaration of *la patrie en danger*.

On 12 February 1793, Saint Just stated what was to become the credo of the revolutionary Jacobin government. 'You must not expect victory to come only from weight of numbers and discipline', he announced, 'you will secure it only through the progress made by the republican spirit within the army.' To achieve victory, the army had to become, in Jean-Paul Bertaud's phrase, a 'school of Jacobinism'. The first to undertake this task of civic instruction were the representatives or deputies-on-mission, who were supposed to raise the political consciousness of the soldiery by arresting traitors, rewarding patriotism, and educating the armies with distributions of tracts, speeches, proclamations, and directives emanating from the Convention.[33] Ultra-revolutionary movements and ideas also infiltrated the army, seeking to win it to the sans-culotte cause by means of the press and, above all, songs. But radical sans-culotte propaganda was less effective than government propaganda, and it failed to reach the mass of combatants. Following a phase of intense activity in the summer and autumn of 1793, it went into decline, notably after the ultra-revolutionary journalist Hébert was arrested in March 1794.

The question we must ask is how far this propaganda influenced the men in the ranks of the republican army and how it was received there. To judge from letters and journals written by soldiers at the time, its themes did reach a relatively large audience and contributed significantly to the politicization of the army, enabling Jacobin ideas and beliefs to take hold, and supporting troop morale by presenting the war aims in terms that were easily understood, that related to personal experience and to individual lives. Propaganda facilitated the assimilation of abstract concepts such as liberty and equality as part of a political education of the people. The battalion leader of the district of Amiens used a 'practical' approach to show his troops why defending the Republic and its values was so important for each of them.

> You have not been grouped together on the orders of some *intendant* or subdelegate, whose ridiculous function authorized them to recruit soldiers of a particular height while relying on pure chance to obtain strength and courage. The homeland summons us, virtuous children obedient to their mother. For this reason, honour will be our guide... Born in villages, we know better than townsmen about the horrors of the feudal regime. We were the 'serfs'. So let us show our former 'masters' that the serfs, the *sans-culottes* will no longer let the rabbits eat their harvest, nor will they pay the tithe.[34]

When soldiers assimilated this propaganda it supplied the ideological fuel that sustained their combat motivation. In something like a plagiarism of the 'Marseillaise', the volunteer soldier Bourgognaux proclaims, 'These fierce soldiers are trembling, and the Republic will triumph with the help of Heaven. Better to die than to surrender an inch. Our cause is just, we shall defend it as we always have, to the last drop of our blood.'[35] Bourgognaux is a far from isolated case. Among volunteer soldiers, and in the early stages of the war when it was a question of defending *la patrie en danger* and the young Revolution, their positive acceptance of the war was in little doubt, especially when they felt that it was a just war.

The early letters of these often very young men, penned with a lyrical, at times naïve enthusiasm, show an unqualified support for the aims of the war. Here is Joliclerc writing to his mother, on 13 December 1793:

> In every one of your letters you tell me that I must get out of the military life whatever the cost... When we are asked to defend the fatherland, we must hasten as I would run to a good meal. Our lives,

> our possessions and faculties are not really ours. They all belong to the nation, the fatherland. I know well that these views are not shared by you or the inhabitants of our commune. They ignore the cries of the outraged fatherland, and whatever they do for it is by force. But I, brought up in the liberty of conscience and thought, always republican in my soul even though forced to live in a monarchy, have the principles of love for the fatherland, liberty, and the Republic etched on my heart, they are engrained there and will remain so . . . I would gladly give three-quarters of all I own for you to share these feelings with me . . . Ah! That one day you may know the price of liberty.[36]

The impact made by the political education of the armies in this early phase of the Revolution (1793–1794) can be measured by comparing the discourse of official propaganda with the spontaneous discourse used by soldiers in their letters. A simple example is eloquent in this respect. One of the most common discourses in Jacobin propaganda, elaborating on the watchword of 'Les tyrans détruits, repos' (when the tyrants are destroyed then we can rest), promises soldiers a bright future following the victory of the Republic. Among the many men who developed on this theme was the prosecutor for the second division of the Armée du Nord when addressing his fellows in arms, in January 1794. 'The benefits of the fatherland will be yours,' he assured them, 'you will have a cherished companion and will enjoy untroubled possession of the fields abandoned by the emigrants and cowards. You will cultivate them with the hands that won victory and you will give us a sturdy progeny worthy of upholding your reputation, your achievement, the liberty of the Republic.' With minor differences, this discourse is repeated almost word for word in countless letters from volunteer soldiers. One such example is that from Tuzest, a *chasseur à cheval* or light cavalryman, to his parents, on 2 January 1795:

> The tyrants will soon be overthrown. With the enemies of the Republic defeated, I shall again know the joy of embracing you and of staying . . . in the bosom of my family. There I shall taste the flood of delights that liberty and equality procure for free men. That is where the farmer will work peacefully in his fields and harvest the sweet fruits.[37]

Another example comes from Jean Villedieu, dated 20 February 1795:

> The armies of the Republic are doing well and soon our enemies will be overthrown. After the tyrants are destroyed, I shall again know

> the joy of embracing you and of staying... in the bosom of my family. That is where I shall taste the flood of delights that liberty and equality will procure to free men. In the haven created by our victory we shall be sheltered from every kind of ill. There the farmer will work peacefully in his fields and savour the sweet fruit; he will enjoy fruitfulness and liberty together. No more ills, they will be over.[38]

IV. The quality of leadership

The cohesion of the campaigning army as a whole and the will and motivation to fight of its individual soldiers also depend on the relations between officers and men, between commanders and troops. Alexander George was the first of several historians to demonstrate the essential contribution of leadership to the individual and collective motivation of fighting men.[39]

The example that an officer sets his men is one of the founding elements of authority. Equally it is a federating element that unites the secondary group through imitation of action. In both literal and figurative senses, a leader, a superior officer is duty-bound to set an example. It may be an example of personal bravura, as when deliberately exposing himself to danger, or a technical example to be imitated, as for instance when showing troops how to execute a particular artillery shot. In their writings officers often use expressions like 'set an example' and 'lead from the front', the suggestion being that their conduct, especially in the moments of greatest risk, was being observed, scrutinized, and ultimately judged by their men. Many officers wrote at length on this aspect of their leadership mission. In his memoirs, written in captivity in 1813, Adolphe de Gauville, a young captain from the West Indies, recalls his own conduct during the battle of Leipzig (when he was taken prisoner).

> I merely did my job, which is no small achievement with raw troops who hardly know how to load their weapons... At fifty paces from us there was a deeply embanked river. I spotted the heads of several Austrian soldiers who were walking crouched down, hiding on the edge of the river, planning to go behind us and catch us in cross fire. I took a sergeant and six men. Seeing their way back cut off, the other lot laid down their weapons and asked for quarter. There were fifteen of them. I prevented any harm being done to them and had them taken to the rear escorted by only one man. My young men took courage from this capture and they were more willing to follow me. I marched in front, pushing back the enemy skirmishers roughly half a league... My battalion followed my movement and marched

> 'in battle formation' at five hundred paces from me... We were approaching the village where the enemy was present in force. I continued to march ahead of my soldiers to guide them and to set them an example. From the shots falling around me and whistling past my ears, it was clear to me that many of the enemy had me in their sights. That did not stop me and I continued on my way, though I took care not to stay long in the same spot.[40]

The 'exemplary' dimension of leadership, the giving of examples to be followed, is central to the relations that form between an officer and his men, so providing the basis for a common, shared experience of war. For the Great War, Emmanuel Saint Fuscien has shown the importance of example for the exercise of authority and for mechanisms of obedience, in both practice and representation (notably writings), with example acquiring a paroxystic dimension from the attention concentrated on the officer during combat and moments of extreme danger. He notes that

> The sources... consider example as central when attempting to describe the authority of combatant officers or to explain the submission of men both in combat and out of the firing line. In 1914–1918, example in combat meant exposing one's body to bullets and shells, encouraging those around one, and visibly accepting danger. By example was understood all conduct suggestive of action, that is, undertaken with the aim of being seen and imitated by others....

He concludes 'Throughout the conflict, influenced by representations that pre-dated the war, men in the ranks and combatant officers put example at the centre of their acceptance of the bond of hierarchy.'[41] This exemplary attitude – in the literal sense of the term – was essential to building a glorious reputation, and many idealistic young officers dreaming of glory and recognition based on personal merit considered it commendable, even desirable or necessary. This is present in the doubts expressed by Octave Levavasseur over leaving active leadership to be promoted to aide-de-camp:

> I did not conceal from myself the disadvantages of accepting it... I would be removing myself from the sight of the battery and the whole Walther Division, used to seeing me always out front on the battlefield, leaving the path of true glory, and the presence of those who were as one with me, to take a different route, more brilliant

perhaps but one often usurped, acquired without the control of obedient witnesses – these were the thoughts that turned me away from the function of aide de camp.[42]

V. The role of religion

Defining the role of religion as a prop for troop morale is not an easy task since soldiers do not usually mention religion in their writings. But are we to conclude from this that the revolutionary and imperial armies were won over to the agnostic principles of the revolutionaries and the Enlightenment *philosophes* who inspired them? Nothing could be less certain. Even in the early stages of the Revolution, when the government's anti-clerical policy was at its most active, the letters and journals of some soldiers reveal a deeply held Catholic faith. But if, as is often the case, generalization is impossible, a few broad points can nevertheless be made with which to sketch out a spectrum of contrasting attitudes and reactions towards religious faith.

French soldiers at this time certainly occupied an unusual position in the religious domain. They were part of a society in which a new regime was pursuing an energetic anticlerical policy to break from Catholicism and to replace it with a secular and civic religion. Unlike other armies of the day, including the British Army, the French Army of the revolutionary period included no military chaplains in its ranks. Open practice of religion was forbidden and until at least 1795 soldiers were not allowed to attend mass. The army did contain a few former priests who had enlisted as volunteers, but they were there as soldiers not as priests and there is nothing to indicate that they continued to exercise even an unofficial pastoral role during their time in the army. Despite the Concordat of 1801, the situation changed little during the Consulate and Empire: military chaplains were still not admitted to the French Army. Indeed, the French Army appeared to be an essentially secular or agnostic institution, something completely without precedent for the period.

An aggressive and violent anticlericalism, rather than *laïcité* or neutrality in religious matters, seems to have characterized the French Army in the revolutionary and Napoleonic wars. Evidence for this includes the pillaging of churches and the virulent commentaries of some soldiers in their memoirs. This is also the picture of the French military that is conveyed by the writings of some foreign soldiers.

It is undeniable that dechristianization was under way and even making significant inroads in French society in the early years of the

Revolution. Soldiers, drawn from civilian society, were no exceptions to this change. The scant respect troops showed for places of worship and above all their failure to express moral condemnation or feelings of remorse or shame when recounting in letters and memoirs the sacrilegious acts they or their companions had committed – plundering, pillaging, destroying churches and religious objects; violent and even barbaric acts (woundings, killings) against priests, monks, and nuns – reveal the state of religious mentalities among soldiers in the revolutionary armies, their complete lack of belief in such concepts as sin or divine punishment, and their lack of fear when committing acts of sacrilege. No attempt was made to protect the clergy from the violence of the armed conflicts, or to respect the sanctity of places of worship.

Dechristianization was not universal, however. Soldiers sometimes admitted, perhaps through chance remarks, to keeping their faith and to counting on divine forgiveness and protection to save them from the dangers of war. Although they continued to observe rituals such as prayers, their religion was usually closer to deism than to traditional Catholicism. Volunteer soldiers who had been influenced by revolutionary propaganda often combined this deist religious outlook with a strong condemnation not of God and religion but of the clergy. Though remaining believers, they adopted many Jacobin criticisms and representations during the Revolution and the Consulate and Empire. In their writings, they depict priests and monks as greedy for power and money, and as hypocritical and dishonest, especially in countries, like southern Italy and Spain, where religion still had a central role in public life.[43]

All through this period, however, the experience of danger and the fear of death could also lead to a renewal of faith. In the early years of the Revolution, there were soldiers who, though deeply attached to the revolutionary cause, admitted to keeping their faith, finding it useful for sustaining their morale in the face of the hardships and dangers of war. One such was the volunteer soldier Joliclerc, who wrote to his mother on 30 May 1794 in the following terms:

> In all your letters you never stop...nagging me to pray to the Lord and his saints. What is the point of asking for rain when my comrade is asking for sunshine? No. I simply say: Thy will be done on earth as in heaven...Let Providence decide, put ourselves in his hands, do all the good we can, and when our time's up, into the hole with us. This God is not as fearsome as our rascally priests told us from the pulpit and at confession. The God I worship is kindly, just and merciful

towards his creatures. But the former priests ascribed all their own vices to him.[44]

Here is the same Joliclerc, writing to his mother from the small Breton town of Josselin, where he was encamped with the Armée des Côtes de Brest, on 5 April 1795, after the re-opening of the churches and the granting of official tolerance for Catholic worship:

> Today, Easter Sunday, two or three masses were celebrated in the town for the first time. I had not been for around two years. It certainly restored spirits among the troops and inhabitants and it will go far to easing consciences. At last we can worship again; only tyranny prevented us from doing so, and today we are in the reign of freedom and virtue.[45]

On the eve of a particularly hazardous battle or after being seriously wounded, a soldier might feel the need for a divine protection and bring to mind some half-remembered prayer from childhood religious instruction. In his memoirs, François Lavaux recalls his reaction when he thought his final hour had come during the siege of Badajoz in the war in Spain:

> From the rampart, the Spanish sent four shells and four cannon shots in my direction. The first shell landed near me in my foxhole, at my feet. I saw it was smoking but I could not put it out. I did not get out of the hole, since if I had come out I would have been in an even worse position. Thinking I was dead, I made my act of contrition.[46]

Personal testimonies on this subject are too few in number to conclude that there was any general revival of faith in the army during the revolutionary and Napoleonic wars – a 'spirituality of combat' comparable to that described by Annette Becker for the Great War. But these isolated examples do serve to qualify the overly simplistic view of a generalized dechristianization of either army or society in France at this time.

VI. War as an individual experience: the role of self-concern in troop motivation

Another key factor sustaining morale and the will to 'stick it out', to keep on fighting, was the survival instinct. In the thick of action, men kept on fighting primarily because they wanted to come through it alive.

François Vigo-Roussillon notes this in his campaign diary at the time of the battle of Aboukir (7 Thermidor Year VII): 'We straight away made ready to fight; there was not a single soldier who did not understand that it was a question of kill or be killed.'[47] Grenadier Guardsman Henri Scheltens makes a similar point in his memoirs, concerning the campaign of France in 1814: 'Each man is fighting his own war; he defends himself and kills as necessary.'[48]

In some cases the power of this instinct was cynically exploited by military strategists to stimulate the fighting spirit of troops. Indeed, this was one of the bases of Napoleonic strategy. 'An army's strength depends not on the number of combatants but on their spirit', noted the young officer Octave Levavasseur, in the section of his memoirs devoted to the Austerlitz campaign.

> The belief in victory leads to victory. Precautions taken for an eventual retreat reveal to the soldier the general's fears and inhibit recklessness and courage. A fighting spirit is better than any fortifications. When a soldier thinks he can fight protected by ramparts, he is good only for defence: he ceases to be the equal of his enemy who, attacking in the plain, has only his chest for a rampart. The Emperor was convinced of these truths. At Austerlitz, a battle he wanted to win at any cost, he took no measures that could have weakened morale or given soldiers the idea of looking to the rear. He knew that a French army that marched into combat thinking of retreat was already half beaten.[49]

Shortages and setbacks led to a wave of discontent in the Republican Army in 1795–1796. Desertion became increasingly common. In his campaign diary, Fricasse records that 'it was during the month of Frimaire Year V... that desertions to the interior of France from the Armée du Rhin et de la Moselle were frequent,' and roundly condemns the traitors:

> They waited until their fatherland needed them most to carry out their plans... They fled before the enemy. But these cowards have been little missed. They were like the venom expulsed from the body of a poisoned man, and they made themselves unworthy of the French name and of the esteem of their comrades.[50]

Even the men who stayed at their posts had lost their initial enthusiasm and morale and showed clear signs of discouragement.

> We poor heroes had long been without clothing and boots, with no hope of obtaining any... We had not received our pay for three months. We celebrated the anniversary of the Revolution. The fête started at six in the morning... A member made a speech recalling at length how the French Revolution had taken place, and how the priests and émigrés had set about preparing a counter-revolution, which we managed to thwart, but that we needed to stay firm in our support for the new constitution. This was the wish of the garrison. We had not made all these sacrifices just to abandon our fatherland to detestable tyrants [though Fricasse adds] It must be said, however, that the joy was not unqualified, on account of the hardships we were suffering. For while this was of course a glorious anniversary for the French people, yet the defenders of the fatherland were short of even essential items. The pay was several months in arrears, no change of clothing was issued, and we lacked almost everything. This cast so much gloom among the troops that the fête was more like a funeral. The speech ended with *Live free or die!* and *Long live the Republic!* These shouts were taken up only by those at the altar of the fatherland; next, they began to sing the *Marseillaise* hymn, taken up by our musicians, but the voices were not wholehearted.[51]

VII. External and material supports for troop morale: the example of alcohol

At an everyday level, several more concrete elements contributed to troop morale, one of which was alcohol. In their letters and memoirs, some soldiers make no mystery of their addiction to drink, often presenting it as justified and legitimate in view of the demands made of them and the dangers and risks they faced. In a letter of 30 May 1794, Joliclerc replies bluntly to his mother's criticisms on this subject.

> Wine is fairly cheap... We drink a few bottles. It angers me to have to talk to you about this, because you practically forbid me to tell you anything about it... Not at all! My drinking has not dishonoured me, and I believe I have more honour than all your drinkers of water who have never said or done anything except with a clear head. And I ask you this: has my drinking got me into any trouble, any danger? Have I been in fights? Has drink ever led me to commit any misdeed? All that has happened is that I have spent what's mine, mine... and sometimes I got a headache. That's what happened. And on the subject of what's mine, I haven't finished spending it yet.[52]

Many other soldiers make passing reference in their memoirs or letters to the habitual heavy drinking in the armies.[53] In his report of 1 June 1793 to the Committee of Public Safety on the taking of Furnes, Carnot, *représentant* of the Convention to the armies, noted that 'The soldiers were all more or less drunk. At every step there were some who fell over.'[54]

The prime function of alcohol was to sustain the morale of soldiers, to give them a few hours' escape from the war's daily routine of hardship, danger, and horror, a way of forgetting the whistling of bullets, the screams of the wounded, the smell of death, and the longing for home. As François Cochet commented for fighting men in the First World War, drink is 'a strong psychological prop for the combatant' and 'drinking blots out the deathly surroundings, rekindles your courage to carry on, makes you forget the absence of loved ones.'[55] In his memoirs, Sergeant François Lavaux recalls his stay at Valladolid during the war in Spain: 'We never had a moment's rest. We were always out chasing the brigands in the mountains. Our sole relaxation was wine, of which we had as much as we wanted.'[56]

Drink was not only a means of distraction and escape from daily life in the army. It could also be prescribed by a doctor as part of the soldier's regular diet,[57] or even employed as a fortifier and stimulant – consumed not to drown men's fears and sufferings but to give them courage or make them oblivious to danger. A fairly common practice in the ranks at this time, it seems, alluded to by several soldiers, was to down large amounts of brandy at the start of the battle, before throwing oneself into the thick of the fighting. This was how Captain Adolphe de Gauville spent the last few hours before the battle of Leipzig.

> At five o'clock we were told that at eight the battalion had to be under arms and assembled, ready to go and take up position. The laughing was over... At eight o'clock we were... in battle order with weapons and packs; a light rain was falling. While waiting for the signal to leave, I went with several of my comrades to an underground café situated just behind the battalion, and tried, with glass in hand, to ward off what the future might hold by enjoying the present. We spent a merry hour in this café making music. It was preparing us for some more music of quite a different kind. At ten o'clock we left and were taken two leagues from the town.[58]

There is a sense in which drink is so much an element of the military identity that it even transcends the political divisions between nations. Drink certainly played a central role in incidents of fraternization with enemy soldiers. On many occasions, combatants of opposing armies spent a few hours sharing wine or brandy, and then resumed combat.

> When battle was about to be engaged, before the firing started, the enemy officers and French officers walked out towards each other, up to the middle of the space separating them. I myself went half the way several times, and after exchanging a few signs, we drank a glass of rum, then returned to our guns. The same thing happened outside Hollabrünn, where the enemy was waiting for us. We set up to the right and left, and were separated from the enemy by a small valley. Opposite my battery, on the side of the hill, at the top of which were the Austrians and Russians, there was the door to a cellar. Guessing there was wine inside, my gunners made signs with canteens to the enemy scouts and slowly approached the door. When they reached it they broke it down and immediately came out with buckets filled with wine. Seeing our soldiers thus supplied, the Austrians and Russians wanted a share of the booty and came down and joined in with them. Thus it was that hostilities were suspended while Russians, Austrians, and French drank of the same wine.[59]

Officially, the political and military authorities condemned the consumption of alcohol on moral grounds (propriety being expected of the soldiers of the Republic). In January 1794, the prosecutor for the second division of the Armée du Nord warned soldiers against the dangers of drink. 'The reign of courage goes together with that of good morality,' he proclaimed,

> Remember, the despots encouraged debauchery and sought to deprave men solely to degrade them, to drag them down into the most vile servitude. Today, the people are sovereign and demands that all its members be virtuous, incorruptible and pure. Can someone who becomes incapable of rational thought, for an instant, be responsible for his actions and for himself?[60]

In certain cases, however, the authorities tolerated or even encouraged the drinking of wine and brandy. Thus Napoleon frequently ordered bottles to be distributed on the eve of major battles, to fortify or stimulate his troops, or on the following day, to reward them. On the evening of 1 December 1805, in a village near Austerlitz, 'the Emperor gave orders for brandy rations to be distributed and ordered the attack for the morning.'[61]

VIII. Conclusion

War is not an exclusively physical experience. The soldier's mind or *esprit*, no less than his body, is subject to constant pressure and challenges. The quality and effectiveness of an army are intrinsically dependent on levels of troop morale, with inevitable implications for the practice of leadership. Building and sustaining troop morale is as much an imperative for the authorities in wartime as are technical manoeuvres and physical exercise. The soldier's mental health, like that of his body, had to be cared for and administered to. For the military authorities the challenges were multiple – those of preventing *mal du pays* and anxiety, countering the enemy's psychological warfare (distribution of tracts encouraging desertion, spreading rumours and false news), and bolstering the tenacity, mindset, and will to fight of the soldiery. Their response took a variety of forms: propaganda and political education, fostering belief in war aims and in the war itself as just, an exemplary attitude displayed by officers, the satisfaction of self-interest (promotion, awarding of honours such as the *légion d'honneur*) and a toleration of excesses judged useful for sustaining troop morale (notably alcohol). Morale was vital to pursuance of the war, and became more so as the years went by and the war dragged on. The patriotic fervour of the early days subsided, gradually giving way to apathy and even opposition, especially after 1795–1796. The predominant view in Year II of a short war was shattered, replaced by one of a never-ending war, with the prospect of peace receding ever further into the future. Discouragement took hold among volunteer and conscript soldiers. Their initial commitment had been patriotic, perhaps reckless, now they needed to find the inner resources that would enable them to 'stick it out'. And for this purpose anything could be used. Examined in the light of original evidence and eyewitness accounts, the motivating factors sometimes presented in sociological or historical analyses as contradictory or incompatible appear rather as complementary and inclusive. It was to every available resource – comradeship, the bonds of collective solidarity, patriotism, political and ideological beliefs, plus the appeal of self-interest (starting with the will to survive) and material supports – that these men turned for the strength to endure the physical and psychological hardships that were their lot.

5
From Individual Experience to Collective Identities

Several generations of Frenchmen were directly caught up in the revolutionary and Napoleonic wars. Willing volunteers or reluctant conscripts, they left their families, homes, regions, and usually their civilian occupation as well, to take up the profession of arms. During their years of service they discovered a hitherto unknown world of long marches and bloody battles, penury and excess (looting, drinking), danger and patriotic or military pride, physical and mental suffering (post-combat trauma, homesickness) and endurance, violence and comradeship, and national hatreds and occasional fraternization with enemy soldiers. The majority of these men had grown up in rural communities that were still largely self-contained and unchanging. In sharp contrast to the civilian life they had left behind, men now gained first-hand experience of far-away foreign lands and peoples.

Men cut off from their families and far from home were naturally drawn to seek out the bonds of shared identity from which to build a group or community that would offer moral and material support. Cohesion and unity were further fostered by contact with the 'other', allowing soldiers to discover what differentiated them from a community perceived to be different and, in turn, what they had in common with members of their own community. A study of the affirmation of collective identity is essential for understanding the true nature of the soldier's experience of war. The concept of 'identity' can be problematic – in its inclusiveness or '*plurale tantum*'[1] (encompassing territorially based attitudes as well as feelings of common belonging based on, for example, class, ethnic or linguistic features, or religion), and in its implication of a conscious awareness by the subject of this sense of identity, which is not always easy to evidence through historical sources – yet it remains a useful and valid concept for the analysis of the collective *mentalités* of soldiers at war. This chapter will thus address the different categories of 'identity' or, more accurately, 'sentiments of identity' experienced by French soldiers and officers during this climactic period of their lives.

I. Local and national identity

The awareness of a sense of national identity or national sentiment requires, in Benedict Anderson's words, the feeling of being part of a national 'imagined community'.[2] Arguably, the same was true for the sense of regional identity as long as it referred to membership of an area larger than a village and thus precluded individual interactions and connections with all members of the community. This emotional feeling of belonging to a common 'imagined community', the strongest antidote to feelings of nostalgia and homesickness or *mal du pays*, could accommodate different levels of collective identity and lead to a 'double' identity, integrating sentiments of both national and local identity.

One of the most basic and most obvious bonds of identity between men is geographical, that of coming from or near the same locality, or of belonging to the same national territory and sharing common mores, food habits, language, and culture. For many historians, the French Revolution is a turning point in the development of a sense of national identity, the matrix of nationalism and national identity in France. However local loyalties remained strong; regional languages or *patois* were still spoken by the vast majority of Frenchmen. The rise of a sense of national identity therefore did not supersede the ancient and deep-rooted local loyalties, it complemented them. Rather than seeing an opposition or contradiction between national and regional identity, we should thus think of Frenchmen of that time as experiencing a 'double identity'.[3]

1. Regional and local identity

What is loosely referred to as 'regional' identity denotes belonging to the same geographical area, a subdivision of the national territory, and recognizing the same landmarks and referents, such as knowledge of localities, roads, and landscapes, use of a regional language, attendance at the same schools, and familiarity with the same weather patterns and local food. It may be narrowly local, based on the municipality, village, or hamlet that a person comes from – the *pays* – or it may encompass a geographical zone (an upland region, a coastal area), a department, a region, or indeed a cultural and civilizational zone such as the south of France or the north.

Military recruitment under the Revolution and Empire was not totally national. In some cases, regiments and companies (principally though not exclusively for volunteers) were still organized on a regional basis, which suited some young soldiers. Much more commonly, companies and regiments were organized on a national or at least cross-regional basis, but even then a regional identity remained strong. Despite the beginnings of a few timid though real expressions of national identity, young soldiers felt themselves to be as much Provençal or Alsatian as they were French.

Coming from the same region was often decisive in the formation of small groups of comrades and played a key role in the sociability of the bivouac and the march. In a letter to his parents dated 7 October 1794, Claude Cornet, a young volunteer soldier from the Auvergne, makes clear the importance of wartime camaraderie and the influence upon it of shared geographical origins.

> I should have written sooner to tell you that I have left the company to which I was attached for rations. It is already a month since I joined the grenadiers company of the 1st battalion of our department. I was tired of being in a company where I had no friends. I did not fail to take advantage of the opportunity that came up. Also, I can't hide it from you, dear father, that the battalion I was in did not have a good reputation: it was full of cowards and fops. At least I shall have the satisfaction of being in the Armée du Rhin with lads from home. The grenadiers company is going to join the battalion in twenty days. I am well liked by the grenadiers and by Captain Frenaye who is from Riom. I shall try to retain their esteem and their friendship... The Captain has made me a small loan, so please send some money.[4]

A regional or local identity could be reinforced by personal acquaintanceship that pre-dated the war and involved other soldiers from the same village or region, or family members and friends. But this was far from being always the case. The war disrupted daily life, challenging familiar standards and longstanding certainties, and so produced changes in established rules of conduct. Men from the same village, who in peacetime might not have mixed on a regular basis or perhaps even avoided each other's company, could in wartime become friends or comrades, brought together far from home by a common attachment to a 'pre-war' existence, to a small locality identified with their families and civilian life. Joliclerc wrote to his mother on 16 Germinal Year III (5 April 1795),

> You reprimanded me, two years ago, when I was back at home. I told you that I was lodging with Michaud, Compte, Fourquier, Girod, Lamy and Vuillet... You said that that made seven drunkards. Well, dear mother, of the seven, I alone am still in the company. Three have been killed and the others are out of action. Lamy the Mason, known to everyone, was recently killed by the brigands. He took a musket shot that went right through him, and he eventually died after languishing for fifteen days. When shall I end up with him and the others? It made me very angry, he was a dutiful soldier.[5]

Later on, under Napoleon, conscription was generalized, leading to a strengthening of the military identity, yet the Consulate and Empire did not see a significant weakening in the regional identity of soldiers. Volunteer and conscript soldiers still felt a need to seek the company of men from their own region. The young Auvergnat Narcisse Faucheur, who had enlisted in 1812, describes in his memoirs his natural inclination to form groups with fellow Auvergnats, as happened in the Bautzen campaign.

> My duties as a quartermaster sergeant had taken me to the far limit of the lines occupied by the VI corps, and on my way I met two sappers of the 22nd Light Infantry regiment. Now, for the last twelve years this regiment was recruited mainly in the Puy-de-Dôme department, so I asked these sappers if their regiment was in the neighbourhood and if it still contained many men from Clermont. They replied that their regiment was not far away and that nearly all the NCOs were from Clermont or thereabouts, and they mentioned several names that were very familiar to me... It was impossible for me to abandon the task I had been allotted, so I wrote my name and rank and the number of my regiment on a piece of paper that I handed to the sappers and asked them to give it to the first NCO from Clermont they met and to tell him how pleased I should be to see some fellow countrymen... Less than two hours later, twenty NCOs from the 22nd Light arrived and bid me accompany them to the mess so as drink to my health and reminisce about our common home country. It was a good quarter of a league to the camp where the division's kit and food stores were, and throughout the journey we did not stop talking

about our families, our friends, and where we came from, so that by the time we got to the mess we were already well acquainted.[6]

Soldiers often formed groups spontaneously with their 'compatriots' – men from the same department or same region, men they had not known before – simply because of the shared geographical origin. Knowing a regional language could be another factor. Despite measures introduced by revolutionary governments to promote linguistic uniformity and modernization, notably through a 'language policy',[7] regional languages and local dialects or *patois* were still widely used in France during and after the Revolution.[8]

In areas of France with a strong ethnic and linguistic autonomy, such as the Basque region, the existence of local populations that did not speak French at all could find this a barrier to their integration in national units. When a project to incorporate the Basque regiments into the main body of the army was being discussed in Year VIII, an officer of the regiments wrote to the First Consul explaining that since Basque soldiers would not be able to communicate in French or to understand orders given in French, they 'would be exposed to boredom, disillusionment, discouragement. Then homesickness would take hold of them . . . and they would end up abandoning the new flags.'[9]

Even in regions of France less marked by a strong cultural autonomy, some soldiers still spoke their regional language much better than they did French, which made communicating with men from other regions difficult and reinforced the tendency to form groups of comrades from the same locality. Here is Moulinet, a soldier from the Auvergne, writing to his parents at Pionsat in the Puy-de-Dôme, on 28 June 1793: 'We are in a region where only beer is drunk as the wine is expensive and not any good. We are in Alsace, and we don't understand any of their language and they can't understand Frenchmen, which makes buying anything difficult.'[10] Moulinet is referring to the civilian population of the region, but the same problems of communication could also arise with conscripts from Alsace or from other parts of France where a regional language was in wide use.

The military authorities made no systematic attempt to stamp out or forbid use of regional languages. Far from it, partly since such action would have been impossible in practice, but also because regional languages could be useful. Bilingual soldiers, able to speak French as well as a regional language, were employed as interpreters in a number of campaigns, where their regional language was similar to the language of the country they were in. This was the case for Alsatian soldiers during campaigns in the Germanic regions,[11] and for soldiers from Provence and Corsica during the campaigns in the Italian states. In 1807, during the campaigns of Eylau and Friedland, the language skills of soldiers from Brittany and Provence were needed to communicate with the local populations: 'Apart from the great difficulty we had just living, we often could not make ourselves understood. By a singular coincidence, the dialects of our soldiers from Lower Brittany and Provence were akin to the local idiom, so that before long relations were established.'[12]

The forming of groups based on a common identity was particularly attractive when such groups offered soldiers a haven of safety and mutual help. Solidarity between men from the same region – 'compatriots' – was customary in the army; it was a means for coping with everyday hardships (by pooling provisions or money), for ensuring letters were delivered to families, or indeed for rising through the ranks and getting promotion. Octave Levavasseur mentions in his memoirs the role of shared geographical origin in securing his promotion to the rank of aide-de-camp to General Seroux in September 1806. Both men were Picards, both being born in the Oise department, and the young officer notes 'I knew him from Montreuil, and had always got on well with him. He was from Compiègne and I was from Breteuil; in the army we perpetuated the fraternal relations that should always exist between compatriots from the same department.'[13]

In some instances a local identity transcended regional divisions and was based instead on a common culture rooted in economic activity or, even more so, the form of habitat. Sharp contrasts could exist between men from the countryside and those from towns and cities, reflected in differences of attitude and behaviour in rural and urban contexts (discomfort due to pollution or 'town air' among countrymen, ignorance of agricultural work among townsmen). The young Fricasse, who enlisted voluntarily in 1792, noted in his journal in August 1792,

> At Metz I got an illness that took me to within an inch of my life. I attributed the cause of this illness to the air of the city... I had always enjoyed the good air of the countryside. Perhaps also the fact of living sixty leagues from home was responsible for these six weeks in hospital.[14]

2. National identity

A link between war and national identity has often been identified for contemporary conflicts. Stéphane Audoin-Rouzeau brilliantly demonstrates how the strong national sentiment of French soldiers in the First World War accounted for their tenacity during those climatic years. But although he acknowledges the specificity of the war and experience of it in the shaping of collective identities and mentalities, alluding to a 'wartime culture', he concludes that the national sentiment expressed by those men 'only completed the "task" begun many years previously. The foundations of French national sentiment between 1914 and 1918 were, to a large extent, already complete in 1870, and must be seen as part of a long-term cultural development.'[15]

In this respect, the revolutionary and Napoleonic wars present a particular interest. Although a national identity began to emerge in France in the eighteenth century and received additional impetus from the ambitious policy pursued by the post-1789 regimes, it was still a limited phenomenon in the late eighteenth and early nineteenth centuries. David Bell has highlighted the importance of the Seven Years' War for developing a sense of national identity in France, showing how it was presented not as a war of religion or a war of succession but as a 'war of nations'. Yet this vision seems to have been restricted to a tiny elite, and to support his thesis David Bell draws uniquely on literary sources, notably propaganda material,[16] not on the private writings of people from lower down in French society. Nationalism and national identity certainly existed in France before the Revolution, but they were essentially a concern for the elite of the nation; for the bulk of the population, notably in the countryside, they had little or no meaning.

From the end of the eighteenth century, and especially from the Revolution onwards, the phenomenon grew in importance. Conscription, the army, and war itself made fundamental contributions to raising national awareness among young Frenchmen in the revolutionary and Napoleonic eras and during the rest of the nineteenth century.[17] Young men from every region of France, brought together in national or supraregional regiments and units, were now deployed across the countries of Europe, where they shared dramatic experiences with comrades from every geographical origin. Not surprisingly, war fought in these conditions helped to promote a sense of national identity among soldiers.

During the Revolution, the sense of national identity was primarily political in nature, particularly among volunteer soldiers. It corresponded to a set of shared values and new beliefs. In soldiers' discourse, the Frenchman was defined above all as the defender of liberty, in contrast to other peoples who were perceived as lagging behind in the march of civilization, modernity, and democracy, like peoples still in slavery. This comes over clearly in a letter from Bravy Soulbost, a young volunteer soldier from the Auvergne who enlisted in the 3rd Battalion of Paris, to his father, a peasant proprietor, on 29 October 1792:

> I have enrolled at Paris in the Volunteers and I am ready to leave to fight the enemies of the fatherland. I was born French and with other Frenchmen I want to share the danger and the glory, and I shall always be careful to respect people and property or to die defending them. My comrades and I, we feel the same. In short, I am devoting myself, my will and my heart, to the defence of the fatherland, and my motto is, Live free or die.[18]

In similar vein, Jean Ataix, also a volunteer soldier from Auvergne, wrote to his father in 16 May 1794,

> Make haste to celebrate. Mont Cenis has been taken; yes, we have taken the mountain they said was so daunting, and without many losses. I mean to say that, including the wounded, we have lost only twenty men... Soon we shall be at Turin. This will not be so difficult for us even though it is said to be impossible to get inside, but for free Frenchmen nothing is difficult.[19]

Under the Consulate and Empire, national identity was increasingly defined in cultural rather than political terms. The militant Jacobinism of the soldiers of Year II declined, partly due to the arrival of a new generation of soldiers, partly also because the authoritarian regime created by Napoleon stifled expression of egalitarian revolutionary political ideals. A political identity gradually gave way to a professional military identity, as mass conscription, longer terms of duty, geographical remoteness, and growing professionalization all tended to reinforce awareness of a military identity. The sense of national identity did not disappear in the Napoleonic period. In fact, it grew even stronger, but it was based less on shared political values and beliefs than it had been during the Revolution. Among soldiers in the Napoleonic period, the sense of national identity was of essentially cultural inspiration, one formed largely in opposition to the 'other', the foreign peoples whose manners, culture, and customs seemed so utterly different to them. A large part of the French Army was now stationed almost permanently in foreign, sometimes far-off countries. A sense of national identity was sharpened when troops discovered what united them, what distinguished them from the population of the countries they crossed and stayed in, and what, over and above regional differences, established the unity of their own people and let them see themselves as belonging to a single nation.

This cultural or politico-cultural national identity had multiple bases. By examining the criteria that French soldiers use in their letters and memoirs to describe the foreign countries they visited, we can identify, by inference, what they considered to be the core elements of nationhood, and thus the bases of their national identity.

Although the criteria vary depending on the author of the letter, diary, or memoir, a certain number of constants are present in their writing. Some of the writers, particularly men who enlisted during the Revolution and went on to serve under the Consulate and Empire, retained a political interpretation, judging foreign societies by the democratic character of their institutions and by the degree of liberty accorded to their inhabitants. For these men, liberty remained the key principle, the true test of how far a country had advanced along the path of progress and civilization. When French soldiers condemned Prussia and the countries of eastern Europe, from Poland to Russia, they were making an ethical or moral judgement on the political and social organization of countries that they considered backward and barbaric. Central to this condemnation was the question of serfdom. For soldiers with Jacobin sympathies and imbued with Enlightenment ideas, serfdom was synonymous with oppression and barbarity: countries where it persisted stood outside the sphere of civilization. In many cases, denunciations of serfdom were all the more vigorous because of its association with labour services and other feudal vestiges observed in France in the not-so-distant past. As during the Revolution, therefore, these soldiers continued to conceive national identity in political terms.

Likewise, the perception of some southern European countries still deeply infused with Catholic religious faith was often biased by a strongly anticlerical or secular outlook, especially among the first generation of volunteer soldiers, imbued with Jacobin anticlerical propaganda. The fact that the Italian and the Spanish clergy took an active part in the defence of their country against the French invaders further increased the hostility of the French military towards the religious elites and their followers. Criticisms of the Roman Inquisition, of the omnipresence and influence of the clergy and of its wealth and corruption, of a deep popular faith that many described as 'superstition' – abound in French soldiers' writings. The French troops tended to assess Italian and Spanish people through the lens of religious attitudes, and defined their own national identity according to Jacobin views of secularism. As Michael Broers has recently suggested, the invasion and ensuing occupation of Italy under Napoleon (though arguably the same was true of the revolutionary period) present an instance of frontal confrontation between religious authority and rational secularism:

> [The French] contempt for every conceivable facet of the religious culture of their *administrés* led the French to see themselves as part of a *longue durée* which pitted the more rational, civilizing forces . . . against the latent barbarism of the hinterlands . . . Here the struggle was perceived . . . as a confrontation between unreconstructed religious archaism and the forces of modernity.[20]

As well as this political and moral perspective on national differences, the discourse used by soldiers introduces other elements from which to construct national identity. From these, a more complex, fuller picture of national identity emerges, one made more tangible and more human – and thus easier for men to assimilate and accept – by the presence of cultural, physical, and social factors.

Soldiers increasingly paid particular attention in their accounts to the differences in physical appearance between inhabitants of the countries they visited. For each country, the soldiers give a description – typically fairly short and thus caricatured and superficial – of the physical aspect of men and women and of their dress customs. This bears out the comments made in Chapter 3 concerning the importance of the body in collective representations and on the formation of a body politic. Joseph Laporte, on his arrival in Egypt, is struck by the difference between France or rather, as he puts it, between Europe and Egypt and has the feeling of arriving 'in another world' because of the otherness of the language, of dress habits (large trousers instead of the European tight clothes, veiled women, tanned faces, coloured turbans on the head . . .) and of the fauna and flora (palm trees, camels used to transport water in the cities . . .).[21]

Another key criterion in the perception of foreigners was physical cleanliness or the lack of it. This was applied to all domains: men, places, housing, even animals. Foreshadowing the nineteenth-century discourse on hygiene, cleanliness was equated with progress and the Enlightenment, whereas dirtiness was associated with bestiality, and any people perceived by the French to be dirty were relegated to the fringes of civilization. What French soldiers saw while campaigning confirmed stereotypes that reveal the power of collective representations. Thus, while Germans and Dutch were usually presented as models of cleanliness and tidiness, the Spaniards, southern Italians, or Egyptians[22] were denounced for being repellently filthy. Grenadier Guardsman Henri Scheltens, unafraid of generalizations or of reiterating stereotypes, confidently proclaims in his memoirs:

> Spaniards in the lower classes are all revoltingly filthy. No water ever touches the inside of their houses, least of all in the countryside, while among the ordinary people, mules, asses, and pigs inhabit the ground floor, so that the smell of the animals gets into the furthermost corners... The peasants never wash their hands.[23]

Another criterion used for comparing countries, and thus for asserting national identity, was economic more than cultural. What soldiers observed of a country's poverty or wealth, and in particular whether the countryside was cultivated, formed the basis for judging a nation's moral qualities, such as its propensity for work and its industrious, hard-working character. Similarly, the prosperity of a city and of its trade and industry was taken as evidence of an advanced civilization, in contrast to the poverty, misery, material shortages, and uncultivated fields that characterized other peoples. The wealth or poverty of a country is sometimes related to external factors (such as geographical situation, climate, soil fertility, or aridity), but more usually it is presented and explained as the logical consequence of human labour or the lack of it, and thus as an element in the national character of a people. This is illustrated by the following extract from Octave Levavasseur's memoirs, concerning his arrival in Spain in 1808:

> Streams with many waterfalls, but no factories to make use of them; on the rocky hilltops, houses or rather eagles' nests, built at the time of the Moors, but on the slopes, none of the villages and isolated houses that animate and enliven a landscape. The land has the potential to produce but is never cultivated. Only sheep and wild bulls wander the uncleared heath. The power of nature is everywhere, and the strength of man nowhere, except in the vicinity of the towns, for the indolent hand of the Spaniard extends no further than this.[24]

Food provides a final unifying element against which to appraise foreign countries, to make comparisons with France and thus to express a sense of national difference. When writing about the countries they visited, French soldiers commonly describe the culinary customs of the populations, the local produce, and the flavour of foreign dishes and beverages. Some, like Chevallier, distinguished two types of

European country: countries where the national drink was beer, and those where wine was more common; his preference was for the latter. During his stay in the Low Countries, in 1811, he noted that in Brussels

> ...'what little wine there is sells for three or four francs a bottle, and is it really wine?...The beer is very good. It comes in several kinds: Louvain beer is pale and light; country beer is strong and thick like chocolate; faro and lambic, the best and the most expensive, is distilled and clear like spirits...The inhabitants, used to living with other nations, are polite though undemonstrative. This comes from the climate, and beer drinkers are never as vivacious as wine drinkers... [At Antwerp] the men spend their time doing trade, smoking tobacco, or drinking bad beer... Beer is the usual drink since poor wine sells for three or four francs a bottle...The men all walk at an unhurried and steady pace, with their heads down, they always seem deep in thought, being slow and unexcitable'. [Pursuing the culinary comparison, Chevallier added that] 'Bread is very expensive, which scarcely troubles the Dutch who eat none or next to none, and who even seem to dislike it. We big bread eaters had difficulty obtaining a small quantity of bread, they would rather give four *livres* of meat than half a *livre* of bread. Although meat is also dear, in a meal for thirty people there are sixty *livres* of meat but enough bread for only two Frenchmen with normal appetites'.[25]

As well as these points of comparison, soldiers sketched out a people's national character by reference to other factors. These varied with the social background of the writer. Soldiers from well-to-do families and those who had received a classical humanist education generally attached much more importance to the arts, culture, architecture, and urban landscapes. Typically, they contrast the large cities with the countryside and small towns, or northern Italy with southern Italy. Others consider the tastes and behaviour of different peoples, making bold generalizations, and defining national types. True to the clichés and representations of the time, the Italian was outgoing, lively, cultivated, cheerful, and musical, whereas the German and most of all the Dutchman was slow-witted, ponderous, melancholy, and hardworking but, lacking any artistic feeling or sense of fantasy, was dull and morose. Chevallier, in his memoirs, exemplifies this approach to the point of caricature. He gives careful definitions of the national types – on occasions presented with a scientific and objective gloss – and claims to want to re-establish truth and denounce stereotypes (such as the supposed alcoholism of the Germans), but ends up asserting the superiority of the French over all other peoples.

> Germany as a whole is a fine country, particularly Bavaria.... Of note in many towns are the grotesque paintings decorating the façades of the houses; these paintings have nothing like the refinement of those in Italy, and come nowhere near those of antique Herculaneum. The architecture of the monuments is inelegant and tasteless, nothing like the Roman monuments that cover Italy. The majority of palaces and gardens are poorly designed... What makes the Germans dull, slow, and severe is that in their houses there is always a hot stove – beer, the smoke of smokers, the stove and tobacco smoke that fill the atmosphere, it must be this that makes the Germans dull and gloomy. Playhouses are rare, and even in the large towns it is difficult to find one; the theatre is extremely feeble and narrow, not to say boring and monotonous; one does not go to the theatre to have a good time... Everything is done in the same way: methodical, slow, one step at a time, without haste, without boldness... The German is hard-working and temperate, but stubborn and ideological...... Because a lot of fermented beverages are drunk in Germany, we think of the Germans as drunkards; I believe, on the contrary, that the majority are most temperate... The language seems extremely harsh to us, it is inharmonious but not as difficult as it looks. The French made themselves reasonably well understood. We were the masters, it is true, and that irons out many of the difficulties over language.[26]

However superficial their judgements, the attempts of French soldiers to analyse what constitutes the essence of a people, of a nation, attest to the emergence of this concept and thus to the affirmation of a national identity that was both real and increasingly democratic. From being the monopoly of a few men of letters, authors of pamphlets and essays in previous centuries, it was now being observed, experienced, and assimilated by ordinary soldiers, men of humble origins, mostly from peasant backgrounds. The war gave these men an opportunity to move beyond the confines of their region or even of their country, and to discover other peoples and other societies; in so doing they perceived what they might have in common with a soldier from a different region. In this way, the war represented a first step in the shift away from a regional identity and towards the affirmation of a national identity.

This comes over particularly strongly when the soldiers are presenting and describing the countries they have visited. In their attempts to sum up differences and communicate them to their family, they use familiar referents, making comparisons with places, monuments, objects, and customs in France. This is how Narcisse Faucheur describes the city of Dresden in his memoirs: 'The Elbe, whose source is in Bohemia, emerges from a gap in these hills and divides Dresden into two parts almost as the Seine divides Paris, and there is a further similarity in that the Elbe at Dresden is roughly the same width as the Seine at Paris.'[27] Faucheur's choice of reference in this example is in itself revealing of the growing sense of national identity. To describe Dresden he compares the Elbe to the Seine and Dresden to Paris, the capital of France, even though he himself, far from being a Parisian, actually came from Clermont-Ferrand in the Auvergne.

The emergence of a French national identity, as yet timid but unmistakeable nonetheless, was also signalled by the awareness of national frontiers, in particular of immediately visible physical frontiers – a river like the Rhine, or a mountain range like the Pyrenees. In their writings, the men often present crossing the frontier and entering France as a moment of general rejoicing, whichever region the soldiers were from, even if they came from the Nord or from the Centre of France. Grenadier Guardsman Henri Scheltens was born in Belgium, one of the states annexed to France. In his memoirs he describes the return to France after taking part in the war in Spain: 'We drew steadily closer to the frontiers of France ... Finally, on 2 March 1812, we arrived at Fontarabie and, crossing the Bidassoa, we stepped onto the soil of France. The troops' enthusiasm as they went over the bridge separating France from Spain was unimaginable. Canteens, pots and mess-tins were all thrown in the river. Try as the officers might, it was impossible to put a stop to this. Everything went in, to an accompaniment of ringing hurrahs of Vive la France!'[28]

Language and habitat were also elements of national cohesion. Several soldiers confessed to feeling immense joy when, at the end of a long foreign campaign, they heard their language spoken and caught sight of the first French village.

II. Cultural identity: membership of minority religions and secret fraternities

Culture and religion could also function as unifying elements, especially in the case of minority faiths with a marginal or persecuted status, or of secret elitist communities. Either because they belonged to a minority religion or because they were part of a community whose founding principle was solidarity between its members, fellow Jews or Freemasons tended to give each other mutual support, and in some situations this cultural identity proved stronger than their national or military identity. Soldiers and civilians, even when of opposing nations, could count on help from men professing the same faith or belief.

Contemporary soldiers were aware of this and some did not hesitate to exploit it by cynically manipulating civilians. A case in point is Imperial Guardsman Picart, who obtained free provisions and accommodation during the Russian campaign by pretending to be a French Jew. The account by his friend Adrien Bourgogne shows the extent to which racism and anti-Semitism inherited from the eighteenth century permeated the collective representations held by French soldiers in the revolutionary and Napoleonic eras,[29] as well as the importance of a shared attachment (albeit fictitious in this case) to a marginal religion.

> We got to the back of the synagogue, next to which was a small house where Picart stopped. He looked left and right to see if the coast was clear and then, pinching his nose, he called out several times in a nasal voice 'Jacob! Jacob!' At a hole we saw appear a face wrapped in a long fur bonnet and wearing a dirty beard. It was Jacob the Jew. Recognizing Picart, he said to him in German 'Ah, it is you Solomon my dear, I will let you in!' The Jew opened the little door and we went into a room – very warm but stinking and filthy. When we were seated on a bench around the stove we saw three other Jews come in and Jacob told us they were his family. Picart knew how to go on with his pretended co-religionists and began by opening his bag, then took out a pair of epaulettes, not of a colonel but a brigadier, some rubbishy stripes, all new stuff, picked up on the Wilna mountain, from abandoned wagons. There was also some silver tableware that came from Moscow. The Jews stared wide-eyed. Picart asked for bread and wine. Some excellent Rhine wine was brought; the bread was not of the same quality, but at that time it was more than could be hoped for. While we were drinking, the Jews looked at the objects spread out on the bench. Jacob asked Picart how much he wanted for it all, to which Picart replied, 'You tell me.' The Jew quoted a price a long way off what Picart wanted, and he said 'No!' Jacob said something higher, and this time Picart, who was beginning to feel the effect of the wine, looked at the Jew... and in reply put a finger on the side of his nose and hummed – not words but the chant of the rabbi in the

> synagogue on the Sabbath. The four Jews also began to sway…and sing verses. Grangier looked at Picart, thinking he was mad…At last Picart stopped singing and poured us some drink. Meanwhile the Jews were talking together about the price of the objects. Jacob offered a higher price but it was still not what Picart wanted, so he began his racket again and went on until agreeing to the price on condition that he was given gold. Jacob paid Picart with Prussian gold coins.[30]

Also important as a unifying element was Freemasonry. A key feature was the mutual help and support that Masons were required to provide each other, mutual help that was especially precious and sought after in time of war. Together with other aspects of Freemasonry (notably its elitist character in the eighteenth century), this explains the strong appeal that the movement had for the military elite of the day, as it did for civilian political and administrative elites. In 1788–1789, France counted more than 100 army lodges, with 690 Masons for 3000 officers in the line infantry, an average of 22.9 per cent Masons among officers with a maximum of 53.2 per cent in the Penthiève Infantry Regiment.[31] On the eve of the Revolution, more than one in five French officers was a Freemason. The Revolution disrupted the hold of Freemasonry in the army, due to the emigration of large numbers of noble officers and to the decree of the Constituent on 6 August 1790 banning 'deliberative associations' from the regiments. By the end of 1790, most of the army lodges had ceased to function.[32]

Freemasonry in the army underwent a revival following the Peace of Amiens in March 1802. That year alone saw the setting up of 12 lodges in the infantry, two in the dragoons, and one in the artillery. This trend continued even when the war resumed. During the entire period of the Consulate and Empire, a total of 132 masonic lodges were created in the army.[33] In the line infantry, an average of 24 per cent of the officers were Freemasons in 1805, and the proportion reached 44 per cent in the 54th Line Regiment. To a large degree, therefore, the cadres of the Imperial Army were Freemasons. In his memoirs, Octave Levavasseur noted the extent to which non-masons like him were marginal in the higher echelons of the military hierarchy.

> When I joined the regiment I was asked if I was a Freemason. Nearly all my comrades held positions in the institution. Young officers wasted no time seeking admission and underwent strict tests, descriptions of which often formed the subject of our conversations at mealtimes. As the real purpose of Freemasonry was concealed from

> the newly initiated and none was made known, of all the officers in the regiment I was perhaps alone in thinking I should keep out of it. Indeed, I mocked my comrades so much that, later on, had I sought to be admitted I would have been pointed out to the whole corps and put through the most gruelling tests.[34]

The reasons for becoming a Freemason were of three kinds. First, the sociability associated with Freemasonry made it valued as a source of diversion. The Blaze brothers – Elzéar, and his younger brother Sébastien, an army pharmacist – both became Freemasons; in his memoirs Elzéar explains the reasons for his decision:

> When we were obliged to spend a long while in a garrison, we had two main ways of passing the time agreeably. If there was a Masonic lodge, we would attend it as a group, or else we'd form one just for us. It is well known that the brothers like to laugh and feast while performing the great work. In many regiments the officers formed a lodge with the colonel as the Worshipful Master.[35]

Beyond this festive aspect, Freemasonry held out the prospect of help between members that made it attractive to ambitious officers. More simply, since equality between brothers was one of its principles, Freemasonry was a way of putting aside hierarchical differences. Sergeant Robert Guillemard lauded its advantages:

> As a reward for my conduct in the engagement of 6 August, I was proposed for the masonic lodge of the regiment, and my admission was set for Saint Napoleon's day. It took place with all the pomp that the circumstances allowed – a hut fifteen feet long and six feet wide, in which you could not stand upright, was used as the temple. After I had made my journeys, which were not very long, undergone the ordeals of water, fire, and all the customary mystifications, received the passwords, signs... and other niceties, the adjutant, our speaker, made me a fine speech, in which he elaborated on the sublimity of the character that had just been communicated to me, by making me a "child of the true light", and all the happiness that I would derive from this. I then took part in a banquet, and you can imagine how delightful it was to hear myself referred to as "my brother" by our colonel and all the officers. I left full of enthusiasm for masonry, of which I became a fervent supporter and for a long time I believed it meant something.[36]

But others, like General François Dumonceaux, who was initiated into the Freemasons at Versailles in 1810, was disappointed with the experience, as he acknowledged in his memoirs:

> Solicited by one of my comrades from the grenadiers, I got myself accepted into a Masonic lodge... I was promised all manner of advantages, in respect of social relations... I was admitted with all the fantastical tests customary on such occasions... I never derived any advantage from my membership of Freemasonry and the only one I ever saw was for the jokers looking to spin their yarns.[37]

In addition to social relations, Freemasonry afforded protection against wartime dangers in encounters with the enemy. Promises of help between members counted for much in these situations, particularly since Freemasonry, like other intellectual movements originating in the Enlightenment, aspired to be cosmopolitan, universal, and supranational. The Masonic bond could transcend enmities and divisions between countries and prove stronger than patriotic and nationalistic ties. For Masons on opposing sides to help each other was not unusual, as shown by the use of Masonic signs on or off the battlefield in case of danger. Octave Levavasseur witnessed this during a battle in Spain: 'We came across some Spanish troops that we charged furiously... When the troops retreated to the village of *** we pursued them there. A Spanish engineer officer was up a belfry, using a telescope to carry out reconnaissance of distant positions. He came down just as we arrived and met me first. He immediately went on his knees and began frantically making Masonic signs', and, Levavasseur concludes, 'In the army, the promise to assist and help each other became very useful; there was fraternization even between enemies.'[38] This was in accordance with the instructions issued by the masters of the lodges. On 30 February 1808, the president of the *Parfaite Amitié* lodge in Brussels asked whether it was not Freemasonry that 'in the midst of the fury of war has often turned the sword of death from an enemy head?' Similarly, the master of the lodge of the 30th Line Regiment drew the attention of the other brothers, 'The Enemy victor, if he is a Mason, becomes their friend as soon as he has recognized them as brothers, and if they... are the victors and they recognize a Freemason among the vanquished... they must become the friend of their prisoner.' During the war Freemasonry became a means of protection – a 'society of insurance against military murder'.[39]

All this was well known to soldiers, and many did not hesitate to make masonic signals to the enemy when their position was desperate. A number of officers mention this in their memoirs. Thus Bouilly notes:

> The power of our fraternal bonds is so great that it even operates between those that the interests of the fatherland set against each other. How could one forget the bloody combat of Trafalgar, where the French navy, obliged to yield to the superior force and the genius of a famous enemy, chose to die rather than fall into the hands of the victor? Nelson had issued the order to give no quarter . . . On the point of being cast into the bloodstained waters, several French sailors remembered the strength of Freemasonry among the Scots. They tried making the first recognized signs and, getting an answer, made the distress signal . . . more than one hundred and sixty of them were carried on board in the arms of the enemy, lavished with care and restored to life.[40]

The help that Freemasons gave each other also crossed the division between the military and civilian worlds. The Belgian grenadier, Henri Scheltens, notes in his memoirs that 'For officers at this time there were great advantages to be had from joining a masonic lodge. It enabled good relations to be established with the leading figures of the towns where you were garrisoned, and was a source of civilian protection in wartime.'[41] Some soldiers admitted to receiving help from foreign civilians who were Freemasons. When Joseph Dembowski, a Pole serving in the French Army, left Saint-Domingue in 1802 penniless and hungry, an American Freemason from Charleston provided him with lodging until he could find a boat to return to France.[42]

III. Military identity

One element of cohesion in an army is the development of a public opinion and a public space specific to the war and to combatants. André Loez has identified this phenomenon for the Great War, showing how acceptance of the fighting in the intensely public setting of the trenches depended on the opinion of fellow soldiers.

> What matters . . . is the public nature of behaviour, when every movement is instantly visible. In the trenches, everyone lived in view of everyone else, in a space where nothing went unobserved and

> nothing remained secret. This made it absolutely necessary to "keep face"...and not add to the dangers of the war itself that of having one's identity called into question...Beneath the public gaze it was necessary to hide one's tears and other signs of emotional distress...It is clear that the visibility of one's emotions imposed a constraint, that "keeping face" was an imperative, and that any course other than "sticking it" was impossible in this public setting in full view of other people...The public setting of the trenches thus had a fundamental role in instilling and sustaining tenacity. Since conduct and demeanour were all instantly visible, any failings in manly courage were noted and sanctioned...This contributed to perpetuating the corporal *habitus* (control of emotions and bearing) and to constructing the identities that kept individuals in the conflict.[43]

Loez relates this public scrutiny of behaviour to the particularities of a place – the trenches – that was specific to World War I, but it was present, too, on the battlefields of the revolutionary and Napoleonic wars. Unlike those of the First World War, battlefields at this time, though often larger than in earlier conflicts, were still usually on a human scale. Thus combatants were subjected to the pressure of group opinion and exposed to the scrutiny of others, the more so since regiments commonly fought in grouped formation, thus bringing together in the same place men who were in daily contact outside the place of combat.

In his memoirs, Narcisse Faucheur relates how in 1812, during his first long expedition from Napoléon-Vendée – the present-day town of La Roche-sur-Yon – to Mainz, and only a few weeks after his arrival in the army and incorporation into the 26th Line Regiment, he went for several days concealing from the other troops the pain he endured during the long marches, weighed down by the foot soldier's heavy pack. He wanted to appear equal in strength and stamina to the others: what kept him going, pushed him to carry on and overcome the pain was not patriotism or republican ideology or personal ambition, but the pressure of the group, the fact of being observed by his fellow soldiers. Anxious to avoid losing face he even took to marching at night in an attempt to keep up with more experienced soldiers.

> I had stout legs and broad shoulders but the skin on the soles of my feet was still thin and delicate like a town boy's,...so that to reach the staging post...I suffered everything imaginable; nothing in the world would have persuaded me to remain in the rear, and were I sure

> of dropping from exhaustion on arrival I would never have broken rank, so full was I of the military pride that is an army's strength and with which it overcomes the greatest difficulties. My colleagues were all old soldiers well tried in the gruelling conditions of the war in Spain; the skin on their feet was like horn, whereas I suffered terribly on account of the roughness of the road. Finally we reached the staging post... Exhausted and in agony, I stretched out on some bales of hay and went to sleep. I woke up two or three hours later and from the pain I was in I knew that it was impossible for me to keep up with the ordinary progress of my colleagues. At no cost did I want to remain in the rear, so I resolved to... march all night stopping as often as I needed to... In the first league I stopped more than ten times, my feet felt as though they were on fire; had I been walking on hot coals I would not have suffered more... At last, when I reached Niort, I was fit to travel with my colleagues... Wanting to make up for the difficulties of the march in the eyes of my comrades, I tried to perform all the small services of good companionship whereby one makes friends, and to prove to everyone that I had also become good at marching, able to withstand bravely any fatigue. I was always careful, when I reached a staging post, to take care of my person so as to always maintain a correct military appearance.[44]

A military identity was also forged from a culture of soldiering that was both physical and mental, composed of gestures, words, symbols, and signs. This identity was sometimes infra-military in that it defined subgroups within the army. In such cases the divisions were by rank (officers and men) and thus possibly along social lines, by generation or age group, by arm, or by regiment.

Social distinctions were not completely abolished in the army. Brun de Villeret, son of a Lozère magistrate from an influential but impecunious noble family, complained that democratization of the army had gone too far and that he had difficulty fitting into a community of men drawn mostly from the lower classes. 'I was posted to Sète in a recently formed company of coastguard gunners', he notes in his memoirs when discussing his arrival in the army in autumn 1794. He goes on, 'The company was composed, even its officers, of men from the lowest class. The captain was a barrel maker, his second in command a tavern-keeper. They were good people and serving with them was not unpleasant. Nonetheless, in such society I could not but feel ill at ease.'[45] Gradually, though, his preconceptions seemed to fade and he was able to overcome social prejudices and find his place in the group, as he shows when relating his arrival in Holland, with the 7th Artillery Regiment, in 1799:

> I was there with a dozen army officers, fine fellows but coarse and uneducated, who in the Ancien Régime would have only made sergeants or corporals. When I first saw them I feared that I was going to suffer. Not a bit of it. I showed kindness towards them and they replied in kind. Far from being hostile towards me, when the situation arose they always gave me more than my fair share of commons and were very pleasant about it... So my time passed agreeably enough.[46]

If acts of kindness could not altogether efface social differences, the army does nonetheless appear as an institution with relatively democratic social relations, where communities and comradeship could develop without regard for social distinctions. Chevallier indicates this in his memoirs, regarding an incident while on leave in his hometown of Versailles, when he met a comrade from the same regiment but of more humble social origins:

> One day, I was out walking with a lady... I met a corporal from the company with an attractive young lady on his arm, we greeted one other and the women turned their heads, though each knew the other, since the corporal's young lady was the forewoman and trusty maid servant of my lady. Neither of them ever spoke about this encounter, and corporal Théroine, today a retired officer, never spoke about it either, and nor did I.[47]

By fostering the soldier's pride and urge to emulate, the *esprit de corps* associated with membership of a particular combat arm makes an essential contribution to the morale and tenacity of combatants. Under the Empire, the Imperial Guard, successor to the Consular Guard, was considered by its members to be the elite of the army. The Imperial Guard enjoyed a degree of independence from the regular army, having its own general staff, separate infantry, cavalry, pontooner and artillery corps, and complete with a regiment of *pupilles* (orphans), *vélites*, and veterans. In his memoirs, Henri Scheltens, a grenadier guardsman, proudly evokes the campaign of 1814, when France was invaded:

> This campaign should be considered the campaign of the Guard. The battles, in the course of which they brought dread and death into the

> ranks of the enemy, are forever memorable for the Guard. More than once their mere presence caused the enemy to retreat. Everywhere their name inspired terror, and they always lived up to the glorious reputation earned in previous campaigns. For as long as men talk of Bar-sur-Aube, Saint-Dizier, Brienne, La Rothière, Vauchamps, Hangie, Montereau, Château-Thierry, etc. these names will stay irrevocably linked to the memory of the Guard.[48]

The same elitist view was held by Imperial Guardsman Chevallier when he discussed the *vélites* corps to which he belonged:

> If the spirit of the Old Guard was distinctive and different from that of the other army corps, the *vélites* also had a distinctive spirit that owed nothing to the other regiments of the army: great pride and military chivalry, great presumption and bravura, great self-esteem and courage, and an immense desire to distinguish oneself. And this privileged corps certainly had great military virtues... Numerous fine and courageous officers, educated and of uncommon valour issued from this seedbed of military talent.[49]

The strong *esprit de corps* that was so characteristic of the Imperial Guard sometimes came under attack from officers and soldiers of other companies, as Octave Levavasseur indicates in his memoirs:

> The Imperial Guard exercised a marked preponderance in the quarters. Contact with it was most unpleasant. Everything seemed to be destined for the Guard. Its soldiers always got double rations. It was the same for services attached to the Guard. One day a convoy of donkeys came before the military *intendant* and the drivers asked for their rations. The *intendant* gave them coupons for ordinary rations, whereupon the drivers exclaimed "We are the donkeys of the Guard!", to which the *intendant* replied, "That's different then, the Guard's donkeys, mules' rations". By its higher status among pack-saddled animals, the mule was to the donkey what the Guard was to the line. This witticism became famous in the line army and was repeated whenever line troops and the Imperial Guard mixed together: "The Guard's donkeys, mules' rations".[50]

A sense of elitism and *esprit de corps* also bound together the groups that formed within the army among graduates of the military schools set up under Napoleon. This elitism and group loyalty could be deeply resented by officers who had not graduated from a military school but had instead 'grown up under the yoke' and climbed the military hierarchy by merit, combat action, and seniority. Divisions sometimes appeared between officers educated in the schools and the others, as Brun de Villeret, a graduate of the École Polytechnique, noted with regard to his posting to the Armée de Hollande in 1799: 'The ranker officers were starting to become disgruntled with the young men from the student corps, who occasionally made fun of their ignorance.'[51]

The soldiers came together for rituals and rites that punctuated their everyday routine, establishing new points of reference to replace those of civilian life and contributing to sociability and group cohesion. They even had a language of their own, a 'barrack room slang',[52] that set them apart from the civilian population. Narcisse Faucheur in his memoirs alludes to the particular vocabulary of the soldier: 'As soon as we got to the barracks, known in military language as "quarters", I hastened to ask for my letters.'[53] Prominent among the soldiers' rituals were festivals or *fêtes*, of which there was no shortage: in the army practically every occasion was an opportunity for festivities, generally with copious amounts of drink. During the revolutionary wars, the 'republican' festivals coexisted with those to celebrate and commemorate French victories; while the former declined under the Consulate and Empire, the latter continued to be as frequent and as lavish as ever. And the troops now had other *fêtes* to celebrate: political festivals – principally the Saint Napoléon, on 15 August – and, once the Concordat reinstated religion in public life, religious festivals, including those to honour the patron saints of particular arms or regiments. The gunners honoured their patron saint, Sainte Barbe, by downing glass after glass in her honour.[54]

One consequence of the development of this professional military identity was a growing distance between soldiers and civilians and the rise of military professionalism.[55] Gradually, this military community and identity tended to become the main reference of soldiers at war: 'Soldiers ended up by regarding the eagle of their regiment as their village's church tower, their regiment as a family, and sometimes their captain as a father.'[56]

Many soldiers in their writings also point out the contrast between their experiences and the daily life of civilians during the war. They had some hardships in common, like rising prices and shortages, and soldiers acknowledged that civilians faced real difficulties; still, they nonetheless thought that this was nothing compared with what they went through in terms of suffering, exhaustion, and danger. Young soldiers, volunteers or conscripts, were often highly critical of their contemporaries who stayed at home. The word *embusqué* or 'shirker' to designate men who found safe and sheltered positions for the duration of the war and thus avoided the hardships of active military service made its appearance during World War I, but the concept and the reality that lay behind the expression existed well before. Strategies for avoiding or limiting exposure to the rigours of war, similar to those used in the First World War and analysed by Charles Ridel,[57] were also deployed during the wars of the French Revolution and Empire. Soldiers who had been in combat were harshly critical of those who managed to avoid conscription.

One way of contributing to the war effort without playing an active role in the war was to volunteer to look for 'republican saltpetre' used in making gunpowder. Many recruiting officers denounced young men who, though they claimed to be occupied in this activity, were in fact living at home.[58] Soldiers frequently made the same charge in their letters. Joliclerc wrote to his mother on 27 January 1795:

> I had a letter from Emmanuel Gaillier. He is outside Mainz, a sergeant. He told me of his situation ... He gave me news of our young men of Froidefontaine. He is no happier about it than me, and he is right. These citizens prefer producing saltpetre to singeing Austrians' moustaches. By Jove, that's where it's really hot. It's easy enough to play the hero when you're sitting next to a nice hot fire. But if we volunteers had done like them, you would all have been robbed in your cottages![59]

IV. Conclusion

The experience of war encouraged an affirmation and, even more, an acceptance and integration of collective identities by soldiers. Collective identities in the plural, because the identities in question were not mutually exclusive but complementary: they could be cumulated and juxtaposed.[60] The same person might consider himself to be simultaneously a Norman, a Frenchman, and a soldier. Regional, national, religious, and military identities were different facets of the same phenomenon: the recognition – fostered by danger, distance, and contact with the 'other' – of what it was that bound that person, an individual, to a given group or community, one whose members had the same values or practices, where he could find a readiness to emulate and help, and where a common experience, like attendance at the same military school for officers, use of the same language by soldiers from a region with strong local traditions, or membership of the same political or cultural organization, formed the bases for similarity in understanding and outlook.

Their individual experiences of the war enabled soldiers to situate themselves in various groups, societies, and communities and to define or redefine the collective identities that linked them together. These identities had a dialectical relationship with war, and more precisely with the experience of war that forms the subject of this book. By conditioning their perception of objects and of men, these identities shaped soldiers' experience of war; equally, however, perception was itself shaped by this experience, by what soldiers went through and discovered in their daily existence.

6
War and the Economy

Soldiers of course bore the brunt of the almost continuous conflict, but civilians were by no means insulated from the events or from their repercussions on economic activity and daily life. Having observed French soldiers in a range of situations – exposed to shelling and battlefield horrors, bivouacked on the freezing steppes of Russia and Eastern Europe, fighting on warships and in the Egyptian desert, or in the scarcely less chaotic and dangerous conditions of field hospitals – it is now time to look at the group that formed the majority of the French population, the civilians. Few civilians had exposure to the physical reality of combat, but all had to endure the war's consequences. The next two chapters are given over to this other facet of war: the 'home front' and the war experience of civilians.

The businessmen of France – merchants, shipowners, craftsmen, entrepreneurs – were the first civilians to feel the full impact when war broke out. Before long, however, the political and military crisis was making far-reaching changes to activity and working conditions in the agricultural sector. In fact, the whole fabric of the French economy would be undermined by a conflict that was unprecedented in scale and duration, and involved massive requisitioning of men, material, and foodstuffs, a disruption or breakdown in communication and exchange, and an increasing militarization of society. Added to which, a succession of monetary and financial crises (several major defeats, notably Trafalgar, precipitated bank and stock market crashes) eroded confidence and depressed consumer spending. First to be affected were the great seaports, but the consequences of military operations and commercial and industrial crises were soon being felt throughout much of urban and rural France.

For the majority of players in the economy, the revolutionary and Napoleonic wars were a period of contraction and of changes in occupation or location. For a tiny minority they were an opportunity for speculation and personal financial gain. Finally, for a significant number they were a struggle for economic survival that sometimes ended in ruin.

I. Agriculture

By its demands on manpower, conscription generated deep discontent in rural France, especially at harvest time. In July 1793, the administrators of the District of Gaillac replied to the Directory of the Tarn department:

> We have received your letter of 4 [July] concerning the workers you requested for Perpignan. We shall carry out the requisition, but we feel that it will serve no good purpose in an agricultural district like ours, particularly now, at harvest time. We have provided the fatherland with so many defenders that their absence is greatly felt and we are short of labour for working the land... How do you think we can supply men without leaving our properties uncultivated; we are ardent patriots but we cannot do the impossible.[1]

A few weeks later, in September, at the height of the grape harvest, they even petitioned the directory of the department for a special measure – the return of the local conscripts to do field work – that was warranted by the needs of agriculture, they claimed. The request was unrealistic and not granted but shows the extent of the repercussions of the war effort in the countryside. 'This is the period when grapes are harvested and seed is sown, and is a most precious time. Would it not be possible to send all our men home for the grape harvest and sowing season?'[2]

The situation was the same in many other rural regions. At Porrentruy, in the Franche-Comté, François-Joseph Guélat noted in his diary on 19 October 1793,

> There were representations from many youths and from their mothers and fathers, requesting exemption from recruitment, based on the law that dispensed all those needed for threshing grain, as well as millers' and bakers' assistants, at the rate of one per master. Rather than risk accusation, none of them were sent off.[3]

One consequence of this situation was the rising cost of agricultural labour. The Law of the Maximum for wages enacted in 1793 to combat inflation, which introduced a 300 *livres* fine and 6 months in prison for any employer found guilty of overpaying his workers, was thus in practice unworkable and indeed actually encouraged a black market in seasonal labour. There were many instances of employers and local authorities being forced to grant wage increases when threatened with strikes by workers unable to live on fixed wages at a time of inflation.

The shortage of agricultural labour caused by conscription was so severe in some regions that the authorities had to intervene. In autumn 1793, the local authorities in Toulouse ordered all citizens to send their domestic servants to bring in the harvest.[4] A year later, the deputies Ingrand and Garnier were sent to the Charente-Inférieure where, on the eve of the harvest in 1794, they issued a decree requisitioning all available labour in the towns and cities of the department to help with the fieldwork necessary to maintain food supplies. In La Rochelle, this measure affected mainly women, who were forced to go each day into the surrounding countryside and who returned exhausted in the evening. Because money was scarce, their wages were paid in kind, in wheat, oats, or wine.[5]

In other cases, garrisoned or encamped soldiers were used in the same way. In his memoirs, Brun de Villeret describes a stay in the Gard in autumn 1794, when he was leading a battalion section of conscripts from his locality:

> The recruitment of young men having seriously depleted the local population... difficulties arose everywhere when it came to bringing in the harvest. The authorities of the Gard asked the camp commander for harvesters, and with my section I was sent to a village called La Calmette. As soon as we arrived we were issued with sickles. I pointed out that those who knew how to use one got on with the work willingly but that I had many youngsters from towns who did not know how to cut wheat for their own use. My observation angered the Popular Society, which informed me that everyone, excepting only myself, had to lend a hand. This was at the height of the Terror and heads were rolling in Nîmes every day. So there was no way of opposing it and all my subordinates were dispatched to farms. The peasants, however, were shrewder than their leaders and quickly saw that they gained nothing by feeding as harvesters people who had never cut a sheaf. They sent back to me all those they found useless for their work... With the harvest over, we returned to camp.[6]

On occasions, prisoners of war were also requisitioned for harvesting. This was the experience of Spanish prisoners in Toulouse.[7] Eventually, when all these measures proved inadequate, some municipalities decided in 1794 to exempt agricultural workers from conscription.[8]

Wheat prices remained high for much of this 20-year period, but the prices of most agricultural products collapsed. The price of land followed a similar course. Farmers faced the twin difficulties of a fall in their standard of living, and a contraction in trade that encouraged them to retreat from production for the market.

The situation was particularly critical in 1793–1794. The measures to control prices introduced after the voting of the Maximum, together with fears of requisitioning, made farmers reluctant to bring their produce to market and created serious problems for the provisioning of urban populations. Farmers who did go to towns and cities were immediately followed and placed under observation by the police and municipal tax agents looking to detect possible fraud, such as illicit or direct sales that bypassed the market.

With sales closely regulated, selling prices subject to a maximum, and payment made in rapidly depreciating *assignats*, farming became increasingly inward-looking and autarkic. Farmers stopped investing in seed and instead bought land or new livestock, thereby avoiding the requisitions of wheat and other field crops. In some cases the agricultural activities of entire regions were modified. In the Charente-Inférieure, as in many other departments, pasture increased at the expense of arable;[9] the latter being especially badly hit by the shortage of agricultural manpower.

Farmers became particularly fearful of requisitioning and reluctant to sell on the market during the *assignat* crisis of 1795. Autarkic impulses, denounced as attempted hoarding by some authorities, were strong at this time, as is revealed by this advice from the Auvergnat volunteer Joliclerc to his mother on 31 August 1795:

> You were very wrong not to make hay from our enclosed meadows. At least we would have had that, whereas with your 2,000 francs you have nothing. I think that you are letting yourself be dazzled by quantity, that you are counting as you did in the old days. Here, though, you wouldn't get a tupenny reaping-hook for 200 pounds. Absolutely no one wants *assignats*, least of all the peasants... Don't be so foolish again as to sell your cheeses! When they are delivered, eat some and put what you don't eat in a dry room. They will keep quite well for a few years... When you have something that you have

> to get rid of, exchange it for iron, wood, cloth, or staples. You have enough *assignats*, I tell you.[10]

Requisitioning was still a source of complaints from farmers under the Consulate and Empire, particularly in the frontier regions. In July 1810, the prefect of Haute-Garonne reported to the minister of the interior about the discontent caused by requisitioning in his department:

> Ever since the start of the war in Spain, the supply officers for Perpignan and Bayonne have been requisitioning hay, oats, grains, oxen, wagons, horses, pack-mules, etc. Doubtless obeying the highest imperative, the War Administration set the price of these supplies well below their market value and then paid for only a small part of them. It is estimated that one million is owed to this department, and if this delay persists it will be unable to pay its taxes! Instead of this system of requisition and arbitrary prices and payments, if there had been one based on purchase, by retaining some of the special war taxes abolished by His Majesty to help his people, there would have been no need to burden a few southern departments with contributions beyond their means. These contributions are nonetheless made, but there is widespread complaint.[11]

If requisitioning and manpower shortages created problems for agriculture, for the fishing communities, notably on the Normandy and Breton coasts, the situation was even more worrying. The frequent presence of British frigates prevented the French fishing boats from taking to sea. The few that were allowed out had to be escorted by soldiers or members of the National Guard, partly to prevent them being stopped and captured by the enemy, though also to ensure that they did not engage in espionage or pass information to the British. Since few troops or National Guards were available for this work, fishing fell to insignificant levels, as was noted by Conseiller d'État Barbé-Marbois during an inspection visit in the 13th Military Division in Year IX. Reaching Saint-Malo he noted that fishing is

> in a state of great hardship... Even around our own coasts, fishing expeditions are suspended or hampered by the English presence and the dangers associated with ease of communication. A bad year has deprived the inhabitants of what the land produces, and the sea, which compensates them with its abundance, is so to speak, forbidden to them.[12]

II. Commerce

The revolutionary and Napoleonic wars had a serious impact on commerce, and from early on most merchants were in no doubt about the desirability of a speedy return to peace. One such was Frédéric Tansard, who ran the Livorno branch of his family's trading house that operated between Italy – chiefly Genoa, Turin, and Livorno – and France. He wrote to his father on 19 November 1794, 'We are led to hope for imminent peace. This would be a most fortunate event, business would revive with a vengeance.'[13] Two years later, we find him complaining about the war's adverse effects on the commercial activity of the family firm:

> Humanity has suffered for so long. Commerce feels the effect of this and getting on with any work grows more complicated every day. The lack of confidence gets worse with the succession of difficulties and unless a strong hand puts a stop to all these troubles I truly do not know what will happen.[14]

International trade, like that engaged in by Tansard, and maritime commerce were especially badly affected by conditions at this time. A case study of maritime trade gives a clearer view of the impact of the war on commercial activity.

These years of war caused a shift in the economic geography of France, initially towards the Mediterranean regions, subsequently towards northern and eastern France. Maritime trade survived in the form of coasting by small craft, but there was a sharp decline in transatlantic traffic. The war at sea, the privateers, and the British blockade seriously hindered commercial shipping. In 1797, the French merchant fleet numbered only 200 seagoing vessels, one-tenth of its 1789 strength.[15] Trade did not cease completely, though. To get around the British blockade, merchants, masters, and shipowners had to use 'neutral' vessels, from countries not involved in the conflict, though these vessels also on occasion came under attack from privateers – from British corsairs, but also, in the Mediterranean, from Barbary Coast pirates, who did not hesitate to attack American merchant shipping. The peace made by the Treaty of Amiens stimulated the economy and benefited business, but the respite was short-lived. By 1803, tension was increasing, and when hostilities resumed maritime trade again collapsed, bringing stagnation and a paralysis of business in many major ports.

The strategies elaborated by French merchants and shipowners to cope with the difficulties caused by the war at sea were seriously threatened by the decree of 21 March 1806 that instigated the 'Continental System'. This prohibited trade with Britain and its colonies and imposed an economic blockade of Britain intended to suffocate its external trade – to which the British retaliated by a blockade of French ports and coasts. The French business community and large sections of public opinion were highly critical of a policy that disrupted economic activity, pushed up prices (particularly of foodstuffs), and imposed significant changes in French dietary patterns. Bourrienne, in his memoirs, is scathing about what he refers to as 'a system of money, fraud, and plunder',[16] and 'a fiscal tyranny that put exorbitant prices on foodstuffs that after three hundred years had become indispensable for rich and poor alike',[17] and again as 'a legislation of customs barriers...a legislation of death that...armed the coasts of the continent against the introduction of sugar'.[18] He points out the absurdity of an economic blockade without means of pressure, without ships to enforce it: 'What was needed was not a decree but fleets; without a fleet, without a navy, it was ridiculous to declare a blockade of the British Isles at the same time that the English fleets were in fact blockading all the French ports.'[19] French commerce thus felt the full effects of Napoleon's naval and economic strategy and the vicissitudes of the war at sea.

1. The Atlantic sector

The early stages of the Revolution brought few changes for French merchants and shipowners. Maritime commerce was not damaged by the political turmoil affecting the country. Economic conditions remained favourable and from 1789 until May 1792 it was largely business as usual. Indeed, for the merchants of France's three great Atlantic ports – Nantes, Bordeaux, and Le Havre – this was a period of prosperity. Compared with the years before the Revolution, there was a considerable increase in the number of ships fitted out for colonial cargoes or as slavers.

This maritime prosperity was ended abruptly by the slave revolt in Saint-Domingue in August 1791. This precipitated the collapse of the island's economy and with it a whole section of French seaborne commerce, based on the colonial markets of the Caribbean. The implications were particularly serious given the large place the colonial sector had taken in the French economy between 1763 and 1789. The share of colonial re-exports in external commerce had risen steadily whereas exports from mainland France had declined; the colonies were also an increasingly important outlet for domestic French products such as textiles. In addition, Saint-Domingue came to occupy a preponderant position within the colonial trade of a number of French ports in the last years of the ancien régime, whereas trade with the Windward Islands (Martinique and Guadeloupe) had stagnated or even fallen both relatively and absolutely.

In Bordeaux, for example, 66 per cent of ships sailing to the colonies between 1784 and 1789 (152 of 230 ships leaving the port annually in the last 5 years) went to Saint-Domingue, and they transported 70 per cent of the total average tonnage of goods destined for the West Indies. The share increased over this period, with the percentage of ships rising from 59 per cent in 1783 to 73 per cent in 1789, while the share of Saint-Domingue in Bordeaux's colonial exports rose above three-quarters, from 75 per cent to 82 per cent.[20]

Colonial commerce was also one of the main activities in Nantes, where it was *the* main motor of economic growth. After the treaty of 1783 and American independence, Nantes experienced remarkable levels of growth. Rennes might have been the political capital of Brittany, but after 1783 Nantes was its economic capital, noted the merchant Ouvrard, who lived there in 1788–1789: 'Everything about Nantes – its maritime commerce, its wealth, energy, and luxury, its fast-increasing population – made it one of the foremost cities of France.'[21] Having become one of the main centres for communication with the New World and for the trade in spices and other colonial raw materials, the city expanded rapidly. One developer, Graslin, even acquired large amounts of land and set about creating an entire new neighbourhood to provide the dwellings and shops needed for the luxury trades and for housing the working population that expansion had attracted. The onset of the revolutionary upheavals produced unease among the Nantes merchants who had acquired their wealth recently, and so who did not yet have a large capital in property. Many of them, expecting the Revolution to take measures against both their capital and their income, decided to invest their fortunes in the colonies by purchasing sugar, coffee, or cotton plantations, thinking that their money would be safe there far from the troubles in France.

The firm of Begouën, one of the largest merchants and shipowners at Le Havre, made substantial profits averaging around 300,000 *livres* per year between 1780 and 1789, most of which had been invested on the eve of the Revolution in colonial debt held in Saint-Domingue. Consequently, the firm felt the full effects of the revolt on the island and the war at sea. François Begouën paints a bleak picture of the situation in a letter of October 1797 to his friend and agent in New York,

Nicolas Olive: 'Unfortunately it is true that the state of affairs on Saint-Domingue offers a far from flattering or even reassuring prospect. It is still shifting ground, as it were, on which nothing can be built with safety.... In her commerce and manufactures, and in the foreign surplus that she used to receive each year, France will feel for a hundred years the great mistake she made in revolutionizing Saint-Domingue, in allowing the destruction of the richest, most useful and most prosperous colony in the world. The damage was done with the speed of lightning...I am getting over the loss, though not without also feeling a most bitter pain. No one in France knows, no one has ever known, what the possession of such a colony is worth for the prosperity of the state', and he added in January 1798, 'The hopes placed in the colonies are truly blighted. The unlucky colonists and all who care about the colonies will just have to be patient, for it looks as though their troubles are not yet over.'[22]

The revolt on Saint-Domingue dealt a blow to an entire sector of the French economy, dislocating the activity of the great seaports and bringing a collapse in the external trade surplus. Its impact was both abrupt and massive: in the space of a few weeks, between April and August 1792, shipowners stopped all shipments and brought their merchandise back from Saint-Domingue. As during any economic crisis, some made fortunes through skilful speculation. Gabriel-Julien Ouvrard, son of an entrepreneur from Poitiers (where he was the owner of a paper manufactory at Clisson), had moved to Nantes in 1788 when aged 18. Initially employed in the colonial trading house of Guertin, Loret et Compagnie, he then ran his own wholesale grocery business in partnership with one of his former employers (*maison* Guertin et Ouvrard) and was well placed to turn the disruption caused by revolution and war to personal advantage. In the early months of the Revolution, when most merchants in Nantes were tying up their money in the purchase of Caribbean plantations, Ouvrard was one of the few to realize that the upheavals in France would soon spread to the colonies and that when they did, their trade would cease. With new supplies of colonial products no longer arriving, supplies already in the metropole would necessarily command higher prices due to their relative scarcity. He concluded that it was those with the largest stocks who stood to make a fortune, not those with their money tied up in the Caribbean. After persuading his associate Guertin that his analysis was right, he also won over to his view some importers in Nantes and the owners of a Bordeaux trading house (Baour frères et Compagnie). Working together, the speculators built up large stocks, which they then sold at a handsome profit in the

2 years following the revolt of Saint-Domingue and the outbreak of the war at sea.

> Most of the capital acquired through commerce was put into colonial property. Sugar plantations earned 10%, cotton plantations 12–15%, and coffee plantations 15–20%. But I felt that the colonies could not avoid being drawn into the agitation affecting the metropole, and that the numerical superiority of the slave population and the distance from France and any help it could provide, left the colonists in an uncertain and dangerous position. The same considerations that turned me away from the idea of acquiring property in the colonies pushed me towards heavy dealing in colonial products. Working in partnership with some Nantes merchants and with Baour frères et Compagnie of Bordeaux, I made large profits in a short space of time.[23]

For Ouvrard, therefore, the maritime war was an excellent opportunity for personal gain. But such cases are few in number and limited to importers. The shipowners and merchants, by contrast, bore the full brunt of the maritime war that cut them off from their source of supplies.

In Le Havre, maritime commerce and shipping languished badly. After the untroubled prosperity they had enjoyed on the eve of the Revolution, shipowners now saw their business collapse. François Begouën, owner of one of Le Havre's leading merchant shipping houses, witnessed the near-total paralysis of economic activity. Commerce was quickly in difficulties. Of the five vessels belonging to the shipowner, one was laid up in December 1789, two others made their final voyage in 1791, and the remaining two returned to port in 1792 and did not leave again during the rest of the war. The other 12 ships – slavers, Newfoundland fishing boats, privateers – in which Begouën had an interest as a shareholder, lay idle throughout this period.[24] In his diary for 15 September 1792, he noted, 'Nothing is selling at the moment, there are no prices quoted whatsoever, no demand; it is true that the bankers in Paris are refusing to give any credit, and our present critical situation blocks all commerce.'[25] He reports the 'huge' bankruptcies among the merchants of Rouen and Le Havre, and notes that although prices had fallen, commodities of all kinds were 'still virtually unsellable'.[26] Faced with such difficult economic conditions, François Begouën decided in 1795 to put his business interests on hold and devote himself to farming. On 26 July 1795 he wrote to Nicolas Olive, his New York agent, 'It must be hoped that a time will come when I can go back to commerce and work with a few good American houses, but at present I am doing no business.'[27]

Outside of the ports, the collapse of maritime commerce resulted in a loss of outlets for large parts of France's industrial, agricultural, and mercantile sectors. Textiles from the West, agricultural products from the Aquitaine basin, wine and many other products were cut off from their export markets in the West Indies. Large sections of the French economy were damaged, as François Begouën pointed out to Nicolas Olive, 6 months after the start of the Consulate:

> I will not conceal from you that you will find traces everywhere of the terrible revolution we are emerging from. Commerce, industry, shipping, former institutions – all are in ruins... You speak of business stagnating in America. That cannot compare with what exists in France where all work is halted, where workers are idle because there are hardly any rich people left, except for a few in the capital; consequently there is no call for luxury craftsmen, any more than for workers in the manufactories or the men who earn a living from the commerce and shipping of our sea ports.[28]

In the regions along the Atlantic coast, every sector of the economy and every social class were affected by the cessation of maritime trade, the ruin of shipping and colonial commerce, the loss of colonial investments and loans, and by the increasingly difficult conditions of maritime trade with the countries of northern Europe. By 1793, the port of La Rochelle contained merely a few laid-up ships; incoming shipments declined in 1792 and were almost non-existent in 1793. The area's winegrowers were also badly affected. The British, traditionally large customers for wine from south-west France, had left the market, the Dutch and Scandinavians had reduced their convoys and purchases to insignificant levels, and customers from the Hanseatic regions rarely came to French ports, following heavy losses of shipping and cargoes to privateers.[29] The only remaining customers of importance in this area were the Americans, who, because they shipped foodstuffs, had the right to take return cargoes of wine and brandy. With colonial trade halted, La Rochelle's sugar refineries were deprived of their raw material, and in 1794, once their stocks were used up, the owners had to shut down their establishments, spelling unemployment for their workers. The glassworks shut in the same year, again because of lack of raw material. Building sites were abandoned, and forges closed down for lack of iron and charcoal.[30]

The salt producers of the Île de Ré were in an even worse plight than the winegrowers and brandy producers, due to a dramatic slump in salt exports. Fishermen on the North Sea and Channel coasts had stopped visiting the Newfoundland fishing grounds, while those operating from La Rochelle had not left port since the start of the maritime war. The 'industrial' demand for salt thus vanished. With their markets gone, the owners of the salt beds had no money coming in, further diminishing the trade between the city and its hinterland, between La Rochelle and the Île de Ré.

2. The Mediterranean sector

The revolt in Saint-Domingue had no direct economic impact in the Mediterranean. Maritime commerce in Marseille continued for the rest of 1792 and the port was actually busier, thanks to the trade diverted from the Atlantic ports. The decline in economic activity in the Mediterranean dates from 1793, from the declaration of war against Britain on 1 February and against Spain on 7 March.

Before 1793, Marseille dominated European trade with the Levant. In 1788, it accounted for 70.2 per cent of all trade between the North African ports and those of Europe (Marseille, Livorno, Genoa, Barcelona, and Malaga). Exports far exceeded imports (respectively 2,820,000 and 1,216,000 *livres tournois* in 1788), and Marseille ranked first in 1788 for exports of oil to the Levant, and second for wool and wheat.[31]

In the eighteenth century, Provence-based shipping enjoyed a near-monopoly in the transport of goods in the Mediterranean. Although the various treaties of peace and of commerce signed between the North African regimes and European states provided for reciprocity in the treatment of ships and merchants in the ports, the reality was very different. The rare North African ships that ventured into European ports, notably Marseille, were subject to a multitude of administrative formalities whose purpose was to delay and dissuade, and ultimately prevent, Arab merchants from selling their goods. Also, in the late seventeenth century, the Morean War (1684–1699) was fought in the eastern Mediterranean between the Ottomans and the Venetians. After pursuing the Ottomans, the Venetians took up position at the entrance to the Dardanelles, from where they blocked maritime communications within the Ottoman Empire between the capital and the provinces (Syria, Cyprus, Crete, Egypt). In 1686, the Ottoman authorities decided to make French merchant shipping officially responsible for commercial transport within the Empire. The practice was continued thereafter, partly on grounds of seamanship – French sailors of the day were superior to their Ottoman counterparts – and partly on those of security, since Muslim shipping came under attack from warships of the Christian states (Venice, Spain, and especially the Order of Malta aided by Maltese privateers),[32] whereas ships under the French flag could sail the Mediterranean in safety.

Through this practice of carrying trade for another party – the so-called *caravane maritime* – the Provençal ships gained a virtual monopoly of the Ottoman Empire's domestic shipping, earning large profits for the Marseille shipping companies.[33]

When maritime commerce in the Mediterranean collapsed in 1793, most Marseille merchants saw their activity decline or even stop completely.[34] Marseille had experienced economic crises in the past: the port was closed for 3 years after the 1720 plague epidemic, and again in 1774 (resulting in 154 bankruptcies in just a few months[35]). Previous wars had also depressed levels of economic activity. Thus ships into Marseille from the Levant and Barbary numbered 243 in 1777, 123 in 1779 during the American War of Independence, and 283 in 1783 when the war ended. But the impact of the revolutionary and Napoleonic wars was altogether more abrupt and far-reaching. There were three reasons for this: first, the emergence of the Mediterranean as the theatre of naval warfare; second, Britain's early achievement of naval superiority and control of the Mediterranean; and third, the siege of Toulon and total destruction of the French Mediterranean fleet by summer 1793. Lacking a military convoy, Marseille shipping was confined to port. Ships entering the port from North Africa declined from 191 in 1792 to 28 between January and June 1793, and remained at that level on average each year between 1794 and 1799. The situation was identical for ships coming from the Levant: from 209 in 1789 their number declined little until 1792 (190 in 1790, 195 in 1791, 190 in 1792), but plummeted in 1793 (51) and 1794 (4), and thereafter made only a very partial recovery (38 in 1795, 33 in 1796, 43 in 1797, 37 in 1798, 10 in 1799).[36]

Disembarking at Marseille on the way back from Egypt early in Year X, François Vigo-Roussillon was struck by the war's impact on maritime commerce: 'Marseille is without doubt one of the finest cities in France. Anything can be obtained there. When we disembarked, the city was extremely busy even though shipping was paralyzed by the war at sea.'[37]

Commerce between Marseille and the Levant did not cease completely, but it declined as port activity diverted to the rival Italian ports of Genoa and, above all, Livorno.[38] Thanks to an unprecedented expansion in *cabotage*, short-haul, and coastal shipping, Marseille was able to maintain indirect commercial ties with North Africa and the Levant. Military and civilian visitors to the city observed the effects of this change in the direction and organization of maritime trade. Early in Year X, François Vigo-Roussillon noted that 'the continental peace was enough to give a great stimulus to coastal trading and internal commerce. From what we saw we could imagine what this trade was like at Marseille.'[39]

The number of small coastal craft, with a capacity of a few tens of tonnes, arriving in Marseille from Liguria and Tuscany, rose rapidly in this period: 548 ships per year on average between 1789 and 1792, 1,106 per year between 1793 and 1799.[40] Evidence of the reorientation occurring in the geography of maritime commerce between Europe and the Levant was also visible at the other end of the trade route, in the Levantine ports. The managers of some French companies in these ports placed themselves under Prussian or Austrian protection so as to have the possibility of sending their goods in neutral ships as far as the ports of Genoa and Livorno, from whence they were sent on to Marseille. For the ports of Liguria and Tuscany combined, the number of ships coming from the Levant rose from 490 in 1789 to 1,483 in 1794.[41]

Yet even coastal trading became fraught with difficulties once the British controlled the Mediterranean and implemented a coastal blockade. This happened in 1793–1795, during their occupation of Corsica, and after 1806, with the economic blockade in response to Napoleon's Continental System. The period 1793–1795 corresponded to the maximum British naval presence in the Mediterranean, when forward and rear bases were established near the French coast. It was a difficult time for all forms of maritime commerce. Short-haul trading between neighbouring Mediterranean ports was still possible, though not with Corsica. In her memoirs, Laure Junot, Duchesse d'Abrantès, relates the experience of her aunt, a Parisian of Corsican origin, in this matter:

> At this time, everyone was trying to add to what little fortune had been salvaged... My aunt calculated quite rightly that she could get profitable results by sending merchandise to the Provençal ports that could then be sent on to Corsica, and by bringing back other goods in exchange. Some time after the siege of Toulon, she sent sheets and cloth to Marseille for forwarding to Calvi. Her agent wrote to say that the English controlled the sea too tightly to attempt to get goods across safely. "Take my advice", he added, "sell your goods at Toulon or at Antibes or Nice. Among the soldiers, twenty out of thirty have

no shirts. Your cloth is excellent and, as the price is quite high, you will make a good sale... Your business should earn a 50% profit."[42]

The duchesse's aunt followed this advice and entrusted her goods to one of her father's former servants, a Corsican now living in the Marseille area who engaged in some trading and coasting with the neighbouring Mediterranean ports.

Another source of difficulty for maritime trade was lawlessness at sea. The Mediterranean at this time was a *champ clos*, a combat area, where all kinds of sea adventurers operated at will. One unexpected consequence of the revolutionary and Napoleonic wars was a reappearance of the Barbary pirates in the Mediterranean. There were several reasons for this. The sharp decline in trade between Marseille and the Levant due to the difficulty in maintaining maritime communications severely reduced the customs revenues of the North African regimes, weakening them economically and threatening the incomes of their leading families. In addition, Napoleon's Italian conquests disrupted trade between North Africa and Genoa or Livorno. In the past, treaties to limit the attacks of Barbary corsairs were made between certain European countries and the North African regimes, the former agreeing in exchange to pay a regular tax. These payments to the regimes ceased when France annexed the Netherlands and incorporated its fleet into the French Navy, and when the Venetian Republic was abolished and its dependent territories annexed. Seeing their income shrink and eager for reprisals, the Barbary pirates, supported by the regimes, resumed their activities. In this way, the pirates benefited from a new freedom of action, since the abolition of the Order of Malta following the French conquest of Malta removed an old adversary that had remained on the offensive right up to its demise: in Tunisian waters alone, the Order's warships and Maltese pirates captured 33 corsair ships between 1770 and 1779, 28 in 1780–1789, and a further 32 in 1790–1798; the captured corsair crews being kept as slaves on Malta.[43] Pirate attacks against French craft, and against those of the Republic's annexed territories and its allies, began in 1798, after the sultan, concluding that by the expedition to Egypt Napoleon had ended good relations with his Empire, had his North African provinces declare war on France. In 1798, the Algiers regency fitted out 27 corsair ships, which captured booty to the value of 1,510,528 *francs or* (the total in prizes during the year). The total annual value of prizes declined thereafter, averaging 150,000–200,000 *francs or*, though the Algiers regency alone still captured goods with a value of 2,136,675 *francs or* in 1812.[44]

The Barbary pirates damaged commerce by capturing cargoes, but piracy was a plague throughout the Mediterranean at this time. On 19 August 1806, Vice-Admiral Burgues-Missiessy, commander of the French Navy at Toulon, issued the following warning to the Marseille merchants through the city's chamber of commerce:

> I have just received a letter from Algiers informing me that several pirate vessels flying the black flag are cruising the Mediterranean, where they are causing heavy losses. I have been assured that they have already plundered various ships and massacred their crews...Two of these boats have already been identified...They are believed to come from the Gulf of the Adriatic. I hasten to inform you, Sirs, of this unpleasant news so that you may make it as widely known as possible and that our seamen may be on the look out lest they run into these scoundrels.[45]

The position of supremacy in the *caravane maritime* that the French had acquired during the ancien régime was thus lost during the Revolution. French ships using the port of Rhodes, for example, numbered 121 in 1776 but a mere eight in Year IV (1796). The insecurity that now afflicted French shipping in the Mediterranean led foreign merchants to end their agreements with the French and turn instead to neutral-country shipowners and masters – to the Venetians, Ragusans, and above all Ionians (Greeks). The French vice-consul at Rhodes, Chépy, informed the foreign ministry on 21 December 1797 that 'Far from improving, the situation gets worse each day for the European caravan. The Ottoman Turks and Greeks have grabbed nearly all the profits of the freight trade.'[46] The diplomat's fears are borne out by the statistics: of 92 ships entering the port of Rhodes in Year VI, more than two-thirds (59) were Greek or Ottoman, the remainder being from Venice (20), or Ragusa (13). No French ship entered the port in Year VI.[47]

The Greek merchant fleet experienced an unprecedented expansion at this time.[48] In addition to the security offered by their shipping, the Greeks were in a position to operate the *caravane* at much lower costs. Michel-Joseph Trullet, *drogman* or interpreter at Nauplion, wrote a report (dated 25 May 1803) bringing the Greek competition to the attention of the French authorities and public, in which he explained how the combination of lightly built and simply fitted ships, together with the low wages of crews recruited mainly from the fishing and farming populations of the islands, enabled it to reduce freight costs substantially.[49] Between 1794 and 1820, growing numbers of Muslims,

North Africans, and Levantines were also involved in the *caravane maritime*.[50]

3. Crisis and reorganization of maritime commerce

The collapse of the Atlantic trade between Bordeaux and Saint-Domingue was initially compensated for by a reorientation of trade to the colonies not affected by the revolt, Guadeloupe, Martinique, and the islands of the Indian Ocean. But the Windward Islands did not escape the war at sea. In February 1793, the British, commanded by Admiral John Jervis, attacked the French possessions in the West Indies, taking first Martinique, followed by Sainte Lucie, Tobago, and, in April 1794, Guadeloupe where British forces occupied Basse-Terre and then the whole island. The French government responded by sending 1000 men led by Corentin de Leissègues, with the mission of bringing the islands back into the French commercial sphere. In Guadeloupe, the French forces recaptured Grande-Terre and, after the British capitulated in October 1794, Basse-Terre, which was evacuated in December. The other islands, however, remained under British occupation, and because of the British blockade the liberation of Guadeloupe did not lead to a re-establishment of trade with France. In the West Indies, there was a sense of isolation and of being neglected by the French government – which admitted in its official documents its inability to spare large numbers of troops from the continent to defend them against the British. In addition, because of the breakdown in maritime communications with France, the islands faced mounting food supply problems. This was the background to the decision to open the ports to neutral shipping. Before long, the islanders had the daily spectacle of 'thirty or forty American ships in the harbour at Pointe-à-Pitre come to distribute across the colony supplies of flour, beef, lard, and salt cod.'[51] The same phenomenon was observed in the other ports of Guadeloupe and Martinique. Although other neutral shipping – Swedish and Danish – traded with the French West Indies, the Americans were by far the most numerous. In the course of the revolutionary and Napoleonic wars, therefore, it was not only Saint-Domingue but all the colonies in the West Indies that gradually slipped out of the French commercial sphere. The British blockade that followed the setting up of the Continental system in 1806 merely accelerated this process.

The loss of communications with the colonies, a prolonged war and an economic blockade, insecurity at sea due to the activities of pirates and the British fleet – all served to disrupt the maritime exchanges and overseas trade on which the prosperity of France's Atlantic ports depended. In Bordeaux, the mood was sombre in the merchant district of the Quai des Chartrons. As the number of bankruptcies climbed, the city's merchants were brought face to face with the economic impact of the war. Even those whose own business was as yet unaffected invariably knew someone, a friend or associate, whose position was critical. Benoît Lacombe, the Bordeaux merchant who had retired to his property at Gaillac, in the Tarn, received a stream of desperate letters from merchants overwhelmed by the 'disastrous storms of commerce'.[52]

But while conditions were certainly difficult, it would be a mistake to think that commercial exchange stopped altogether at this time.[53] In the Atlantic, no less than in the Channel and Mediterranean, it continued thanks to *cabotage*, both on short-haul routes using local masters and low-tonnage ships, and on European and transatlantic routes using neutral shipping. The worst affected by the crisis were thus the shipowners, who were fitting out hardly any ships. In some cases, the ports avoided ruin by the recourse to neutral shipping. At La Rochelle, in 1795, the port received 35 American ships of mixed tonnages, ranging from three-masters down to luggers, and including fishing ships from Newfoundland with cargoes of salt fish to sell. In the same year, ten Scandinavian ships (Danish and Swedish) also visited the port, bringing wood and salt fish, and taking return cargoes of wine, and in particular salt for preserving fish. The year 1795 thus brought economic recovery for the salt producers of the Île de Ré. One of their number noted in November, 'The price of salt has risen to 1,200 *livres* [the average was 800] on the Seudre, a result of foreigners having chartered large numbers of ships without having purchased cargoes beforehand.' The salt producers also found outlets in France itself, in the departments of the Nord, when the Channel fishing fleets resumed expeditions to distant fishing grounds.[54]

After the Committee of Public Safety authorized shipping by ostensibly neutral nationalities, French merchants also used neutral ships to transport their own goods from port to port, operating what resembled a maritime *caravane*. Thus it was that the La Rivallière family firm of La Rochelle chartered an American ship, the *Argonaut*, in 1795 to deliver its goods to Dieppe.[55]

The merchant community greeted with enthusiasm the rumours in 1800 which suggested the imminent conclusion of a peace treaty with Britain. Benoît Lacombe wrote to Garrigou, a former employee who had become his partner at Bordeaux, in October 1800, 'The maritime truce that we are led to hope for will mean a lot of wine leaving your port, and it will not be long before the wines of Gaillac are again favoured over those of Cahors.'[56] As the rumours of peace gained in force so Lacombe grew increasingly hopeful and he returned to the theme repeatedly in his letters. 'Prices would rise if the hopes for peace were confirmed', he noted, 'Our wines are just lying here and they will never fetch good prices until people's minds are set to rest over political affairs, and if peace or a maritime armistice are delayed, a way will have to be found for disposing of them.'[57] Ten days later, on 23 December, he was getting himself and his nephews ready for business to pick up:

> I think that if we have peace as is forecast, and if the harvest is as bad as we are told it will be, you will make great profits; let us do the best for our interests... Important events are preparing, after our most recent victories, will the coalition of the Northern Powers give us an armistice or peace? It is reasonable to think that we could have one or the other, in which case we are sure to have an outlet for our wines...[58]

The Peace of Amiens did indeed produce a sharp upturn in business affairs. Merchants returned to their offices, ships took to the seas again, and contacts were renewed with customers and middlemen. At Bordeaux, 200 ships were fitted out. At Le Havre, François Begouën began construction of the *Eurydice*, a new merchant vessel that he planned to send to the Angolan coast. In a letter of 16 July 1802 to a New York agent, Samuel Ogden, he spoke of his optimism and related how in the last two months (May and June 1802) no fewer than 300 fully laden merchantmen had come into the port, blocking the quays and filling the warehouses with a great quantity of goods of all kinds.[59] In the south-west, Benoît Lacombe, like many others, responded eagerly to the prospect of resuming business in the Atlantic port; he went back to live in Bordeaux between 1801 and March 1803.

The peace, however, was short-lived. From 1802 tension was again rising. Anticipating the resumption of hostilities, the merchants hastily scaled back their operations. The war at sea began again in May 1803, cutting communications and aggravating the crisis in the French ports. The merchants in France's Atlantic ports were forced to withdraw from the colonial trade. Facing attacks from British privateers, an increasingly dominant role for the Americans in trade with the West Indies, and a new rising on Saint-Domingue, the future looked increasingly bleak.

A new period of contraction had begun and the merchants concentrated their efforts on trying to recover their goods and funds from the other side of the Atlantic. Benoît Lacombe told one of his managers on 9 June 1803:

> Conditions have changed greatly...Now we are at war, with only troubles ahead. Whenever will there be peace? You must be concerned about what has become of your possessions in the colonies... I think about it every day. Have you any satisfactory news? Do you think our government will be able to keep Saint-Domingue or that it can hold out against the fierce Africans?...If there is something at sea [a ship returning to Bordeaux with its cargo], what can be done to get it here? I cannot say, not knowing when or how this wretched war will end. Give these friends [Laffite] the instructions that you consider appropriate for my interests, write to M. Réaux in Louisiana about what they have of mine, and to M. Saulnier at Ile de France [present day Mauritius]. Do what you think appropriate for my interests, using neutral ships or others. I am too removed from events to judge what needs to be done.[60]

But this proved impossible. With large amounts of transatlantic shipping being lost to pirates and privateers, communications were irretrievably broken. No shipowner now dared risk making the crossing. Moreover, 'with insurance rates as they stand, there is no hope of being covered, so the capital would be at stake.'[61] Like many merchants, Lacombe failed to recover the sums he had invested in the West Indies.

Having returned to Gaillac, Lacombe wrote in July 1803 to his nephews who had stayed in Bordeaux to execute the buying and shipping instructions that he sent them from Gaillac, warning them of the need to run the family business carefully and intelligently. 'You have an avalanche of bankruptcies in your locality. Although they are not important, it is not just the humble honest folk that are being ruined, and I fear that in such disorder some old established firms might be forced under, there being no resisting the force of circumstances. It saddens me to see Bordeaux going into liquidation and many firms no longer trading, the unfortunates are to be pitied...These are dreadful times', and he concludes, 'take in your canvas and try to keep out of the turmoil'.[62] Caution was required at this time. The letters between Lacombe and his foreign customers, in Amsterdam and Rotterdam, are full of references to the 'wretched doings' [sunken ships, lost wine][63] occurring in waters henceforth 'exposed to the rapacious English'.[64]

Apart from the fragile and short-lived recovery that followed the Treaty of Amiens, for the great seaports of France and their hinterlands, the period 1792–1815 was one of economic decline and commercial stagnation. Benoît Lacombe lamented on 23 March 1805,

> I am not doing business of any kind. Outlets are so scarce and consumption so low that my grapes may as well be destroyed, nor is there any demand for our vinegar-making plant. The proprietors are most unfortunate, since the costs of planting and of barrels exceed the value of the production. If this continues we will all be reduced to misery.[65]

Soldiers travelling through these regions were struck by the depressed state of commerce in the ports. One such was Cosme Ramaeckers, on route from Nantes to Spain in December 1807, who noted in his journal, 'Nantes would benefit from a prosperous commerce, though in this it is like Bordeaux and other trading cities. It must be hoped that our ports will one day be free.'[66]

A sense of war-weariness was apparent among the shipowners, merchants, and all who depended on overseas trade for their livelihood, sooner than in the French public at large. By 1803–1805, after more than 10 years of economic crisis, even convinced republicans and patriots like Benoît Lacombe, alarmed at the prospect of financial ruin, were calling openly for peace. Writing on 7 June 1805 to his old friend Fagedet, whose Bordeaux merchant firm was in difficulty, he noted 'For a long while I have been telling you that business is in a bad way and will remain so; only peace can revive commerce.'[67]

If Bordeaux's merchants and winegrowers were to compensate for the collapse of maritime commerce and stave off bankruptcy, they needed to find new outlets for their products. Like the merchants of Marseille, Lacombe initially turned to *cabotage*, trading along the Atlantic coast.[68] But the activities of British privateers limited the scope for this trade, and demand in Bordeaux and its surrounding area was insufficient to form a viable market. The merchants needed alternative outlets. Lacombe was among those who, from 1810 onwards, sought new markets in the interior, in the upland regions of the Massif Central. Thus the war effectively imposed a fundamental reorientation in the geography of commerce. Lacombe turned away from the Atlantic and concentrated instead on supplying the rural populations in the region extending from Albi up to the uplands of the Auvergne and Cantal, for which Gaillac served as the staging post. His wines no longer travelled the high seas but along stony roads and earth tracks: 'The people from the upland regions are keen to get the young wines', he noted on 4 February 1810, 'But as a contingency solution it is unsatisfactory, since the inhabitants of these regions buy very cheap wines and are indifferent to the quality.'[69]

Maritime commerce in the Mediterranean was also reorganized at this time, chiefly through the development of short-haul trading and, for the largest ports, through the use of neutral shipping. In the small port of Menton, for example, which officially became part of France on 4 March 1793 along with the rest of the principality of Monaco (after French troops had entered Monaco on 29 September 1792), the bulk of port activity took the form of short-haul trading on the Provençal and Ligurian coasts. Most of the ships that operated out of Menton were of low tonnage, and all were owned by their captains. In all, the commercial fleet of Menton comprised some 30 vessels (roughly half the size of the 70-strong Nice fleet). During the ancien régime, it sustained a continuous and large-scale trade with Mediterranean ports from Marseille to Livorno, as well as a range of northern European ports including Hamburg, Copenhagen, Posen, and Warsaw. Like the largest Mediterranean ports, Menton was badly affected by the revolutionary and Napoleonic wars and by the economic blockade. Coastal trading, though possible to begin with, became increasingly difficult as a result of the British blockade. Merchant seamen were subject to endless administrative formalities. Every ship coming into port was automatically put in 'quarantine for observation' if during its sailing it had been in communication with corsairs, even if it had not come from a suspect country.[70] The seafarers also had to contend with requisitioning, restrictions on sailing, and surveillance measures. In 1810, the *Conservateur de la Santé* or public health officer at Menton even decided to tighten the restrictions in the aftermath of manoeuvres by the British Navy that he judged suspicious: 'The enemies currently cruising in our locality have few scruples about the means they employ: they use anything that they think can serve their hatred and inflict losses and misfortunes on France.'[71] He believed that the British had attempted to spread contagion by covering the beaches with goods 'infected with the plague'. These fears were fuelled by a rumour going round the Mediterranean to the effect that the British had already left contaminated products on the beaches at Bormes.[72]

Like their counterparts in the Atlantic ports, merchants and shipowners in the Mediterranean were forced to use 'neutral' ships for their transatlantic and northern European commerce. The nationalities chosen for this depended on the port and in some cases reflected trading links formed before the war. At Menton, long-haul commerce was handled exclusively by Danish shipowners. But Danish merchantmen were irregular visitors to the port of Menton, and economic activity in the region was seriously damaged by the disruption of trade and maritime communication due to the war. In the Mediterranean, as at Bordeaux, the war was associated with shrinking markets and lost outlets. Menton's mayor, Jérôme Monléon, commented in 1810 that 'The trade in our lemons, that were sent as far as the Baltic ports before the arrival of the British pirates, is currently limited to the port of Marseille.'[73] Trading conditions were such that producers sometimes held on to their crops until they could be distributed using *cabotage* or neutral shipping. But if products were kept for too long they went bad, with a complete loss for the farmer. In late February 1814, nearly three-quarters of the lemon trees in Menton were touched by frost. What made it more serious was that 'all the fruit that should have been collected in October was still on the trees when the frost occurred.'[74]

Thus the consequences of the war at sea were not limited to maritime commerce but were felt in all areas of economic activity – agrarian, industrial, and artisanal production – in the coastal regions.

III. Industry

Relations between industry and war in France at this time were complex. The war, of course, created new demands and new markets, to satisfy military needs. But this was not usually enough to offset the negative consequences of the conflict, such as shortages of labour and raw materials, breakdown of communications with foreign countries and loss of markets, tight credit, and economic and financial crises. For the majority of industrialists, as for farmers and merchants, the revolutionary and Napoleonic wars were primarily a period of hardships and exacerbated difficulties.

In many instances the war caused industrial production to slow down or even to stop. Producers lacked the necessary fuel and raw materials such as soap and wool. After the revolt of Saint-Domingue and later as a result of the blockade under the Continental system, raw material shortages reached unprecedented levels. With the start of the war in Spain, textile producers suffered as a result of the disruption to supplies of oils and vegetable dyes.[75] In Normandy, the famous *Aigle* pin manufacture that had employed more than 3000 workers before the war was completely moribund in 1800–1801, owing to the scarcity and high price of its main raw material; deliveries of the brass wire traditionally supplied by Sweden were interrupted by the war at sea. When Conseiller d'État Fourcroy was sent on mission to the 14th Military

Division in Floréal Year IX to assess conditions in this part of the country, he reported that more than 50 *Aigle* workshops had closed in less than a year, since the last Caen fair in Floréal of the previous year.[76]

Some raw materials, though still available, became so expensive – notably because of high import duties – that it was virtually impossible for producers to use them and still make a profit. Visiting the 19th Military Division in Year IX, Conseiller d'État Najac reported that the total output of the muslin and printed cottons manufacture at Tarare, which produced 10–12,000 *pièces* annually before 1789, had fallen by more than half as a result of the heavy duties on imported cottons.[77]

Other problems facing entrepreneurs in these years included the tight conditions for credit, the erosion of confidence in the *assignats*, and above all the high cost of borrowing that severely curtailed investment. Nor did conscription deprive only agriculture of labour. Industrialists too complained about labour shortages and the consequent upward pressure on wages. This was the experience of the Toulousain entrepreneur Boyer-Fonfrède. He had to relinquish his premises in the convent of the Jacobins – intended as the site of his new cotton manufacture – when it was requisitioned for the army, had his cotton supplies impounded in the port because of the blockade, saw his English textile experts imprisoned, and also lost all his work force to conscription during the revolutionary wars.[78]

Industry also suffered badly from the loss of outlets brought about by the war on land and at sea, by the fall in consumption, and the contraction of the domestic market. Several years of war left France in a deeply worrying economic situation, as emerges from the reports prepared by the *conseillers d'état* sent on mission to the military divisions in Year IX. These paint a sombre picture and show that industrialists and merchants in every region, like the population at large, were unanimous in wanting a rapid signing of a peace treaty. Marseille before the Revolution had been a prosperous, bustling city, whose port handled 3000 ships a year, but 'this splendid state of affairs has vanished. The causes are the excesses of the Revolution and the maritime wars,' recorded Conseiller d'État Français de Nantes, before adding,

> I visited the merchant community who were assembled at the Stock Exchange. A few days later, during a celebration held in my honour by the merchant community [attended by 150 guests], I was asked to pass on its wishes to the government... and to request a Chamber of Commerce, the abolition of duties, and peace.[79]

In Brittany, the cloth manufacturers whose goods had been exported to Spain, Portugal, and the colonies were barely active since the loss of these markets due to the war. Meanwhile, 'the town of Lorient, formerly enriched by America and Asia, is today ruined. The traders who used to send ships to the Indies, are reduced to a petty retail trade that barely suffices to support their families.'[80] One consequence of this state of affairs was a significant increase in crime across the region, when those without work turned to brigandage.

Most of the manufactures in Normandy had either closed or were working at very low levels. Lacemaking at Alençon and Argentan had practically ceased by Year IX. Production of cloths, like those of Vimoutiers, which before the war had been exported to Britain and the colonies, and where annual production before 1792 had been worth 4–5 million *livres*, had fallen by more than one-third since the start of the war at sea.[81] In the Charente-Inférieure, more than half of the paper mills had stopped producing by Year VI, on account of the loss of foreign markets.[82] An identical situation was observed in the Paris region. The rising number of bankruptcies stemmed from reduced consumption, requisitioning, discrediting of the *assignats*, the Terror 'which drove capital to ground', and most of all from the war that halted exports. Conseiller d'État Lacuée agreed that manufacturing would become extremely active again if the war at sea was concluded peacefully.[83]

The situation was equally dramatic in the Rhône. According to an enumeration in 1788, Lyon had 14,777 looms for silk fabric manufacture, 9335 of them in operation. By Year IX, only 5000 were active. Likewise, hat manufacturing that employed 8000 workers before the Revolution had only 1500 by 18 Brumaire, while at Tarare, the manufactures of muslins and printed cottons had laid off more than half of the 3000–4000 women and children they had employed before 1798.[84] In eastern France, finally, at Mulhouse, nearly half of the calico manufactures had gone bankrupt: of the 25 or 27 that existed before the Revolution, only 15 remained by 18 Brumaire.[85]

The industrial and commercial crisis induced by the war led to a dramatic increase in unemployment and poverty. And because the ancien régime economy was still based largely on outworking, much of it in the countryside, the effects of this state of affairs were not limited to town dwellers. Once the war had started, the Legislative Body began to receive petitions from the central administrations of departments, in which they invoked the widespread impoverishment of the population to obtain a reduction in taxes. On 1 Fructidor Year VI, the central administration of the Aude informed the Legislative Body that since the start of the war at sea and the collapse in production of the cloth formerly exported to the Levant, more than 20,000 workers were without work and bread, and 'nineteen-twentieths of the population have scarce the resources to feed themselves with maize or chestnuts... Many are clothed in rags... Not a winter goes by that a number of inhabitants are found dead of hunger in the highland areas.'[86]

However, war could also sometimes have a positive impact on the economy. The army and the war economy absorbed a proportion of the unemployed. Raoul Hesdin, the Parisian wood engraver, noted in his diary in December 1793 that Paris had large numbers of unemployed and that the only group with regular work were those working for army contractors.[87] While this was certainly an exaggeration, it was true that the army provided many jobs in wartime. In Toulouse, it was indeed the largest single employer in Year II: 762 men were employed in administering food supplies, in gun crews, military hospitals, and boot manufacture; 1000 in shoe manufacture and in the arsenal; and 122 as masons, carpenters, and labourers in the canon foundry. When added to the two largest military employers – the artillery park and military transportation – and the conscripts provided by the city (some 1500 men in spring 1793), the total of some 4500 men represented a substantial proportion of the male labour force in a city of between 50,000 and 60,000 inhabitants. Not all of those working for the military would be French civilians though, since the army also used prisoners of war as labourers. Moreover, military workshops were extremely unpopular, especially while the Wage Maximum was in force: artisans and labourers could earn higher wages in the private sector, whereas in the service of the Republic they were expected to work unpaid overtime as an act of patriotic generosity.[88]

However, during the Napoleonic times, the continental blockade, by protecting some industries from foreign (especially British) competition and by establishing a measure of protectionism through high taxes on imports, contributed to the recovery or even the development of some industrial branches such as silk industry in Lyon. The number of crafts (*métiers*) in activity, which had fallen to 2500 during the revolutionary turmoil, rose to 11,000 between 1809 and 1813.[89]

The effects of the war were generally positive for military and war industries. In Saint Etienne, only one-third of the local workforce worked for the *Manufacture impériale* (the state manufactory of war armament) in 1800. This figure rose to four-fifths in 1810 (4000 men in total).[90]

In some cases, the war industries even made a significant contribution to revitalizing a region's industrial structure. At Montauban, for example, the main sectors of economic activity, milling and textiles, had both been depressed for a number of years. The milling industry had not recovered since the bad harvests of 1788, 1789, and 1791, and the textile industry lost its West Indian outlets in 1791. The state filled the role of substitute market in this region, so that by 1793 the war industries had revived the local economy. The conversion of industry began in winter 1792. On 11 November, braid maker Blaise Rémusat was awarded an important contract to supply the battalions of the Lot with 1600 cockades at 3 *livres* a dozen.[91]

The war created numerous market opportunities for industrialists to produce uniforms, blankets, weaponry, footwear, food, and the like. At Strasbourg, orders issued by Napoleon for the production of 500,000 biscuit rations a year led to the development of a temporary industry in the city in Years XIII and XIV, when 15,000 rations were produced daily.[92] Some naval dockyards also benefited from military construction projects. The number of dockyard workers in Toulon thus rose from 2000 in 1783[93] to 9500 in June 1794, and then to a record level of 12,000 in the autumn.[94] But the impact of military purchasing on the local economy was not unreservedly positive: war commissaries often bought at prices that reduced the potential profit for producers, and the army was frequently late in paying contractors for goods and services.[95]

IV. Conclusion

The wars of the revolutionary and Napoleonic eras thus had a heavy impact on the French economy, with consequences in both the short- and long-term. Several reasons can be given for the importance of the conflict in the economic sphere. The length of time it lasted, and above all the fact that its main actors were civilians – recruited as citizen-soldiers, volunteers, or conscripts – resulted in a haemorrhage of the nation's prime human resources, the more so since those called upon were first and foremost young, able-bodied men. The ever-increasing number of conscripts leaving for the war inevitably created a growing manpower shortage at home, both in the countryside and in the urban workshops and manufactures.

Together with this drain on population went a forcible withdrawal of material resources for the needs of the army, which added to the shortages of items such as food, fuel, oils, dyes, that had affected farms and businesses since the start of hostilities. Businessmen also suffered from the disruption the war caused to land and sea transportation. This took the form of costly delays, but also of material losses when ships and cargoes were sunk by enemy action, and convoys were attacked by deserters who had taken up highway robbery.

The situation was particularly critical for the many shipowners and merchants active in maritime commerce, especially in long-distance trade with the West Indies and America. Trade between France and her West Indian islands practically ceased after Saint-Domingue was lost in 1798 and the British Navy stepped up its presence in the waters around Guadeloupe and Martinique. A few years later, the imposition of the continental blockade made conditions still more difficult for firms engaged in overseas trade and for their many subcontractors, and indeed for the maritime economy in general.

These years of war, in fact, set in train a broad, long-term shift in the organization of the French economy. The Atlantic seaboard that had long been the centre of French economic development, based on colonial trade, now underwent a relative decline that favoured, initially, the Mediterranean regions, and in the longer-term, the inland regions of northern and eastern France. If the latter regions also suffered from the war's repercussions, they were at least partly compensated for this with the new outlets offered by the Napoleonic Empire's territorial expansion, and in particular with the presence of troops and garrisons that provided livelihoods for a number of tradesmen and industrial producers.

But if it is undeniable that some businessmen did make a profit from the events and even in some cases grew rich, for the overwhelming majority of farmers, shopkeepers, merchants, artisans, and manufacturers, the war was a period of crisis and trouble that left few sectors untouched. The result was a slowdown in economic activity accompanied by a reorientation away from exports and towards the home market, as well as widespread bankruptcies and changes of occupation. Most of those caught up in it, while still admitting to patriotic feelings of national pride at the news of the great French victories, soon acquired, even if they did not openly profess, strongly pacifist views, which they retained for the major part of the nineteenth century, a sentiment that was reflected in a speech made by Napoleon III to the merchants of Bordeaux in October 1852.[96]

7
Civilians in the War

Farmers and businessmen were not the only civilians to experience the effects of the war in daily life. The length and scale of the conflict meant that the French nation in its entirety would be affected. After analysing the consequences of the war for the economy and for all those engaged in economic activity, it remains to present a more complete and detailed overview of the impact of the revolutionary and Napoleonic wars on French society by observing how the war made its effects felt in the daily life of civilians. This forms the subject of our last chapter.

From late 1793 until 1814, of course, the civilian population of France had no direct contact with the violence, horror, and danger of war. This fact frequently led soldiers to contrast their own experience with that of their contemporaries who stayed at home. On one side were men who had been plunged into the harsh reality of war, on the other civilians who had been spared these years of almost continuous conflict. Assertions that the concrete experience of war is impossible to put into words or communicate to a civilian audience abound in the memoirs of soldiers from this period and quickly became a commonplace of the literature of war. Many officers and men felt that their experience of the war set them apart from civilian society, that a hermetic barrier now separated the civilian and military worlds, which arguably supports the view that the revolutionary and Napoleonic wars were a major turning point in the evolution of relations between civilians and soldiers and in the position of the army in French society.[1] The duration of the wars, the soldiers' distant postings, and the professionalization of the army and of warfare itself all fostered the emergence of a strong sense of military identity in this period. But we should not rush to conclude that there was a clear, straightforward contrast between the front and the rear, between the soldier and the civilian. The daily life of civilians was also transformed during the long years of war: by the all-pervading presence of the war in public life, by the shortages, high prices, and other difficulties in daily life, by requisitioning and the war effort in general, by the economic fallout from the military situation, and, after 1814, by a direct, physical experience of battle and participation in combat.

Studying the consequences of the war for French civilians in their daily lives, along with the material and in some cases physical involvement of civilians in the war, contributes to our analysis of the nature of the conflict, since the involvement of civilian populations is among the criteria usually used to define 'total war'. Some historians have argued that although war in the early modern period and, even more so, in the nineteenth century (especially the wars of the 1860s), did affect civilian populations to varying degrees, the overall impact of war on the 'home front' remained limited. Thus Nicholas Atkin asserts that

> during the early modern period... unless the fighting was close at hand, civilians could still put war aside and almost out of mind.... Whereas in previous conflicts, the populace had managed to put the fighting out of mind, in World War One civilians came to *know* that they were at war. This was evidenced in the appearance of food and material shortages, the extensive mobilisation of labour forces... the exhortations of government propaganda... and the threat of death.[2]

Despite their significance and centrality, however, the civilian experience of war and the impact of war on civilian daily life have been largely neglected by historians. The provocative question raised by Maris A. Vinovskis ('Have social historians lost the Civil War?'[3]) about the lack of social studies on civilian life during the American Civil War could apply equally well to the historiography of the revolutionary and Napoleonic wars. The recent interest of historians in civilians and the home front in Europe during the two world wars of the twentieth century has not prompted similar studies for the nineteenth century. Although it is impossible to identify a general or 'average' civilian experience of the revolutionary and Napoleonic wars, since this depended on and was conditioned by a range of factors (including age, gender, occupation, location, and proximity to borders), the issue of the impact of war on civilians must be addressed to assess the all-encompassing character of this war, the mobilization of both the military and civilian populations. Over and above this conceptual issue, an analysis on these lines gives insight into the impact of the revolutionary and Napoleonic wars on French civilian as well as military society, while comparing the wartime experience of civilian and military populations (some elements being common to both) increases our understanding of the short- and long-term consequences of these wars for the French nation and French society.

I. News of the war

When France declared war on Austria on 20 April 1792, the news was solemnly announced in every town and village of France. How civilians heard of the start of hostilities is recounted in many of the diaries, notebooks, and memoirs they wrote in the revolutionary era. Parisians got the news on the same day. Thus Nicolas Célestin Guittard de Floriban, a bourgeois *rentier* from Champagne, who was born in 1724 and who had lived in Paris since 1769, noted in his journal on 20 April 1792,

> Today 20 April 1792...the National Assembly met...at five o'clock and after lengthy debates the declaration of war was decreed. France is to draw up her manifesto and send it to all the European courts, to inform all the sovereigns and peoples of her reasons for declaring war on the King of Hungary.[4]

The news spread more slowly in the rest of France. It took a few days to reach a small town like Chinon. The saddler Claude Bailly noted in his diary on 29 April 1792, 9 full days after war was declared, 'At Chinon it was announced that the French have declared war on the foreign countries that harbour émigrés without good reason, which means for us a great war with the foreign powers.'[5]

A few months later, the declaration and promulgation of the *patrie en danger* in July 1792 gave civilians clear evidence of the conflict's gathering momentum and deepening nature and drew them directly into the war effort. The news caused a sensation and is related in all the contemporary writings of civilians. In Paris the promulgation and announcement on 22 July was made with great pomp and circumstance intended to impress the civilian population and the foreign powers. According to Guittard de Floriban it provoked a wave of patriotic euphoria:

> So many young men came forward that in the eight amphitheatres more than 10,000 people enlisted and more again will be enlisted today. It's a form of madness; everyone wants to enlist. Patriotic zeal is at its height. Nothing like it has been seen before in the history of

> the world. No one fears for his life. Foreigners cannot avoid saying that there has never been a nation like the French nation. Everyone wants to march against the enemy. Death is no longer feared. The young men enlisting all do so with unprecedented joy...[6]

The *patrie en danger* was announced slightly earlier at Chinon, on 19 July 1792, though it was repeated on 5 August. On the first date, 'the fatherland was declared to be in danger. All the members of the municipality and district, the clerks and magistrates, and the full National Guard remained on duty day and night.' Following the publication and posting of this announcement by the local authorities, a ceremony was held on 5 August, similar to that described by Guittard de Floriban for Paris, though the patriotic zeal was distinctly less marked in rural localities and small towns:

> On a rostrum erected next to the town hall, all the district administrators, municipal officers and magistrates assembled to announce in the presence of the National Guard that the fatherland was in danger: a small flag with the words *Citizens, the fatherland is in danger*... was then paraded through the town.... The municipal officers got down from the rostrum to ask in all the ranks if there were any men willing to go off to defend the fatherland. But no one stepped out from the ranks except young fellows of four foot ten, who willingly enrolled, some fifty of them, and who went up on the rostrum to swear the oath of loyalty.[7]

The visibility of war in everyday civilian life was already striking at the time of the declaration of the *patrie en danger* and the call to volunteers, and it did not diminish in the years that followed.

Throughout this period of conflict, the French civilian population followed the war closely. The better off and the literate tried to get hold of newspapers whenever possible. In Paris and in the main cities, the latest news of the war, and particularly of victories, was delivered in public 'spectacles' at the theatre and the opera.[8] In the smaller towns, the municipal council or more often the popular society were usually important centres of sociability and sources of information. During the revolutionary years, peasants and artisans of a middling condition, like the saddler Claude Bailly, paid regular visits to the Temple Décadaire of their locality to listen to public readings of the 'news'.[9] Civilians, especially those with soldiers or officers in their family, followed the course of the war by reading the press, notably the *Bulletin de la Grande*

Armée. Jean Tailhand, a gendarme in the 7th Division of Army of the Sambre-et-Meuse, ended a short letter to his parents on 8 December 1794, with these words: 'I'll spare you the details about our armies; we are on one side of the Rhine, the lackeys are on the other, and every now and then we fire at each other. You will know the progress we have made, you see it in the bulletins.'[10]

Volunteer soldier Fricasse recollected how the inescapable presence of the war in the public sphere and notably in the newspapers, influenced him and his decision to enlist in the army. On 24 August 1792, he went to the *chef-lieu* of the Jura, the former Franche-Comté, where young men from all the communes in the department were required to go to form a battalion of volunteers. Quilliard, his employer, had offered to pay for a replacement for the army if need be, so as to keep him in his service as a gardener and avoid his going off to war, but Fricasse decided on his own initiative to enlist in the departmental battalion:

> We were in town where all the villages of the canton had come together. [...] By one o'clock in the afternoon several National Guard companies composed of one hundred and sixty men were still short of the required number. One of those was my own company and I found myself filled with a long held desire. So many times the papers had given me the news that our army was pushed back and beaten everywhere. I was burning with impatience to see for myself these things that I found impossible to believe [...] Whereupon, to do my duty I went up to the head of the company and asked them if they thought I was fit to enter the battalion. From every side the shout went up: 'Yes, We can find none better than you!' So then I was registered by the captain and the justice of the peace.[11]

But news of the war was badly distorted by the time it appeared in the public press, especially in the *Bulletin de la Grande Armée*, so much so that a popular saying was *menteur comme un Bulletin* or 'a liar like the *Bulletin*'. Civilians were aware of the distorting effects of propaganda and censorship. The Comtesse de Boigne recalled in her memoirs how they 'had to guess the elements of truth in the lines of the official narratives which, almost always, disguised it... For example, the battle of Trafalgar was never communicated to France in an official report; no newspaper, as a consequence, mentioned it and we heard about it only through clandestine channels.'[12] French civilians tried to counter the omissions and half-truths of the official propaganda by asking officers and ordinary soldiers for full and accurate information on the course of the war. As well as newspapers and gazettes, the letters in which soldiers and officers related their daily existence and the latest military developments, or described the foreign countries they visited, were also read aloud in public or in front of several families. Jean Ataix, the volunteer soldier from the Auvergne, wrote to his father on 16 May 1794: 'Please tell much of this on my behalf to my grandfather Peyrard, and to our neighbours, relatives, and friends.'[13]

When soldiers and officers related the military situation in letters to their family this was often in response to what civilians expected and requested, as is shown by a letter that Jacques Tuzest, a light cavalryman also from the Auvergne, wrote to his parents on 2 January 1795: 'Regarding all the news of the war that you ask me for, I will just say that the armies of the Republic are doing well, and the tyrants will shortly be overthrown.'[14]

The efforts of the civilian population to follow the course of the war as closely as possible through newspapers and personal accounts contributed to placing the war at the centre of public life and making it, in the process, an element of national unity and identity.

II. War and the daily existence of the French people

1. War at the centre of the public sphere

The war quickly established itself as the central theme of public life, thanks to the omnipresence of the army and to the celebration of battles. A round of festivities, victory commemorations, banquets, and military parades punctuated the calendar; civilians flocked in droves to be dazzled and delighted by lavish, grandiose spectacles featuring large numbers of men and horses. In his journal, Guittard de Floriban describes in detail the fête held in Paris on 30 December 1793 to celebrate the victory at Toulon. He emphasizes the strong impression produced by the sheer numbers of soldiers and weaponry in the procession – a detachment each of cavalry and sappers, two platoons of gunners, 50 drummers, two detachments of Paris guards, colour-bearers and torch bearers, 22 cannons, representatives of the political, judicial, and police authorities – and the glorification of the army by the special place accorded to the wounded veterans presented as heroes of the nation.

> The procession was very large and very long. I was on the former Pont Royal. The procession started to go past at three o'clock and continued until after half-past four.... A float of the Revolutionary

> Army had twelve wounded defenders of liberty, surrounded by forty young girls dressed in white holding laurel branches.... Then came the fourteen floats representing the fourteen armies, each containing twelve wounded soldiers from each of these armies. Each float was accompanied by gunners with cannon, platoons of troops and young girls as on the first float... The victory float, the last, bearing the nation represented by a stock of arms with the Statue of Liberty atop.... Positioned around this float were fifty invalid veterans and one hundred *sans-culottes* in red caps.... It proceeded thus from the Tuileries to the Champ de Mars, where hymns were sung at the altar of the *patrie*. It was a superb procession.[15]

A few years later, the celebrations in Paris for the victory at Marengo inspired Bourrienne to describe scenes of jubilation and grandeur akin to those Guittard de Floriban had observed, and to note that their purpose now was also to raise the standing of the army in society:

> On that day there was an immense throng on the Champ de Mars and at the Temple in honour of Mars... Medals were distributed with great ceremony to five invalid veterans designated by their comrades as being the most worthy to receive this honour... The most remarkable thing about this *fête* was... after the ceremony at the Invalides, the arrival at the Champ de Mars of the Consuls' Guard, newly returned from Marengo. I was at a window of the Ecole Militaire and I cannot forget the commotion, like an electrical discharge, that produced cries of enthusiasm when they appeared. When these soldiers marched past the First Consul they were not wearing fine uniforms like on parade days. Leaving the field of battle at lights out the next day, they had crossed Lombardy, Piedmont, Mont Cenis, Savoy, and France, all in the space of twenty-nine days. Their appearance was marked by the weariness of a long journey, their skin tanned by Italy's June sun, and their arms and clothes reduced to the wretched state that attests to bloody combat. A faithful representation, should you wish to have an idea, is to be found in the tableau that M. Gérard has placed on one side of his painting of the battle of Austerlitz.[16]

Large-scale public celebrations of great victories became a regular occurrence under the Consulate and Empire. In addition to their grandiose and prestigious character, these fêtes were a source of distraction for the civilians who attended them in droves, providing entertainment, games, dancing, as well as banquets and distributions of food and drink.

Constant, Napoleon's first valet, mentions in his memoirs the public festivities in Paris in 1805 to celebrate the victory at Austerlitz, observing that 'as usual, there were free shows in all the Paris theatres... games, distribution of victuals, illuminations.'[17]

The prestige of the army and the glory of the 'grande nation' that successive conquests enhanced were also celebrated in bricks and masonry. New public buildings, typically large and grandiose in conception, went up in Paris, architectural testimony to the brilliance and military glory of Napoleonic France. Napoleon wanted to make Paris into the enlightened and majestic capital of his fast-growing Empire, a new Athens; to this end the city was turned into a construction site as new thoroughfares, new bridges, new squares, new statues came to adorn the public space of its inhabitants. Count Bourrienne, who at the time was private secretary to Napoleon, refers to this architectural policy in his memoirs, pointing out its political character and the close link that existed between urban building and military glory, between the role of civilians (architects, workers, etc.) and the indirect contribution of the military (supplying raw materials like lead taken from the enemy), between glory and national identity, and between architectural policy and commemoration of the war.

> In the Place Vendôme, bereft of the statue of Louis-le-Grand, a magnificent column was raised, decorated with bronze conquered from the Austrians after a three-month campaign; long stretches of embankments were built on both banks of the Seine to channel the course of its water... The Pont d'Austerlitz, Pont d'Iéna, Pont de Saint Cloud and Pont de Sèvres generated new communications between the two banks of the Seine, and magnificently revitalized existing ones. The old Louvre was completed and the spire of the Invalides again appeared in the sky, shining and golden, just as it was in the reign of the great king. The inscription in honour of Louis XIV was... put on the triumphal arch on the Boulevard Saint Denis, even as another triumphal arch, on a gigantic scale and dedicated to the Grande Armée, was being built to be in full view of the sovereign's residence... He considered that nothing was too fine, too majestic to embellish the capital of the country he wanted to make the foremost in the world. After war, this was what his ambition needed most. Indeed, the two ideas were inseparable in his mind, in that the work of conquest remained incomplete so long as there was no monument to transmit the memory on to posterity. Glory, always more glory, that is what he wanted for France and for himself.[18]

Alongside the collective glorification of the army by honouring its victories with lavish public festivities and building public monuments, the government sought to raise the prestige of the military in civilian society by glorifying individual soldiers. During the Revolution and particularly during the Empire, soldiers enjoyed a favoured status in French society. Those recently back from the fighting, in particular, could expect a place of honour in recognition for their zeal and patriotic sacrifice in defending their compatriots. Guittard de Floriban noted in his journal for 10 August 1794:

> A *fête* with illuminations was held today in the Tuileries to commemorate that day. The Opera was present and played and sung twelve arias. An iron cage was set up on a pool, and surrounding it were fleur-de-lis tapestries and heraldic scrolls of France. Every disabled soldier in Paris was invited to this *fête*, where they were given the best seats in front of the tribune.[19]

The honoured place accorded to soldiers in French society also found expression in urban development. In December 1799, Napoleon gave Percier and Fontaine the task of making the Invalides into 'the Elysée for warriors'.[20] A few years later, a British chaplain, the Reverend Dawson Warren, vicar of Edmonton and unofficially attached to the British diplomatic mission in Paris during the 1801–1802 peace negotiations, recorded in his diary for 16 January 1802 a visit he had made to the Hôtel des Invalides. A French military officer visiting it at the same time as Warren had stopped in the sanctuary where 'on each side upon the wall are inscribed in gold letters the names of those citizen-soldiers to whom honorary premiums have been awarded for military merit.'[21]

The militarization of remembrance had begun earlier, of course. In 1793, as hopes for a quick victory faded and casualty figures climbed, the government had sought to bolster troop morale with periodic commemorations of soldiers' heroic deeds and official remembrance of fallen soldiers.[22] But it was under Napoleon that this phenomenon assumed its greatest proportions.

A specifically military identity gained in strength during the Consulate and Empire. The professional education officers received in the newly founded military schools improved their prospects for advancement, and the granting of a number of advantages and honours confirmed the rising social status of soldiers. As military careers acquired more prestige[23] they attracted growing numbers of young men, all the more so since war offered an opportunity for rapid upward mobility.

This was what young Maurice Dupin, a volunteer light infantryman, assured his mother, in a letter of 7 Pluviôse Year VII:

> Dearest mother, you long for peace, while I dread its coming. The war is my only means of bettering myself. If it begins again, I shall become an officer easily and honourably. Decent conduct in action is enough to get you promoted on the battlefield. What a thrill! What glory! My heart leaps just to think about it![24]

The appeal of a military career for young men reached new levels under the Empire, as Herbillon recalls in his memoirs:

> Sent to the lycée at Reims on a half scholarship, I left at the end of term in 1811 having been a mediocre student but full of the ideas current at the time of the Empire. Everything filled our young heads with a taste for things military: the readings in the dining hall, comrades back from the army, our military-style walks, our uniforms, our hats with their long plumes. We aspired only to be soldiers, wearing an epaulette was to us the summum of happiness; all we wished and desired for was to be second lieutenants.[25]

The strength of this appeal under the Empire, at least until the retreat from Russia and the reversal in military fortunes, was reinforced by the popularity the army enjoyed in civilian society and by the special attentions lavished on soldiers. Octave Levavasseur made this clear in his memoirs when describing his return to France after the Austerlitz campaign in 1805:

> Paris, like France as a whole, was in raptures. The valiant army that had kept up such a pace for three months and then defeated the combined armies of Russia and Austria was praised to the skies. Proud of their victory, the officers and men were fêted in every public place. They were surrounded by attention and admired by the whole of Europe. The sight of my arm in a sling further added to the interest I personally aroused.[26]

The prestige of a military career rose in the early years of the Napoleonic wars thanks to a series of victories that could not fail to flatter national pride.[27] Commenting on Parisian public opinion in 1805, Comte Miot de Mélito, a Conseiller d'État at the time, noted the marked change in civilian attitudes towards the active resumption of the war in 1805 following the news of the great victories in the autumn and the official handing over of the flags of the conquered countries at the senate, which alleviated the gloom caused by the economic difficulties and the financial crisis.

> The unexpected and rapid successes generated an enthusiasm that quickly won over all shades of opinion until only admiration remained.... Issues of the *Bulletin de la Grande Armée* appeared in quick succession and, almost every day, announced a new victory that drew attention away from all other thoughts. The news of the victory of Austerlitz, which reached Paris on 20 Frimaire [10 December], and the thirtieth *Bulletin* that gave details of the battle, had the people in raptures... At a time when bundles of conquered flags were unfurled to adorn the vaulted ceiling of the Palais du Luxembourg, when all the elements that flatter the vanity and pride of a people with a taste for glory were combined to console it for lost freedom... the inebriation was general and no fears for the future tarnished it with bitterness: the time for reflection had not yet come. The eager crowd packed the streets along which travelled the procession carrying the flags that the Emperor despatched to the Senate.[28]

Yet the prestige of the army, the splendour of the parades and processions, and the patriotic pride at the news of great victories formed only one aspect of the civilian experience of the war. Many Frenchmen resented conscription and tried to avoid it. During the first 2 years of application of the Jourdan Law (1798–1800), over one-third of those called up either dodged the draft (refractory soldiers) or deserted on their way to the front,[29] and this resistance to conscription remained high during the Consulate and the Empire. This provoked disorder in civilian communities because police forces (*gendarmes*) were sent in cities and villages to arrest refractory men or deserters, and frequent riots and clashes occurred when the local community defended the refractory or his family. Furthermore, the presence of deserters in woods and remote places was unsettling and worse, as some of those armed deserters turned to crime.[30]

There were also many instances where civilians had their daily lives severely disrupted by events in the military sphere. They had to get used to living with threats of invasion – whether founded or not – and with rumours, outbreaks of panic, and advances by enemy forces.

When, as sometimes happened, civilians were directly exposed to the sight of a battle or a battlefield, the effect on them was no less traumatic than it was on soldiers. Children were perhaps an exception to this, to judge from those who later admitted to not having grasped the reality of what they witnessed. A good instance is the young Aurore Dupin, the future George Sand. With her mother she followed her military father during the war in Spain and was able to observe fighting at close quarters.

> At the window one evening with my mother, when the sky was still lit by the setting sun we saw it crossed by lines of fire, and mother said to me: 'Look, it's a battle, perhaps your father is in it'. I had no idea what a battle really was. What I saw looked to me like a huge firework display, gay and triumphal, a *fête* or tournament. The noise of the cannon and the great arcs of fire delighted me. I watched it like an entertainment, eating a green apple. It was then that my mother said to someone, I don't recall to whom: 'How happy children are not to understand anything!'...The next day or the day after that, we were driving along by the battlefield when...I saw a place completely covered in formless wreckage, like a life-size version of the massacre of dolls, horses and wagons that I made at Chaillot with Clotilde....My mother covered her face and the air stank. We did not get near enough to these grim objects for me to realize what they were...A wheel struck something that broke open with an odd cracking noise. My mother held me down in the bottom of the wagon to stop me looking. It was a dead body. I saw several more after that, scattered along the way. But I was so ill that I don't remember being deeply affected by these horrible sights.[31]

2. The difficulties of everyday life: hardship, scarcity, and inflation

Even civilians living in remote areas of France, far from the sight and danger of battles, and who had been spared the conscription of a close relative, could not forget that their country was at war, or put the war out of mind. In the Massif Central, in Provence, or in other regions safe from the direct threat of invasion and occupation, the impact of war was felt indirectly – in the same way that the reality of war hit the relatively spared north as well as the ravaged south during the American Civil War:

> Even civilians unrelated to soldiers knew they were at war; they were reminded when they could not afford shoes, or when the local shopkeeper demanded more for his flour with each passing week. Even in corners of the Union remote from military conflict, the Civil War touched civilian lives, sometimes in shattering ways.[32]

One way in which the revolutionary and Napoleonic wars wrought far-reaching changes in the daily lives of French civilians was by modifying established patterns of lifestyle and consumption. A major preoccupation for the French people at this time was the dramatic increase in the cost of living, especially of foodstuffs.

Large-scale requisitioning for the army, the shortage of labour for the harvest (with most young men away at the war), the commercial blockade, and transportation problems – all contributed to make foodstuffs, notably grain and hence bread, increasingly scarce and thus increasingly expensive. For French civilians, the war was synonymous first and foremost with high prices, shortages, and the threat of famine.

Claude Bailly, the saddler in the small town of Chinon in central France, noted in his diary on 9 September 1793:

> I think the war will be followed by famine, due to the high price of victuals. In Chinon, a pound of butter costs two *livres*, a dozen eggs twenty *sous*, a pint of wine two *livres*, a pound of meat one *livre*, a pound of bread five *sous*, a pound of leather seven *livres*, a pair of shoes fifteen *livres*, and so on for every piece of merchandise. Judge from that how people keep going and pay the taxes, with the time that's lost through guard duty and the other interruptions that never stop.[33]

The situation was still more worrying in the cities, beginning with Paris. Nicolas Ruault, a bookseller and publisher in rue de la Harpe noted in his diary on 5 March 1793 that for the second time in less than a year, Paris grocery shops had been pillaged by the population.[34] In Paris, scenes of pillage were followed by dearth in the summer of 1793. Guittard de Floriban noted in his diary on 10 September 1793:

> Today at last there is bread in all the bakers' shops and the people still set on assembling as a crowd have been dispersed. It was pointless, since there was bread for whoever wanted it today. I hope that this time we are out of the crisis we were in. We have eaten some terrible bread. I was ill from it twice, and I only went without once. This began on 10 July and lasted until today, 10 September. So for two months without a break we have had great difficulty getting bread.[35]

For the majority of the civilian population, daily life was conditioned by the problems of food supply. Long queues in front of bakeries became an increasingly common sight. Guittard de Floriban had witnessed this between July and September 1793:

> You had to be at the bakery doors by four in the morning. Some people were there from midnight, others spent the night there, which made it even more alarming. Yet everyone got bread. Everyone lived. So all those who went crowding round the baker's were shown to be mistaken.[36]

Another observer struck by the sight of long queues was Raoul Hesdin, the Parisian wood-engraver working for the Committee of Public Safety. Comparing his privileged position with that of the majority of Parisian civilians, he wrote in his diary on 6 January 1794:

> We, who are not obliged to queue at the baker's doors – thanks to my employ, I am exempt from this, and a bare sufficiency of bread is delivered together with meat and vegetables at my lodging daily – have very little conception of the sufferings of those who are. The queues are somewhat differently regulated in different sections, but my host's daughters, who take it in turn to go, are often waiting from 4 after midnight till 8 or 9 in the morning.[37]

A year later, on 14 April 1795, bookseller-publisher Nicolas Ruault could again note in his diary the unsettling appearance of this mass of people who spend 'each night at the doors of the bakeries to obtain, after a wait of five or six hours, half a *livre* of biscuits per head or half a *livre* of poor quality bread'.[38]

The new rulers of France responded to the threat of widespread and prolonged famine by taking an interventionist course, passing the Maximum laws of 4 May and 29 September 1793 that limited first the price of grain and then of all essential foodstuffs. These laws were intended to control price rises and guarantee food supplies for the citizenry. In many parts of the country, however, the result was panic buying and unrest, together with law breaking and the development of a parallel or black market. Often the Maximum made the shortages worse, as Claude Bailly noted on 17 October 1793: 'The Maximum was fixed for all commodities and eight days later the traders had nothing left to sell.'[39]

Eloy Leclerc, a sergeant major in the free company of grenadiers from the Puy-de-Dôme, noted the perverse effect produced by the Maximum when he was garrisoned at Strasbourg in June 1794:

> A few months back, when foodstuffs were not subject to the law of the Maximum, they were easily obtainable... But since the authorities applied the laws of the Maximum, a few *décades* [the ten-day 'week' of the revolutionary calendar] ago, there is nothing to eat or drink in the taverns. Most of these have shut up shop on the poor excuse that they can find no wine, bread, or meat to buy.[40]

The negative effects of the Maximum were aggravated by regional disparities. The law was applied with a strictness that varied between departments, thus making the situation even worse in departments near those where the Maximum was not applied since producers could sell their grain for a higher price in the neighbouring departments. This happened in 1793 when grain producers from around Toulouse (Haute-Garonne) sold much of their output in the Gers and Tarn departments.[41]

The government then attempted to regulate food supply by rationing. On 6 January 1794, Raoul Hesdin noted:

> Paris is on ration like a besieged city, each person receives from his section a baker's card, and is thereby entitled to receive from the baker, at the maximum price, as much bread as the municipal officers consider sufficient for him... This ration varies weekly.[42]

But the problem was not really solved, as Claude Bailly observed. In February 1794, the saddler of Tours wrote,

> Alas, in our region, though it brings tears to my eyes to say it, I see that many people will perish from famine. Commissioners have been appointed in each canton to distribute grain and ensure that each person gets a pound of bread per day. A card must first be obtained from the Municipality, then armed with this wretched card you can fight with the rest at the bakers' doors to get your pound of bread, which is what happens every day.[43]

Shortages and rises in food prices and in the cost of living were the common lot of civilians throughout the long years of war. They often voiced their complaints, especially in a year like 1795 marked by galloping inflation and financial crisis; the *assignat*, which had dropped to one-quarter of its nominal value by the end of 1794, continued to slip in 1795, down to less than one-twentieth of its face value by the summer of

1795.[44] Young corporal Alex Gosse wrote to his mother on 19 February 1795:

> If I have waited so long before writing to you, it is to spare you the postage on letters, for we are at such a critical time that there may not be enough money to live on. I have seen many letters from home and am surprised how people are able to live. From these letters I learned that the *septier* of grain was selling for up to 210 *livres*. I wondered how you are managing on such a small income. Would that it was within my power to send you some money, but the *assignats* are worth so little that hardly anyone will accept them.[45]

Nicolas Ruault observed the rapidly deteriorating situation in Paris. In his diary for 11 May 1795 he notes the introduction of austerity level rationing – 'for three days now the amount distributed is one or at most two ounces of bread per head plus a spoonful of rice' – and expresses his fears for the future, concluding that at this rate, 'the French will be a people of beggars' in no time.[46]

Food shortages and rampant inflation claimed most victims, especially during the winter months, among the urban poor. At Toulouse, for instance, the number of deaths in the working-class neighbourhood of Saint-Cyprien was 40 per cent higher in 1795 than in the bad year of 1789.[47] The situation in the north of France was worse and mortality rates even higher in 1795–1796.[48] Levels of civilian mortality were also increased by the upsurge in suicide, which was particularly marked during the economic and financial crisis and near-famine conditions of 1795, conditions which were exacerbated by the fact that the winter of 1794–1795 was the coldest in France in nearly a century. In Paris, Nicolas Ruault noted in his diary on 11 May 1795, 'The most impoverished are beginning to despair. Not a day goes by without some of them ending their lives. Some leap from the upper floors of houses, others throw themselves from bridges in broad daylight', and added, 'These tragic adventures are never discussed in the Convention, and the public papers dare not relate them.'[49]

Food supplies, particularly for urban markets, remained problematic all through the 20 years of war. Food scarcity threatened periodically, particularly since bread and meat prices continued to be fixed by the government under the Consulate and Empire, with the result that it was not always in the interest of farmers to sell their produce.

Across France, in the Auvergne and the Haute-Garonne, in Paris as in Touraine, the price of basic necessities rocketed and the civilian population felt the full impact of the war's effects.[50] A wide range of products was affected. In the small town of Porrentruy in Franche-Comté, the markets were empty in February 1794 and the inhabitants lacked butter, soap, oil, and sugar.[51] Wood, requisitioned in mass quantities for the navy, became increasingly scarce and expensive. Rioting was a frequent occurrence in the wood and coal markets of the larger towns and cities. The Parisian wood-engraver Raoul Hesdin noted in his diary in January 1794 that 'the most disorderly scenes are... enacted by the River Seine, where no regular queues are possible for those who wish to provide themselves with slender rations of wood or coal for fuel.'[52] In much of the country, wood and coal merchants had to be escorted through the streets to protect them from being attacked and having their supplies stolen. Forests were raided and tree stumps hacked out for burning as fuel. In Toulouse, the inhabitants of the Île de Tounis made nocturnal expeditions across the river to remove fences, doors, and entire summerhouses from the gardens of the villas on the opposite bank.[53] Yet despite such expedients and the growth of a black market, French civilians remained chronically short of firewood and coal, a situation reflected in higher levels of disease and mortality.

The problems of food provisioning were exacerbated under the Empire by the continental blockade set up in 1806. Following the Berlin Decree (21 November 1806) that placed heavy duties on the small amounts of colonial produce still reaching France in neutral shipping, these items became all but unobtainable. Nicolas-François Mollien, the minister of finance, noted in his memoirs the resentment of civilians in 1810 over the dramatic rise in the price of cotton and dyestuffs (that doubled between 1806 and 1810) and, even more, in that of coffee and sugar (that increased four-fold over the same period).[54] The civilian population thus gradually learned to go without imported commodities that had become an increasingly common part of everyday life during the eighteenth century. In this way the war brought about a profound change in French lifestyles, patterns of consumption, and customs, principally where food was concerned, necessitating the recourse to substitutes, mostly mediocre in taste. Coffee was replaced by chicory, cane sugar by beet, and chocolate by an insipid concoction. The authorities pretended to be unaware of the problem. Antoine-Claire Thibaudeau recorded Napoleon's opinion on the matter: 'It was objected that if coffee became too dear, people would get into the habit of consuming powdered chicory and that when peace came the habit would adversely affect consumption of coffee from the French colonies. The Emperor did not share this fear...'[55] But rising commodity prices and the enforced change in diet made a deep impression on contemporaries. For many French people the war was synonymous with shortages and austerity. The famous writer on gastronomy, Brillat-Savarin, mentions a novel aspect of his personal experience during the Napoleonic wars: 'During the war', he recalls, 'cocoa was rare and very expensive. All efforts to replace it were in vain, and one benefit of the peace lay in ridding us of the various dark brews that one drank from politeness but that were no more chocolate than an infusion of chicory is moka coffee.'[56]

3. Mobilization and the war effort

Increasingly, between 1792 and 1815, the French people lived their lives at a tempo set by requisitioning, conscription, extraordinary taxes, and other elements of the war effort. In some cases, preparing the country for the war mobilized entire local populations, which was as the government had instructed. Speaking for the Committee of Public Safety, Barère set out the programme for material mobilization on 23 August 1793:

> All citizens are indebted to liberty. Some owe it their craft, others their wealth, these their expertise, those their labour... Every physical and moral ability, every political and industrial resource is put to the service of the fatherland. Every metal, every element is won to its cause... In this we are as one: the metalworker like the law maker, the physician like the blacksmith, the scholar like the labouring man, the armourer like the colonel, the arms manufacturer like the general, the patriot and the banker, the needy artisan and the rich proprietor, the craftsman and the cannon founder, the military engineer and the manufacturer, the countrydweller and the citydweller, all are united together, all are brothers, all have their use... Thus all are requisitioned, though not all will march; some will make arms, others use them; some will prepare the foodstuffs for the combatants; others see to their dress and basic needs... Arms! Arms and food! This is the cry of necessity.[57]

Following Barère's report on the project for a decree on the *levée en masse*, the first article of the decree of 23 August 1793 assigned a specific function to civilian non-combatants. Married men not concerned at this early stage by conscription would forge arms and transport supplies. The civilian sphere would gradually be militarized, put at the service of the army and the war effort, with public places turned into workshops for making arms and the soil in cellars washed to extract saltpetre (Article 2).

These mobilization orders created an *élan* of patriotic fervour and were enthusiastically followed by the sans-culottes and by broad sections of the population. In some cases, indeed, they were anticipated upon. After withdrawing to his properties at Gaillac (Tarn) at the start of the Revolution, Bordeaux merchant Benoît Lacombe had been elected president of the town's popular society. As early as May 1793 he was urging the municipal council to provide financial and moral encouragement for the local inhabitants' war effort:

> Hasten the making of pikes, citizens, for the law says each patriot must have one. Order the handing in of all hunting rifles . . . With the enemy invading our frontiers it is no time for thoughts of pleasure and calculations of financial interest . . . Citizens, set up workshops, build forges, fill your storehouses with iron and steel, and at your command let the armourers, blade makers and locksmiths of your district flock to the *chef-lieu* and make the instruments for our defence and the triumph of the Republic. The fire of the furnace will symbolize our love of liberty, while the ringing of the anvil and the shrieking of the file will rouse those who fail to keep their eyes open to the dangers facing the fatherland. Select the most intelligent of the workers and put them in charge of the workshops, and if there are none in your area, recruit some from outside. The armourers and locksmiths will preferably deal with gun repairs, while the cutlers and other blade makers will be asked to make bayonets and pikes.[58]

Actively encouraged by its popular society and municipal council, the small town of Gaillac became a centre of intense activity, turning itself into a military workshop: 'the women span and wove day and night for the soldiers; fields were hastily planted with flax; a saltpetre factory was established; the coopers, blade makers, and cobblers – before long the municipality paid for a shoemaking workshop – set themselves to serve the State under siege.'[59]

Similar developments occurred at Nantes, where two female citizens appeared before the Central Committee of the Department on 13 May 1793 to deliver a petition in which they set forth that 'some women republicans are offering to mend at no charge the clothes of the volunteers if the administration will indicate to them a locale where they could decently perform this worthy and valuable work.' The Committee replied by voting its thanks and placing at their disposal the great vaulted hall of the old Jacobin religious community.[60]

The ambitious programme of material mobilization bore fruit: in Year II it permitted the arming and equipping of the 14 armies of the Republic. Subsequently, however, after Brumaire Year III, national mobilization was gradually abandoned in favour of private enterprise. The national armouries were replaced by private concerns, and the same change affected the production of saltpetre and the supply of uniforms.[61]

If patriotic labour in the workshops producing munitions for the army was a short-lived phenomenon, all through this 20-year period the French population was directly concerned by the requisitioning necessary to keep the war machine functioning: food for men and horses, arms and uniforms for soldiers, and, most of all, money. On 17 May 1793, the Directory of the Department of the Tarn informed the municipal administrations of the type and scale of the requisitions they were subject to: 'You are requisitioned to supply 555 shirts, 370 pairs of lisle or cotton stockings and 370 pairs of lisle socks. You are to allocate this quota between all the municipalities in your jurisdiction ... The municipalities of the towns will search out their townswomen who can knit.'[62] In many localities, the orders for material requisitions were strictly applied, since the inhabitants feared being treated as suspects if they disobeyed. Thus at Porrentruy, women and girls from all occupations and social backgrounds assembled at the town hall on 31 October 1793 to make up lint, bandages, and compresses for the wounded, a task for which they were requisitioned to the sound of the drum: 'all were drawn to this work by the fear of being treated as suspect persons,' noted the bourgeois rentier, François-Joseph Guélat.[63]

From its early stages the war also intruded into the daily universe of the French people through the enlistment of thousands, and ultimately millions, of men for the defence of their country. To begin with the government relied mainly on volunteers, but the number of soldiers fell short of requirements and before long conscription had to be introduced. The war became a concrete, tangible reality for civilian populations when men folk left the commune in large numbers. The initially limited form of conscription was rapidly extended; the effects were felt in households across France, who now saw fathers, husbands, and sons leave for the front. Not merely the families of volunteers and conscripts, but the whole of society was affected. Parents whose sons escaped conscription in one ballot lived in fear that they would draw a *mauvais numéro*, an unlucky number, the next time around. Practically everyone had a relative, friend, or neighbour who had been called to fight far from home. Local populations assembled for the departure of successive batches of conscripts from the commune. When soldiers sent letters to their families they frequently included news about the welfare of the other conscripts from the same commune, news that would be passed on to the families concerned. In a real sense the war was a collective event, less national than regional or local, one that tended to bind communities together around shared destinies, expectations, and anxieties.

A large proportion of privately owned horses in both town and country were requisitioned for the needs of the army. Guittard de Floriban noted in his diary for 2 September 1792 that 'all the houses keeping horses as draught animals or mounts were visited. Today all these horses have been taken as dragoon horses in the cavalry for drawing cannons and pulling wagons.'[64] These measures produced a sharp rise in the price of horses, as Gabriel Abot de Bazinghen, a noble landowner in the Boulonnais region, observed. In January 1795 he recorded in his diary that the price of an 8-month-old foal had risen to 1800 *livres* and that of a mare to 3000–4000 *livres*.[65] The army also required large amounts of transport material, and sometimes the men to operate it. In Alsace, between 15 Fructidor Year XIII (2 September 1805) and 15 Vendémiaire Year XIV (7 October 1805), requisitioning involved more than 3000 horses, plus more than 500 wagons, 1500 carts, boats, carters, and bargees.[66] Requisitioning on this scale had an adverse effect on the public transport used by civilians, already made more difficult by the poor state of the roads (due to shortage of funds), a situation reflected in the significant increase in journey times.

The manufacture of arms and ammunition generated considerable requirements. Saltpetre used for making the gunpowder needed for cannons and muskets was the object of a right to search, and was requisitioned in the cellars of individual householders. In Paris, Guittard de Floriban made the following entry in his diary on 20 February 1794:

> Our cellar was searched today for saltpetre. Cellars, outhouses, stables, storerooms, across Paris, were all searched. The earthen floor is removed to a depth of two or three inches and put in barrels, where water is poured over it, which, running through the earth, washes out the saltpetre.[67]

Requisitions continued throughout the war, under the Consulate and Empire as during the revolutionary period. They were not limited to foodstuffs but concerned every area of the war economy: the government could appropriate any item of use for military provisioning, sometimes making a small payment in return. In 1794, the parents of children under 14 – too young to be conscripted for the defence of French territory – were required to contribute to the war effort and the Republic by handing in at their local town hall a *livre* of rags, for making paper and *assignats*. In practice, however, this measure was hardly ever applied, since few households had the means to supply what was asked of them.[68]

Since the war effort needed specialist skills and expertise, workers in key industries were also subject to requisitioning. Between 1 and 20 April 1794, all the saddlers of Chinon were requisitioned and regrouped at Tours to make saddles for the cavalry.[69] Tailors, seamstresses, and shoemakers were requisitioned in most regions in 1793, and in subsequent years in Normandy,[70] Franche-Comté,[71] and elsewhere. They were required to make and supply their local council with fixed weekly quotas of garments and footwear for the troops. Artisans and workers requisitioned for the needs of the armies were under orders to work only for the government and faced a stiff fine for any infringement. In his diary for 31 December 1793, François-Joseph Guélat noted that cobblers 'dare work only for the troops since they risk a fine of 100 *livres* the first time they are caught working for other people'.[72] The result was a sharp rise in the cost of shoes, and civilians increasingly had to make do with clogs: 'lined clogs sell for 10 *livres* the pair. Our ladies, both old and young, are already wearing them, to set an example.'[73]

Blacksmiths were another group of specialist workers widely requisitioned for the service of the armies.[74] In some cases, workers requisitioned for their key skills were even brought together outside their own region. On 15 July 1803, all French naval carpenters living on the coast or in regions not far from it, such as Touraine, were requisitioned and sent to locations chosen by the government for constructing ships and barges for the invasion of England. Included with them were workers in the fields of naval shipbuilding and ropemaking.[75]

Requisitioning also concerned the bells from public buildings such as schools and, linked to the dechristianization policy, those from the majority of churches, which were to be melted down for the manufacture of cannons. The removal of church bells in towns and villages often ran into strong opposition from the local populations. On 23 October 1793, a large contingent of soldiers had to be sent to the village of Bure, in the Franche-Comté, 'to force the inhabitants to permit the removal of their bells'.[76]

One consequence of the war of which contemporaries were fully aware was the increase in taxes. Claude Bailly noted in his diary for 28 August 1803, 'The expense of the war is to be paid over three years, as of Year XI, at a rate of six *liards* per *livre* of tax.'[77] Guittard de Floriban saw his tax bill for 1793 rise to 237.6 *livres*, prompting him to comment on 15 January 1794 that 'This is truly a burden for me.'[78]

In addition to taxes, civilians contributed spontaneously to the war effort, to the funding of the army, by means of *dons volontaires* or 'voluntary gifts'. Guittard de Floriban recorded his gift of five *livres* in his diary on 17 March 1793:

> Today all members of the Luxembourg Section under arms, aged from 18 to 80 years, met as companies at the Saint-Sulpice Seminary. There were eighteen companies. From there we went to the Jardin du Luxembourg. It started to rain and we sheltered under the Luxembourg arcades. Each company appointed two commissioners to receive the free gifts that everyone gave. This was not compulsory. The money is to equip the Section, which numbers 168 men. Paris is supposed to supply 12,800 men. I gave five *livres*.[79]

Again from choice, he gave two new shirts to the Revolutionary Committee of his section for his 'brothers in arms' (total value 44 *livres*), some money on 27 January 1794 for the wives of the volunteers from his section away in the army, and 50 *sous* on 28 January to equip the horseman raised by the section.[80]

Some gifts made at this time were the genuine and spontaneous product of free choice, and as such attest to the patriotic fervour of a part at least of the French civilian population. In other cases, however, they had a strong compulsory character, given that the list of citizens who made gifts was read out in public by the local authorities and that few people dared to give nothing and thus risk being treated as suspect persons. In this perspective, the 'voluntary gifts' resembled a tax in disguise, and if the call on the good will of the citizenry proved so successful this was partly because of the government's role in its organization, as François-Joseph Guélat noted in the Franche-Comté in March 1794. On 8 March, commissioners from the representatives of the Convention at Strasbourg, of Public Safety and of subsistences, demanded fodder, corn, oats, garments, shoes, boots, coats, hats, and stockings, needed for the volunteers of the Army of the Rhine and Moselle, 'stating that all these objects, along with the cobblers and other workers, were requisitioned and that the utmost severity would be shown towards anyone who did not comply', after which, on the next day, 'people promptly delivered to Quiquerez and L'Hoste, the commissioners of the popular society, gifts of coats, shirts, boots, shoes, etc.', and on 10 March 'the list of patriotic gifts of linen, clothing, and *assignats* was read out at the popular society.'[81]

III. The war comes to France

The Allies had invaded a few French departments in 1793, but thereafter, for around 20 years, the war was fought on foreign soil, sometimes at great distance. France's civilian population suffered the repercussions of the war and its economic consequences, but did not have to face the fear, the violence and destruction that were the concrete reality of combat, attack, and invasion. This privileged position of the civilian population, compared with civilians in other continental countries, many of whom suffered repeated movements of troops across their territory, ended with the partial invasion of France in 1814. The same thing happened again in spring 1815, following a short interlude of peace during the First Restoration and the Hundred Days (March–June 1815). In this last section, contemporary testimony from two merchant families, one in Normandy, the other from Marseille, and both with family members in Paris, is used to examine the experience of civilians when their home country became the theatre for war, and the impact of the invasion on daily life and economic activity in the regions affected.

From early 1814, the advance of enemy troops in the Palatinate and Belgium and the retreat of the French Army caused alarm to spread through much of the French population. Concern was fuelled by military news, the threat of a typhus epidemic, the inadequate defences, and the spread of alarmist rumours.

Economic activity was severely disrupted by events in the military sphere and by the crisis of confidence that they provoked in business circles and in public opinion. Stock market prices collapsed at the start of 1814, and government funds, after rallying slightly, resumed their downward course.

As the allies moved closer and the threat of invasion became a distinct possibility in eastern France and Paris, many civilians took to the roads and sought safety in more distant regions, such as western France. This was the case for the Begouën family, shipowners from Le Havre. As early as 19 January 1814, Jacques-François Begouën was urging his son-in-law to get his family away from Paris, and bring his wife and children back to Le Havre, to avoid being caught up later in the flood of refugees: 'Events may move faster than you imagine... You must be on guard for the floods of women and children who, should public unease grow, will all try to leave at once, thus making transport impossible.'[82]

That prediction proved correct, since 1 month later Begouën noted that 'all these people pouring into Normandy from Paris should at least push up the price of food and in particular of grain in our region, the *pays de Caux*. A small comfort to be drawn from a great misfortune.'[83] The war and the invasion precipitated a vast movement of population, just as it had in 1793, when part of the population of Collioure had to leave the town ahead of the advancing Spaniards.[84] Once again, many civilians were forced to abandon their homes and seek refuge in areas away from the theatre of war.

With the exodus of population came moves to protect property (by hiding or burying belongings[85]) to prevent it from falling into enemy hands and being lost to its owners. From March 1814, the roads and lanes of northern and eastern France were choked with a mass of refugees on foot or in carts, dragging along the few objects they had had time to take with them. Those who, like the Begouën, had left much earlier were able to prepare and take their most valuable possessions with them. André, Jacques-François Begouën's son-in-law, took the silverware and jewellery when he led his family to safety in Le Havre. In February, Begouën feared an invasion of Normandy and urged his son-in-law to take new precautions: 'I advise you, my friend, do not put off taking and hiding at Valasse, with all possible prudence and discretion, our silver and your wife's jewellery and diamonds; put my mind at rest on this point...'[86] Valuables that could not be removed were usually hidden carefully before setting off.

By February and March 1814, the French people lived in fear of an invasion. Jacques-François Begouën, who stayed on in Paris, might try to reassure his family who had taken refuge in Le Havre, but could not always conceal his fears. On 16 February he confided:

> Between ourselves, though, we are in a crisis, on the edge of the chasm, so to speak. The great enemy army of 100,000 men is still intact; I doubt whether the Emperor has more than 60–70,000 men... It pains me more than I can express to see that our successes are talked about less than they are written about. The widely-held view is that they will merely put off our agony and that we will not avoid the cruel humiliation of receiving the visit of these *Messieurs*. I have no hope left. In spite of our successes the enemy is still advancing and we are still retreating, ... However founded the confidence in the Emperor's genius and in the bravura of our troops, it is impossible to envisage without strong feelings the possible results of such a struggle before the walls of Paris... We are in the final phase. In only a few days we shall be saved or lost...[87]

From February, this grim situation was reflected in the economy. Already weakened by 25 years of war, economic activity slowed even further as the threat of an invasion became reality. Credit became scarce and the markets collapsed. On 20 January, the funds were down to 46 francs, producing a wave of panic among savers. On the previous day, the Banque de France was besieged by a large crowd of people all wanting to withdraw their savings. On 19 and 20 January alone the bank paid out 5–6 million francs, before a measure was taken to stave off bankruptcy by limiting to 500,000 francs the amount that could be paid out in a single day.

The start of 1814 saw a growing number of failures among banks and manufactures, including established banking houses like that of the Perier brothers.

With business interests waiting to see how the crisis would end, the economy went into a state of hibernation. In February, when Jacques-François Begouën went to his notary to raise a loan, he was informed that nothing could be done for the time being, while everyone waited to see how the situation would develop and whether Paris would fall into the hands of the enemy. 'When I saw my notary this morning,' he records, 'he told me that the terrible present circumstances made all further business unthinkable, that it would necessarily have to be postponed… I always considered a loan to be indispensable; it would surely have been concluded already were it not for the singular circumstances we face. Let us hope that before the March payments are due the crisis will be alleviated so that I can borrow. I say alleviated, if we triumph, or if we are granted peace, or if the hateful events do at least occur in a civil manner and with a degree of moderation. I realize how vague and uncertain all that sounds and I groan inwardly at the thought.'[88]

The course of events speeded up in March. Part of France had already been invaded. An Austrian force of 80,000 had invaded Burgundy and from there was heading south via Lyon. Paul Aymard, a 14-year-old schoolboy at the time, recalled in his memoirs the sight of the battle and of the refugees fleeing the surrounding countryside and suburbs on 21 March 1811 to look for a safe place in the city centre. After being led by their teachers up the hill of Calvière to 'watch, with scarcely need for a telescope, the heroic fighting taking place', they had started to walk down the hill back to the city centre when they saw the nearby countryside of Vaise, filled by a great crowd of wounded men, women, and children that stretched as far as the Lyon city gates.[89]

A few days later, with the allies at the gates of Paris, refugees streamed in from the surrounding regions and Parisians braced themselves for occupation, as Jacques-François Begouën made clear in a letter to his son-in-law on 28 March:

> The Emperor is a long way off and the enemy is already at the gates of Paris. Rumours were flying around this morning, especially in the Saint-Martin and Saint-Denis *faubourgs*, after the arrival of an immense crowd of country folk, women, children, horses, carts and baggage, fleeing from Meaux and Clayes that the enemy seems to have reached with forces that outnumber ours. There seems no doubt that this evening the enemy is at the village of Ville-Parisis, six leagues from here. Another piece of bad news is that the Austrians are in Lyon, which has capitulated, and there is concern about Toulouse. It is all most alarming and dispiriting.[90]

The next morning Begouën gave him some more precautionary advice about the famine that he believed would inevitably accompany an occupation of France.

> Last night we expected to hear the call to arms. But although nothing happened, there is no concealing the high state of alert. I think that a lot of troops were moved last night to the sector where they are arriving... Another piece of advice I have for you is to stock up at Le Havre on potatoes, vegetables, rice, and in particular flour. I predict that within three months and perhaps much sooner, we are going to experience shortages approaching famine proportions. Ask Votte to send you a few sacks of flour and to save all his other grain for me. Perhaps Maugis will also be so good as to keep back two or three sacks of wheat for us, to provide against emergencies... Think carefully about all that and don't overlook anything. These are exceptional and grave circumstances, and this point must be fully appreciated so as to anticipate everything that can be anticipated by human prudence.[91]

On the same day, the Comtesse de Boigne, after seeing wounded French soldiers heading towards hospitals while she was walking in the Jardin des Plantes, witnessed the arrival of the population of the suburbs in the centre of Paris:

> The [*boulevards*] were overflowing with the population from the countryside and towns around Paris. They walked among their cows and sheep, and their few pathetic belongings. They were crying,

> lamenting, talking about their losses and their fears... I was starting to think that war is ugly when seen close up.[92]

On 30 March, the allied forces were at the city gates. Begouën observed,

> The roar of cannon was heard at intervals throughout the morning. It is said that the enemy is attempting to take Montmartre and the high ground dominating Paris... They also say that he is at Vincennes and controls Saint Denis.... Yesterday evening the enemy was at Bondy, coming in along the road from Meaux, and apparently spreading out to the right as far as the road from Senlis... There are differing accounts of what is happening and it is difficult to know. They say that our side is fighting well and that our artillery has been highly effective.[93]

The same day, a few streets away from where Begouën was writing, the Comtesse de Boigne watched the allied bombardment of Montmartre from the windows at the top of her house in rue Neuve-des-Mathurins. Then, with her cousin, she set about preparing her house for a potential siege, storing several days' food, putting out all the lights, and closing the curtains.[94]

Business was at a standstill. All shops in Paris were closed on 30 March. The situation was similar in other French cities directly at threat. Artillery officer Edouard Lapène witnessed the extraordinary transformation of the city of Toulouse on the eve of the battle of 10 April 1814:

> Fear was deeply rooted and you could see everywhere men struck by stupor and discouragement... All the expensive shops, and they were quite numerous in this town, shut down, and expensive items, which until then were exposed to the curiosity or the need of the public, were removed and carefully hidden. No trade or commercial activity. State offices, courts stopped working. Some of their members, as well as the richest landlords, left the city.[95]

But Lapène also noticed that theatres were often full, as the Toulousains who had stayed in the city tried to escape their everyday fears and problems, and that squares and avenues were peopled by 'curious, idle men who [were] craving for news'.[96]

This eagerness for news was shared with the Parisians and all the inhabitants of cities bracing for an invasion. The inhabitants of Paris could hear, on 30 March, the cannon and the noise of the fighting at the city gates, at Belleville, Saint-Denis, and Montmartre, though they remained eager for any news, however insignificant, right up to the moment on 31 March when the capitulation was made public.

In many instances civilians were firmly encouraged or even requisitioned to join the National Guard to defend their city. This often involved doing day or night patrols, which was not to the taste of everyone, as is clear from a letter sent by an Alsace merchant from Strasbourg, Desboiges, to a Marseille oil and soap merchant, Puget *fils*, on 15 May 1814.

> Between 3 January and 12 April, we remained completely blockaded, and as the garrison was small we had to do the service jointly with the troops and mount the guard every three days, which was not at all pleasant in the hard winter we had this year. If you have not experienced a blockaded city it is hard to form a true idea of what it is like, especially of the stories that circulate all the time. Three and a half months passed in this way and fortunately the enemy did not dare undertake the siege of the locality, where the entire garrison, including the Fort de Kehl, numbered only 7–8,000 men. I am not sorry to have stayed there through all those difficult times, but I can tell you that in the same circumstances I would not let myself be shut in again.[97]

The arrival of the allies on French soil, first in 1793–1794, then again in 1814 and 1815, led to devastation and destruction. Civilians were wounded and even killed in bombardments, and buildings and houses were destroyed. Dollet, a businessman from Cambrai, wrote on 13 July 1814: 'Our city received a bombardment that went exactly by the book. Three hours of heavy shelling, then the assault, and twenty-four hours of pillaging. We were fortunate enough that our homes suffered no mishap.'[98]

Not all the towns and cities that were bombarded were anywhere near as fortunate. The material impact of warfare at this time can be measured from the report drawn up in Pluviôse–Ventôse Year X by Conseiller d'État Fourcroy on the situation of the city of Valenciennes, which had undergone 43 days of siege and bombardment several years earlier (24 May–24 July 1793).

> Forced by insistent requests from the inhabitants of Valenciennes to go to inspect the ruins that remain in their city, I recognized that one-third of the houses had been brought down during the siege,

> that only one-quarter of these houses had been rebuilt, that the compensation payments to rebuild the rest, though often decreed and promised, were still awaited, and that the city's finest monument, the General Hospital,... where the inhabitants sheltered from the enemy bombs, had been badly damaged and left unrepaired since the siege.[99]

The material destruction caused by the assault and bombardment of fortifications and cities was not the only negative effect felt when the theatre of operations shifted to France itself. The arrival of large numbers of enemy soldiers was accompanied by brutalities against inhabitants, acts of pillage, and the plundering of fields and crops – committed by men of all ranks, including officers and even generals.[100] For some of the allied forces, indeed, such actions were revenge for the exactions committed against their own countrymen when French armies had invaded and occupied their countries.[101] A report sent to the Legislative Body in Year IX by the members of the central administration of the Alpes-Maritimes, one of the departments invaded in 1793, gives some idea of the consequences of war and invasion for the civilian population: 'Olive, chestnut and other trees cut down or damaged, vines torn up, flocks taken, poultry destroyed and often the wretched possessions carried off. Even whole villages have been plundered and ransacked, and houses in town and country entirely destroyed.'[102]

Another consequence of the invasion, in 1815 as in 1814, was acts of violence by foreign soldiers against French civilians. Couzineau Huard, a merchant in Saumur, wrote to Puget *fils* in Marseille on 11 August 1815, about the allied military occupation:

> We are demoralized by our circumstances and position, though still very lucky to be situated on the left bank of the Loire, where we are garrisoned only by the remnants of the hapless French army, which is well behaved, whereas on the opposite bank... even our *faubourg* is occupied by the Prussians, whom a few people were describing only a month ago as our liberators. A very different language is used today, especially by those who have them staying in their homes. Pillage, theft, rape, and, frequently, the torching of houses in the countryside are the rewards they dish out to our unlucky neighbours. A large proportion are already ruined, injured, and crushed by their misfortunes and it cannot be long before the remainder go under in

> turn ... I am deeply sorry for you if the Allies who are to occupy your department behave in the same way as those we have here.[103]

On 31 March 1814, France capitulated. A few days later, with part of the country occupied by the allies, a new sovereign, Louis XVIII, was put on the throne. The people of France greeted the peace favourably, despite the price they had to pay for it (lost territory, and the partial occupation of the country). A merchant, Pottin, who was the agent in Normandy for the Puget family in Marseille, wrote to Puget *fils* from Abbeville on 4 June 1814:

> I am writing ... against the noise of two hundred cannon fired to celebrate the peace that has finally brought consolation to humanity and given commerce the security it needs. The treaty encloses France within narrow limits but that must be accepted given the wretched and shameful state to which we were reduced.[104]

The Comtesse de Boigne expressed similar sentiments, albeit more tinged with sadness, patriotism, and even national awareness, at the spectacle of the foreign occupation of Paris: 'Every now and then, the silence was broken by the sound of the troops from the Allied forces, as they were talking to each other as they patrolled the hills surrounding us. This foreign sound made me realize for the first time that I had a French heart.'[105]

One year later, however, with Napoleon's return to France and to power in March 1815, the war began again. As in the previous year, the allied armies invaded France, and civilians relived the drama of spring 1814.

The letters exchanged during the Hundred Days between the Marseille merchant Puget and his agents or customers in a number of French cities show the extent of the war's repercussions for commerce and for the economy in general, which in some regions was entirely paralysed, and illustrate the local variations in conditions and thus in civilian experience of war.

Waljean Puget, in charge of the Marseille house, wrote to his father, manager of the Paris subsidiary, on 1 April 1815: 'We have had no letters from you since that of the 21st ... We are impatient to know what effect the latest news [Napoleon's return] has had on business; in our market it has been devastating.'[106] His father's reply, 2 days later, depicts a situation identical to that in Marseille: 'Business is languishing as before.

Colonial wares are dropping in price but finding few buyers, soap is depressed at 1.95 francs and if we decided to sell off we could only do so below the market price.'[107] Twenty days later the situation had worsened and Puget *père* observed, 'We are not selling any [soap]. There is no demand for the product. The same applies to all commodities. Business has never been so totally moribund... Circumstances are unfavourable for commodities of whatever kind.'[108]

In mid-May, Puget noted the worsening economic crisis caused by the war, together with a fall in government funds produced by the crisis of confidence[109] that continued in June.[110] There was growing disquiet as the allies advanced, and by mid-June economic activity in Paris was at a standstill. 'Business has been suspended all week,' noted Puget *père* on 24 June, 'Yesterday and all last night the National Guard was out... The shops in the Palais-Royal and rue Vivienne were closed yesterday.'[111] Three days later, on 27 June, he confirmed

> Our position is unchanged as regards business, by which we mean that no one is doing any – we would have difficulty quoting you the price of an article. A collapse is expected within a couple of days... The Chambers are taking strenuous measures to defend the capital. Today or tomorrow the Saint-Denis plain is to be flooded... The roar of cannon can be heard at Saint-Denis.[112]

On the next day the businessman felt that the final act, whether victory or surrender, was at hand: 'This morning the allied advance-guards are at Luzarches, Senlis, and Corbeil... Let us hope that the end comes without violent repercussions. No business has been done since the 19th.'[113] On 30 June, Puget *père* related to his son the latest rumours circulating in the capital,

> As I write to you the rifle and cannon fire is no longer to be heard, but between three and eight in the morning there was fighting before the walls of Paris. It is one in the afternoon and all is quiet. Some people claim that we have pushed the enemy back, others say that a capitulation is being negotiated... I have just been assured that the capitulation is being prepared and that there is an armistice until 4 o'clock.[114]

A few days later, however, there was still no news of a capitulation and Puget *père* was becoming worried by the protracted uncertainty and its impact on trade and on his business: 'We are surrounded on all sides.

This unhappy state cannot last for long. Business is interrupted, shops are closed, though payments are still being made...'[115]

Despite the worrying situation for business, the disruption of the economy led to enforced inactivity that fostered a general idleness and almost festive atmosphere. 'Not for a long while have the promenades been more splendid' wrote Puget *père*.[116] On 8 July the capitulation was signed and, he noted, Louis XVIII returned to Paris amid demonstrations of joy: 'The entire population lined his route. From Saint-Denis to the Tuileries, everyone was shouting "Long live the King"... people danced in the streets, and embraced with total strangers.'[117]

IV. Conclusion

Soldiers emerged from the long years of war physically battered, wounded, and in some cases mentally scarred by what they had seen or done. But the civilian population had not been entirely insulated from the harsh realities of war. Its daily existence was transformed and profoundly disrupted. The government might play up the conflict's positive and glorious aspects, offering the people frequent festivities and lavish celebrations of the great victories, but for French men and women the war was much more synonymous with shortages, rising prices, requisitioning, and higher taxes.

The lot of the civilian population altered decisively in 1814 when part of France was invaded and battles began to be fought on home soil. From being a distant reality whose repercussions and economic and human consequences were felt at second hand, the war became an immediate and tangible threat. Civilians now got used to hearing the rumble of guns; on occasions they even witnessed the fighting. In early 1814 and again during the Hundred Days, soldiers and civilians were brought together in a common purpose and struggle.

Though situated in a different register to that of the military, civilians' experiences of war made it possible for them to relate to what was lived by soldiers, who themselves came from civilian backgrounds. When the letters that conscripts or volunteers exchanged with their families mention the rise in the cost of living and the depreciation of the *assignats*, the point is sometimes made that they too suffer from the high cost and scarcity of foodstuffs. Experience of war takes many forms and cannot be restricted to that of fighting men, even though they are its actors, direct witnesses, and main victims.

Directly or indirectly, the long years of war affected every part of French society, disrupting and weakening its civilian as well as military components. The French nation emerged from them transformed and injured. In the immediate post-war period, the requests for pensions from war veterans had a parallel in the wave of petitions to local government from civilians requesting financial compensation for the losses they had suffered during the war and occupation. The revolutionary and Napoleonic wars had a deep and lasting impact on French society and appear as a founding moment in the birth of the young post-revolutionary nation.

Conclusion

The revolutionary and Napoleonic wars, by their scale and duration, by their geographical extent and sheer massiveness, and by the technical and strategic transformations they ushered in, mark a major stage in the evolution of western warfare. Their contribution to this process of change and to the birth of 'total war' has been demonstrated here by the appearance of several factors: the trend to massive battles, the formation of an army of citizen soldiers, the ideological dimension taken by the conflict, the perception of the enemy as forged by patriotic sentiment and ideology, and the far-reaching impact of the war on civilian society.

For these reasons the revolutionary and Napoleonic wars may be considered the first example of total war, before the American Civil War and the German Wars of Unification, which have long been viewed as marking the birth of this new type of warfare.[1] On many points, of course, they differed from the great conflicts of the twentieth century. In the technological sphere in particular, despite some significant progress, they remained close to ancien régime wars. The change and innovation happened elsewhere: in the enormous increase in the size of armies, bringing with it a new military economy (manpower so plentiful was more expendable), and in the ideological dimension of the conflict, introducing a new perception of the enemy and reinforcing the desire to destroy him completely, a desire reflected in a more frequent and more decisive role for battle. These wars marked the demise of the aristocratic tradition of war: a limited and formal practice of war had no place in societies whose political life was more democratic and where war was an instrument of politics. This evolution of the art of warfare cannot be divorced from a broader political and cultural context and must be related to the changes that took place within France at this time.

The military transformation was not directly perceived or given any theoretical or verbal expression by the soldiers who actually participated in war. The majority of them had no experience of earlier conflicts and hence no means of comparing their experience with the practice of war in the ancien régime. Most, however, convey the change implicitly in their writings through references to the war's intense brutality and violence, to the absence of rules of conduct (notably in guerrilla fighting), to the constant danger (quite unlike in formal, limited war), and to the scale and generalized nature of a conflict that mobilized vast armies and raged simultaneously at different points across continental Europe and beyond.

Besides these general reflections on the evolution of the art of western warfare, the wars of the revolutionary and Napoleonic eras were a central, defining event in the lives of ordinary people in France and in many other countries too. The wars left a lasting mark on several generations and lived on in memory thanks to the oral and written narratives that survivors produced through much of the nineteenth century.

The principal actors and observers of this event were, of course, soldiers, and for that reason they have been given pride of place in this book. The men in question were a mix of young and not so young, officers and rank and file, volunteers and conscripts, and came from urban or rural backgrounds and from every region of France. Their transformation into professional soldiers imbued with a strong sense of shared purpose and identity was typically a short, brutal, and, for most of those concerned, definitive process. Many who faced the harsh realities of battle – fear, wounds, disease, death – were left deeply scarred, physically and emotionally, by their experience.

The civilian population, though less directly affected by the long years of war, was not spared or left unscathed. The war rapidly established itself as the main preoccupation and subject of discussion. It assumed a central place in public life, a position reinforced by the propaganda of governments under every regime but especially the Consulate and Empire, which sought to associate the army with glory and prestige by celebrating its famous victories and according soldiers an honoured place in society. Civilians whose close family, friends, or neighbours were serving under arms tried to follow the course of the war through the accounts that soldiers gave in their letters, or through the news-sheets. Civilian participation in the war effort also came about through the mobilization of material resources, requisitions, 'voluntary' gifts, and higher levels of taxation. Civilians may not have shared the fear and danger of the combatants, but they too had their lives and daily existences transformed by the military action and suffered from its economic consequences, most notably inflation and shortages.

In 1814, and again in 1815 during the 100 Days, French civilian experience of the war finally merged with that of soldiers. The theatre of operations was no longer remote and abstract: it was in France, and for civilians in the regions invaded by the Allies war became a concrete reality. During the days and weeks of invasion and occupation, the inhabitants of these regions lived with the noise of combat and cannonades, with the effects of evacuation, pillage, and violence, and with the collapse of economic activity.

The war that wrought deep, profoundly unsettling changes on French society played a key role in the development of feelings of common identity. The formation of an army of citizen soldiers marked a break from ancien régime tradition, and among its most important effects was that of reinforcing national identity, a trend further encouraged by young soldiers' contact with foreign societies and peoples in the course of campaigning. The national identity that made its first timid appearance among French soldiers during the Revolution was primarily political in nature. Soldiers saw in France the embodiment of values proclaimed by the revolutionaries, beginning with liberty and political – if not social – equality. The volunteer troops of the 1790s were dedicated to defending political and moral values rather than a territory or their fellow countrymen. National identity, as they saw it, meant commitment to an abstract political concept, with France as the setting for the realization of the new revolutionary values. When expressed in soldiers' letters and other writings this political conception of national identity was made sharper and more dramatic by the use of an emphatic style and formulas borrowed from *sans-culotte* propaganda, and by the presentation of the military action and combat in moral terms. French soldiers were engaged less in a war between rival nations, than in the struggle of good versus evil, truth versus error, light versus darkness, modernity versus archaism, and, in the words often used by soldiers, the defenders of liberty versus the slaves of 'tyrants' and 'despots'. In the eyes of her soldiers, therefore, France was less a country or a people or culture, and more an abstract political entity, the incarnation and expression of new values.

The essentially political conception of national identity adopted and expressed by volunteer soldiers in the 1790s coexisted with as yet undiminished local identities. These men were citizen soldiers in the full sense of the term: they retained a strong attachment to civilian society. Few planned on a military career; most viewed their time under arms as a temporary situation, lasting a season or two, until the peace was signed and they could go home to their region of origin. Because the men thought their period of service would be short and, more importantly, be followed by a return to their native region, local identities remained strong, sustained by the regional basis of army sociability and by the letters that flowed between soldiers and their families, requesting and supplying news of 'home'.

During the Consulate and Empire, the political form of national identity is affirmed less clearly in soldiers' writings. Increasingly it gives way to a new form of collective identity, centred on the army itself: that of the professional soldier. When soldiers of all ranks admitted feeling a boundless admiration for Napoleon, their veneration was inspired less by the Emperor and head of state than by the commander-in-chief and troop leader. Time and again soldiers refer to Napoleon's presence among his troops during the war; in contrast to civilians, ministers and many other sovereigns, he knew and shared the dangers and the daily existence of his officers and men. The latter delight in describing the times Napoleon spent in their midst, relating his love of uniforms, his qualities as a strategist, his physical stamina, and his concern for their welfare. The admiration that soldiers under the Consulate and Empire professed for Napoleon betokens not a strong sense of national identity, but rather the growing consciousness of a specifically military cohesion and identity, of shared destinies and experiences, all of which were embodied in one man, who also offered social advancement and success through a military career.

Quite how much conviction and sincerity lay behind the expressions of commitment to the political and moral values of the Revolution found in so many letters from officers and in particular volunteer soldiers in the 1790s is difficult to gauge. What is certain and significant, however, is that this previously recurrent militant discourse, strongly influenced by *sans-culotte* propaganda, practically disappears from soldiers' writings in the Napoleonic period. This seems to point to a major change in motivations and war aims among these men, as well as a shift in their view of national identity. From being abstract and political under the Revolution, the sense of national identity became more concrete, based on culture rather than on politics, under the Consulate and Empire.

Related to the development of a professional identity among soldiers in the Napoleonic period, the sense of local identity, evidence of a durable attachment to civilian society and to one's place of origin, began to weaken, tending to be replaced by a national identity constructed with profoundly felt cultural, physical, and emotive elements. Men were more likely now to make their career in the army, serving for many years, often far from France: in the process they developed a group identity and a sense of belonging to a military world that distanced them even more from the concerns and cares of civilian society. And as they became cut off socially and physically from their origins, so there was greater scope for a sense of national identity to be forged through conflict with the enemy and through contact with foreign countries and peoples. A striking illustration of this new sense of national identity was the joy that soldiers felt and expressed when, on returning to France, they saw French villages and heard French spoken. Even soldiers who were not from the south, but who came from Normandy, Flanders, or the Auvergne, felt they had returned home once they had crossed the Pyrenees and again set foot in France. This response seems to me clear evidence for the growth of a sense of national identity among French soldiers during the Napoleonic wars, an identity that continued to develop and strengthen during the nineteenth century and of which one of the main agents remained the army.

Compared with what is observed for the military community, the direct impact of the war on the foundations and essence of civilian society was much slighter. The established categories of collective identity survived intact over these 20 or so years. The turning point here was 1814. The invasion of French territory by enemy troops and the local population's contact with foreign armies, often in a context of fear and violence, prompted a withdrawal into a protective collective identity and an upsurge of defensive nationalism. Many civilians recorded in their diaries and memoirs that they first felt themselves unequivocally French when their region was invaded and occupied. But the broader picture is not quite so simple or clear-cut and more detailed study shows that invasion and occupation did not produce a sense of national identity that was unanimous, universal, or exclusive. Some civilians, motivated by war-weariness or by political and social opportunism, welcomed the Allies with enthusiasm and even gratitude. For these individuals, considerations of personal interest or political opinion (anti-Bonapartism, royalism) were stronger than those of patriotism and nationalism; they saw the foreign soldiers not as invaders but as liberators: the return to peace, prosperity, and material well-being had required foreign intervention, not the ideal conditions for the development of a strong sense of national identity.

Even the civilians who were distressed to see foreign troops tramping across their country, in some cases plundering it, did not always respond by recognizing a national community united around the preoccupations and interests of a shared destiny. Invasion and occupation revealed instead the great diversity of local situations, to the benefit of local rather than national identity. Invasion and occupation, first in 1814 and again in 1815, did not affect the whole of France, and civilians in the invaded areas fared very differently from the inhabitants in the centre of France, which was untouched by these events. In addition, the nature and effects of invasion and occupation varied between regions and in particular between Allied armies. The British gained a reputation for respecting property and people in the areas of France they occupied, mainly in the West.[2] The Prussians and Russians, by contrast, seemed determined to avenge themselves on French civilians for the brutalities committed by the French Army in their countries. In fact, the lot of civilian populations depended on where they lived and on the nationality of the occupier. The sense of national identity that appeared spontaneously among civilians in the early days of the invasion, based chiefly on patriotism and a defensive reaction, gave way in the weeks of occupation that followed to a heightened sense of local identity, as comes over clearly in the correspondence between civilians in different regions at this time.

The peace treaty was signed in April 1814, and followed, after war resumed in spring 1815, by the Treaty of Paris in November of that year. France was reduced to the frontiers of 1792 and parts of French territory were to be occupied for periods of from several months to several years. But while the signing of the Treaty of Paris put an end to hostilities, it did not signify a return to pre-war conditions. French society, both civilian and military, emerged deeply battle scarred and exhausted from more than 20 years of war.

The economy of the country was weakened, and there was now the additional burden of the indemnity for civilians in the occupied areas, war debt repayment, and the cost of reconstruction. The invasion and occupation had a lasting effect on the mentality of inhabitants in the frontier regions. At the time of the July Revolution in 1830, an irrational fear spread through many of these regions that, as in 1814 and 1815, the other European sovereigns, acting in support of a legitimate overthrown sovereign (Charles X) and against his more liberal successor (Louis-Philippe), would intervene militarily against the liberal regime in France and again occupy French territory. Fuelled by collective and individual memories of 1814 and 1815, these fears of an invasion following the July Revolution were particularly strong in the frontier departments, prompting requests for public funds to equip National Guards capable of defending their region and compatriots should the need arise.[3]

Another legacy of the years of war – one that illustrates the role of the invasion in reinforcing a sense not of national but of local identity among the civilian population – was the move to commemorate individuals or groups of civilians for their actions during the invasion and the *Campagne de France*. Public recognition, and in some cases decorations, rewarded those concerned: men of substance and other local dignitaries who had opened their homes to peasants or sacrificed some of their own wealth to pay for requisitions and protected inhabitants from the brutalities of the foreign occupying forces; mayors who had remained in their post through the turmoil, acting as mediators and peacekeepers between occupants and residents; or lone individuals responsible for acts of bravery that had protected citizens from the occupant. The war fought in France also prompted collective actions of civilian defence. These became part of local history, preserved in an oral heritage, celebrated and commemorated all the more for being the cornerstones of a strong local identity.

If many civilians strove to preserve and keep alive the memory of these years of war, this was even more of a preoccupation for the soldiers who had actually taken part in them. The war was a central and in many cases traumatic event for the several generations of men involved in two decades of fighting. Most came back deeply affected both physically and mentally. Nor did their personal experience end with the fighting. The trauma caused by what they had seen, experienced, and in some cases done, could not be wiped out by the signing of a peace treaty. For large numbers of them the war did not end in 1815: it continued for the rest of their lives.

Many were disoriented by the return to civilian life and had difficulty adjusting. Most elderly and disabled veterans experienced deep financial problems after demobilization, 'in the lower reaches of civil society'.[4] Moreover, their personal experiences seemed at times to set them apart from the world of civilians. One consequence of this novel social and human situation was the development in nineteenth-century France of informal communities of former soldiers. As a corollary of the change in the social composition of the army initiated by the Revolution, former servicemen emerged as a new and distinctive group in French society. Under the ancien régime, the army – limited in size and above all composed of professional soldiers, mercenaries, some of them foreign – had existed outside the civilian sphere. By contrast, when the Napoleonic Wars ended, Restoration France faced the problem of reintegrating into society hundreds of thousands of Frenchmen who had spent much of their youth in the army, possibly serving in remote foreign countries, members of a military community with its own codes of conduct and whose ethos was alien to civilians. Recourse to the citizen soldier and the incorporation of over a million young civilians in the army thus had a paradoxical result: at the same time as it helped to anchor the war and its outcome more firmly in French society, it also created a new social category, one defined not by social or political criteria – like class, occupation, or regional origin – but by a shared experience of war, combat, and battle that helped to cut them off from the civilian world. Given the scale of the conflict and the sheer numbers of soldiers, this community of veterans, former combatants, and *demi-soldes* – those who were decommissioned on half-pay when the war was over – was inevitably highly visible in post-Imperial France, particularly during the celebration of that most political of festivals, Saint Napoleon's day (15 August), under the Second Empire.[5]

Large numbers of soldiers from the Napoleonic armies chose – or were forced – to go into retirement when the Bourbons came to power. But this did not mean that they were ready to put the war and its memories behind them. The post-war years saw intense sociability among former soldiers. They got together to talk and remember, informally at first, then in more structured societies once the Law of 1850 authorized the creation of societies for mutual welfare.[6] The network that was formed was highly active and its meetings kept alive the memory of the war. In 1851, the 'Famille militaire', a provident society for former officers, non-commissioned officers, soldiers, and sailors, had a constitution containing the following passage:

> Creation of a provident and friendly society for all dismissed, discharged and retired soldiers from the wars of the Empire down to the present day, was a worthy project to occupy the attention of the old servants of France. The glorious remnants of the Grande Armée claim this honour. Those who spilt their blood on the final battlefields of our great wars, the heroes who survived these immense struggles and whose decimated ranks contain fewer men each day, wanted to leave their brothers of the young Army a testimony of their affection ... It is the wish of the founders of the *Famille militaire*, the officers, NCOs and soldiers of the *Grande Armée*, that the bond that unites the heroes of our glorious fatherland should not be broken by the end of service, discharge, or retirement ... The former servants of the state will recognize each other, come together,

> and at every point of France, form the rear-guard for our youthful regiments.[7]

The memory of the revolutionary and Napoleonic wars was also perpetuated in written form. In response to requests from family and friends, or at the onset of old age, many former soldiers set about writing their memoirs, sometimes supplementing their personal recollections by use of contemporary documents (letters or campaign diaries), and always giving pride of place to the wars that were the pivotal and in some cases most traumatic event of their existence. The production of memoirs was encouraged by a demand from both public and publishers, stimulated by an appetite for personal testimonies about events judged to be of historical significance among a generation affected by the prevailing mood of Romanticism with its exaltation of the individual.

The revolutionary and Napoleonic wars were a decisive event in the history of Europe and a turning point in the art of warfare in the West. In addition, and arguably more importantly, they were a crucial event in the lives of millions of individuals and had a profound effect on succeeding generations. Much of this experience, civilian as well as military, was transmitted to future generations in the form of letters, diaries, memoirs, and other private writings produced during or after the events. These writings have provided the basis for this study. Using them, I have sought to capture the full impact of the events, not at the highest level of political or military history but at the level of the men who lived through them, and to relate and understand the human experience that played out on the bloody threshold of the modern period, in the mud and slaughter of the battlefields, on the decks of warships and privateers, as well as in less dramatic settings, in merchants' offices and at bakery doors.

Notes

Introduction

1. Jean-Paul Bertaud, *La Révolution armée. Les soldats-citoyens et la Révolution française* (Paris: Robert Laffont, 1979), p. 11.
2. Annie Crépin, *La conscription en débat ou le triple apprentissage de la nation, de la citoyenneté, de la République (1798–1889)* (Arras: Presses de l'Université d'Artois, 1998), and the same author's *Défendre la France. Les Français, la guerre et le service militaire de la guerre de Sept ans à Verdun* (Rennes: Presses Universitaires de Rennes, 2005).
3. Gunther Rothenberg, *The Art of Warfare in the Age of Napoleon* (Bloomington, IN: Indiana University Press, 1980), p. 134.
4. Jeremy Black, *The Age of Total War, 1860–1945* (Westport, CT: Praeger International, 2006), pp. 1–2.
5. Jean-Yves Guiomar, *L'invention de la guerre totale, XVIII–XX siècles* (Paris: Le Félin, 2004), pp. 13–14.
6. John U. Nef, *La route de la guerre totale* (Paris: Armand Colin, 1949), pp. 62–3.
7. Albert Soboul, *Les soldats de l'an II* (Paris: Club français du livre, 1959), pp. 203–10.
8. Rothenberg, *Art of Warfare*, pp. 11–30, 95–124.
9. John Lynn, *The Bayonets of the Republic: Motivation and Tactics in the Army of Revolutionary France, 1791–1794* (Urbana, IL: University of Illinois Press, 1984).
10. Roger Chickering, 'Total war: The use and abuse of a concept', in Manfred F. Boemeke, Roger Chickering and Stig Förster (eds), *Anticipating Total War: The German and American Experiences, 1871–1914* (Cambridge: Cambridge University Press, 1999), pp. 13–28, 14.
11. David Bell, *The First Total War: Napoleon's Europe and the Birth of Warfare as We Know It* (Boston, MA and New York: Houghton Mifflin Company, 2007).
12. Annette Becker and Stéphane Audoin-Rouzeau, *14–18: Retrouver la guerre* (Paris: Gallimard, 2000).
13. Stéphane Audoin-Rouzeau, *1870: la France dans la guerre* (Paris: Armand Colin, 1989), and the same author's 'French opinion in 1870–1871 and the emergence of total war', in Stig Förster and Jörg Nagler (eds), *On the Road to Total War: The American Civil War and the German Wars of Unification, 1861–1871* (Cambridge: Cambridge University Press, 1997), pp. 393–411.
14. Alan Forrest, *Napoleon's Men, The Soldiers of the Revolution and Empire* (London and New York: Hambledon Continuum, 2002).
15. Bell, *First Total War.*
16. Forrest, *Napoleon's Men*, p. 21.
17. Carine Trevisan, 'Lettres de guerre', Revue *d'histoire littéraire de la France*, 103/2, 2003, pp. 331–41.

18. Forrest, *Napoleon's Men*, pp. 40–7.
19. Rémy Cazals and Frédéric Rousseau, *14–18: Le cri d'une génération* (Toulouse: Privat, 2003), p. 22.
20. This represented a departure from the literary 'rule' of the journal, an element in the tacit 'autobiographical pact' linking author and reader and based on a unity of time and place, with one paragraph for the events that took place in one day and, usually, in one place, and introduced by a descriptive heading. See Philippe Lejeune, *Le pacte autobiographique* ([1975] Paris: Seuil, 1996), and by the same author, with Catherine Bogaert, *Le journal intime: Histoire et anthologie* (Paris: Textuel, 2006).
21. Forrest, *Napoleon's men*, pp. 24, 51–2.
22. Cazals and Rousseau, *14–18*, p. 22.
23. Frédéric Briot, *Usage du monde, usage du soi. Enquête sur les mémorialistes d'Ancien Régime* (Paris: Seuil, 1994); Madeleine Bertaud and François-Xavier Cuche (eds), *Le genre des mémoires, essai de définition* (Paris: Klincksieck, 1995).
24. Briot, *Usage du monde, usage du soi. Enquête sur les mémorialistes d'Ancien Régime*; Bertaud and Cuche (eds), *Le genre des mémoires, essai de définition.*

1 Battle Experience

1. Erwan Porte, 'Représenter la guerre: la peinture de bataille au Dépôt général de la guerre. Le cas des aquarelles de Bagetti sur la campagne d'Italie de 1796–1797', DEA thesis, University of Paris-1, 2004.
2. On the recent concept of 'culture of war' in the historiography of military conflicts, see Stéphane Audoin-Rouzeau and Annette Becker, 'Violence et consentement: la culture de guerre du premier conflit mondial', in Jean-Pierre Rioux and Jean-François Sirinelli (eds), *Pour une histoire culturelle*, (Paris: Le Seuil, 1997), pp. 251–71.
3. Jean Colin, *Les Transformations de la guerre* (Paris: Flammarion, 1911), p. 206.
4. Gunther Rothenberg, *The Art of Warfare in the Age of Napoleon* (Bloomington: Indiana, 1980), p. 61.
5. Rothenberg, *Art of Warfare*, p. 61.
6. Carl von Clausewitz, *On War* [1815] (London: Penguin Books, 1968), p. 219.
7. Rothenberg, *Art of Warfare*, pp. 61–2.
8. Combatant numbers (all nations together) in the main battles of the Napoleonic Wars: Austerlitz, 160,000; Jena, 128,000; Eylau, 132,000; Friedland, 180,000; Eckmühl, 160,000; Essling, 145,000; Wagram, 320,000; Moscow, 247,000; Berezina, 160,000; Lützen, 225,000; Bautzen, 192,000; Vittoria, 140,000; Dresden, 260,000; Kulm, 132,000; Leipzig, 420,000; La Rothière, 140,000; Ligny, 150,000; Waterloo, 150,000.
9. Octave Chevallier, *Souvenirs des guerres napoléoniennes* (Paris: Hachette, 1970), p. 116.
10. John Lynn, *The Bayonets of the Republic: Motivation and Tactics in the Army of Revolutionary France, 1791–1794* (Urbana, IL: Illinois, 1984), pp. 241–59.
11. Saint-Just, 'Rapport sur le gouvernement Révolutionnaire', in *Moniteur*, 18, p. 106.
12. A. Soboul, *Les Sans-culottes parisiens en l'an II* (Paris: Seuil, 1968), p. 654.

13. Quoted in C. Richard, *Le Comité de salut public et les fabrications de guerre sous la Terreur* (Paris, 1921), pp. 193, 729.
14. Quoted by A. Soboul, *Les Soldats de l'an II* (Paris: Club français du livre, 1959), p. 209.
15. For example, Francis-Joseph Jacquin, *Carnet de route d'un grognard de la Révolution et de l'Empire* (Paris: Clavreuil, 1960), p. 27 (September 1799) and p. 32 (May 1800); Chevallier, *Souvenirs* (in 1813), p. 262.
16. John U. Nef, *La Route de la guerre totale* (Paris: Armand Colin, 1949), p. 62.
17. Nef, *La route*, p. 59; Soboul, *Soldats*, pp. 208–9.
18. Soboul, *Soldats*, pp. 203–10.
19. Hubert Camon, *La Guerre napoléonienne. Les batailles* (Paris: Chapelot, 1910), p. 5.
20. Letter from Pierre Valleron, 29 August 1794, in René Bouscayrol (ed.), *Cent lettres de soldats de l'an II* (Paris: Aux amateurs de livres, 1989), p. 121.
21. Jacquin, *Carnet de route*, p. 25.
22. Narcisse Faucheur, *Souvenirs des campagnes du sergent Faucheur* (Paris, 2004), p. 194.
23. Rothenberg, *Art of Warfare*, p. 62.
24. François Vigo-Roussillon, *Journal de campagne* (Paris: Editions France Empire, 1981), p. 14.
25. Jacquin, *Carnet de route*, p. 27.
26. Paul Gerbod, 'L'éthique héroïque en France (1870–1914)', *Revue historique*, 54, October–December 1982, 268, 409–29.
27. Fricasse, *Journal de marche d'un volontaire de 1792*, Brussels, n.d., 1st ed. (Paris, 1882), p. 30.
28. Fricasse, *Journal*, pp. 20–1.
29. Letter from Joliclerc to his mother, 30 May 1794, in Joliclerc, *Lettres*, pp. 169–70.
30. Claude Simon, letter of 28 March 1793, in Emmanuel Delorme, *Correspondence de Claude Simon* (Grenoble: Allier, 1899), p. 77.
31. Joliclerc, letter to his uncle, Hôpital d'Amiens, 25 September 1793, in Joliclerc, *Lettres d'un volontaire, 1793–1796* (Paris: Perrin, 1905).
32. Letter from Piot to his mother, Dahn, 29 May 1793, and letter from Louis Valeyre to his parents, Frickenfeld, 18 June 1793, in Bouscayrol (ed.), *Cent lettres*, pp. 94, 106.
33. Letter from Joliclerc to his mother, 30 May 1794, in Joliclerc, *Lettres*, pp. 171–2.
34. Narcisse Faucheur, *Souvenirs des Campagnes du sergent Faucheur* pp. 198–9.
35. Faucheur, *Souvenirs*, p. 174.
36. Letter from Gilbert Moulier to his father, La Rochelle, 6 August 1793, in Bouscayrol (ed.), *Cent lettres*, pp. 238–9.
37. Octave Levavasseur, *Souvenirs militaires* (Paris: Plon, 1914), p. 35.
38. Letter from Julien Martin to Jacques Martin, Thonne le Thil, 29 September 1793, in Bouscayrol (ed.), *Cent lettres*, p. 53.
39. Letter from Bravy Soulbost to his father, Metz, 3 February 1793, Bouscayrol (ed.), *Cent lettres*, p. 86.
40. Letter of Antoine Jabouille to his father, 11 October 1793, Bouscayrol (ed.), *Cent lettres*, p. 37.
41. François Lavaux, *Mémoires* (Paris: Dentu, n.d. [around 1880]), p. 92.

42. Levavasseur, *Souvenirs*, p. 23.
43. Dominique Larrey, *Mémoires et campagnes* (Paris: Tallandier, 2004), vol. 1, p. 369.
44. Levavasseur, *Souvenirs*, p. 23.
45. Letters from Denis Fourrette, 28 August 1794 and Gaspard Bousset, 9 August 1794, in Bouscayrol (ed.), *Cent lettres*, pp. 55, 120.
46. Letter from Claude Combes to Albert *fils*, 5 Prairial Year III, in Bouscayrol (ed.), *Cent lettres*, pp. 214–15.
47. Alan Forrest, *Conscripts and Deserters: The Army and French Society during the Revolution and Empire* (Oxford: Oxford University Press, 1998), p. 4.
48. Charles Pierre Lubin Griois, *Mémoires du général Griois, 1792–1822* (Paris: Plon, 1909), vol. 1, p. 51.
49. Letter from François Mireur, 28 August 1792, in Jean Lombard, *Un volontaire de 1792* (Paris: Savine, 1892), p. 141.
50. Letter from Piot to his mother, 29 May 1793, in Lombard, *Un volontaire*, p. 94.
51. Faucheur, *Souvenirs*, p. 170.
52. Vigo-Roussillon, *Journal*, p. 14.
53. Vigo-Roussillon, *Journal*, p. 203.
54. Octave Levavasseur gives the reasons for this: 'In the artillery companies, each gunner has a distinct task. One blocks the vent, another loads, a third fires, a fourth aims, etc. The idea that one might be killed sooner, when taking the place of an absent comrade, had the effect that none were ever missing from their post on days of combat; they enforced this themselves and a gunner who failed in his duty in these circumstances would have been driven out in disgrace. This obsession had its advantages: the gunners stuck to their artillery pieces as to their mistresses and would have considered it great misfortune had they been taken from them' (Levavasseur, *Souvenirs*, pp. 56–7).
55. Chevallier, *Souvenirs*, pp. 117, 75.
56. Letter from Piot to his mother, 29 May 1793, in Lombard, *Un volontaire*, pp. 95–6.
57. Letter from Claude Simon to a friend, Bienne, 17 September 1792, in Delorme, *Correspondance*, p. 32.
58. Larrey, *Mémoires*, vol. 1, p. 48.
59. Chevallier, *Souvenirs*, p. 116.
60. Levavasseur, *Souvenirs*, p. 103.
61. Chevallier, *Souvenirs*, p. 264.
62. Adrien Bourgogne, *Mémoires* (Paris: Arléa, 1992), p. 98.
63. Jean-Marc Bussy, 'Notes de Jean-Marc Bussy, appointé voltigeur. Campagnes d'Espagne et de Russie', in A. Jullien (ed.), *Soldats suisses au service étranger* (Geneva: A. Jullien Editeur, 1913), vol. 6, pp. 219–312, 239.
64. Henri Scheltens, *Mémoires d'un grenadier de la Garde* (Paris: Editions du grenadier, 2004), p. 69.
65. Claude Barrois, *Psychanalyse du guerrier* (Paris: Hachette, 1993) and Louis Crocq, *Les traumatismes psychiques de guerre* (Paris: Odile Jacob, 1999).
66. François Lebigot, 'La folie et la guerre de 1914–1918', *Médecine et armées*, 23, 2, 1995, pp. 203–6; Symposium on shell shock in *14–18: Aujourd'hui, Today, Heute*, 3 (Paris: Noesis, 2000); Peter Leese, *Shell Shock: Traumatic*

Neurosis and the British Soldiers of the First World War (New York: Palgrave, 2002); Jay Winter, *Shell-Shock and the Cultural History of the Great War*, special issue of the *Journal of Contemporary History*, 35, 1, January 2000, pp. 7–11.

67. François Lebigot et al., *Le traumatisme psychique: rencontre et devenir* (Paris: Masson, 1994).
68. Junior elite troops generally made of sons of military or orphans of military.
69. Bourgogne, *Mémoires*, p. 178.
70. Bourgogne, *Mémoires*, p. 178.
71. Bourgogne, *Mémoires*, p. 180.
72. Robert Guillemard, *Mémoires de Robert Guillemard, sergent en retraite, de 1805 à 1823* (Paris: Delaforest, Bossange, Baudouin, 1826), p. 37.
73. Levavasseur, *Souvenirs*, p. 106.
74. Stéphane Audoin-Rouzeau, 'Pratiques et objets de la cruauté sur le champ de bataille', in *14–18: Aujourd'hui, Today, Heute*, 2, pp. 104–15, and idem, *Combattre (1914–1918)* (Amiens: CRDP, 1995).
75. Joanna Bourke, *An Intimate History of Killing: Face to Face Killing in Twentieth-Century Warfare* (New York: Basic Books, 1999).
76. Antoine Prost, 'Les Limites de la brutalisation: tuer sur le front occidental en 14–18', *Vingtième siècle. Revue d'Histoire*, 5, January–March 2004, pp. 5–20.
77. Chevallier, *Souvenirs*, p. 95.
78. Blaise Cendras, *J'ai tué* (Paris: G. Crès, 1919), pp. 147–52.
79. Evelyne Desbois, 'Vivement la guerre qu'on se tue! Sur la ligne de feu en 14–18', in *Terrain*, October 1992, 19, pp. 65–80.
80. Chevallier, *Souvenirs*, p. 66.
81. Bourgogne, *Mémoires*, pp. 112–13.
82. Levavasseur, *Souvenirs*, p. 34.
83. George L. Mosse, *Fallen Soldiers: Reshaping the Memory of the World Wars* (Oxford: Oxford University Press, 1990).
84. Annette Becker and Stéphane Audoin-Rouzeau, *14–18: Retrouver la guerre*, (Paris: Gallimard, 2000), pp. 51–2.
85. Jean-Paul Bertaud, *La Révolution armée. Les soldats-citoyens et la Révolution française* (Paris: Robert Laffont, 1979), pp. 160–1.
86. Quoted in Soboul, *Les Soldats de l'an II*, p. 209.
87. Fricasse, *Journal*, pp. 38–9.
88. Larrey, *Mémoires*, vol. 1, pp. 371, 378.
89. Fricasse, *Journal*, p. 41.
90. Louis-Joseph Bricard, *Journal du canonnier Bricard, 1792–1802, Publié pour la première fois par ses petits-fils Alfred et Jules Bricard* (Paris, 1891), p. 150.
91. Reynald Secher, *Le Génocide franco-français: la Vendée* (Paris: Presses Universitaires de France, 1986).
92. Jean-Clément Martin, *La Vendée et la France* (Paris: Seuil, 1987) and, with Xavier Lardière, *Le massacre des Lucs: Vendée 1794* (Vouillé: Gesté, 1992).
93. Letter from François Bravy Benard to his brother, Saumur, 2 September 1793, in Bouscayrol (ed.), *Cent lettres*, p. 241.
94. Quoted in Chassin, *La Vendée patriote*, 4 vols (Paris, 1893–1895), vol. 4, p. 251.
95. Quoted in Chassin, *Vendée*, vol. 4, p. 256.

96. Letter from Joliclerc, 25 January 1794, in Joliclerc, *Lettres*, pp. 155–6.
97. Joliclerc, Letter of 27 April 1794, in Joliclerc, *Lettres*, p. 162.
98. Joliclerc, Letter of 27 April 1794, in Joliclerc, *Lettres*, p. 163.
99. Ibid.
100. Jean-Marc Lafon, *L'Andalousie et Napoléon. Contre-insurrection, collaboration et résistances dans le midi de l'Espagne (1808–1812)* (Paris: Nouveau Monde éditions, 2007).
101. Henri Scheltens, *Souvenirs d'un grenadier de la garde* (Paris: Giovanangeli Editeur, 2004), p. 32.
102. François Vigo-Roussillon, *Journal*, pp. 236–7.
103. Letter from François Dugarel to his father, Marcel, 9 Ventôse Year III, in Bouscayrol (ed.), *Cent lettres*, pp. 248–9.
104. Michael Jeismann, *La Patrie de l'ennemi. La notion d'ennemi national et la représentation de la nation en Allemagne et en France de 1792 à 1918* (Paris: CNRS Editions, 1997).
105. Fraternization often occurred over food and drink, with soldiers from each side drinking a glass of rum together before the fighting or, less commonly, leaving the battlefield 'to share a drink' (Levavasseur, *Souvenirs*, pp. 46–7).
106. Letter from Bravy Soulbost to his father, Paris, 29 October 1792, in Bouscayrol (ed.), *Cent lettres*, pp. 84–5. My italics.

2 The War at Sea

1. Nicholas Rodger, *The Command of the Ocean: A Naval History of Britain, 1649–1815* (London: Penguin, 2004); Brian Lavery, *Nelson's Navy: The Ships, Men and Organization, 1793–1815* (Annapolis, MD: Naval Institute Press, 1989).
2. August Thomazi, *Les marins de Napoléon* (Paris, 1978).
3. Jean Meyer and Martine Acerra, *Marines et Révolution* (Rennes: Ouest-France, 1988), pp. 154–5.
4. William Cormack, *Revolution and Political Conflict in the French Navy, 1789–1794* (New York: Cambridge University Press, 1995), pp. 109–18.
5. Michèle Battesti, *Trafalgar: Les aléas de la stratégie navale de Napoléon* (Paris: Economica, 2004).
6. Pierre Lévêque, *Les officiers de marine du Premier Empire*, 2 vols (Paris: Editions du Service historique de la Marine, 2003).
7. Piers Mackesy, *The War in the Mediterranean, 1803–1810* (London, 1957).
8. Louis-Antoine Fauvelet de Bourrienne, *Mémoires de M. De Bourrienne, Ministre d'Etat: sur Napoléon, le Directoire, le Consulat, l'Empire et la Restauration*, 10 vols (Paris: Ladvocat, 1829), vol. 7, p. 84.
9. Bourrienne, *Mémoires*, vol. 7, p. 92.
10. Bourrienne, *Mémoires*, vol. 7, p. 90.
11. Letter from Joseph Bonaparte to Napoleon, 7 November 1805, in *Mémoires et correspondance politique et militaire du roi Joseph* (Paris: Perrotin, 1855), vol. 1, p. 315.
12. Gabriel-Julien Ouvrard, *Mémoires de G.-J. Ouvrard sur sa vie et ses diverses opérations financières* (Paris: Moutardier, 1826, 3rd edn), vol. 1, p. 30.

13. For a critique of Choiseul's naval reforms see James Pritchard, *Louis XVI's Navy, 1748–1762: A Study of Organization and Administration* (Kingston: Queen's University Press, 1987), pp. 212–14.
14. Jonathan Dull, *The French Navy and American Independence: A Study of Arms and Diplomacy, 1774–1787* (Princeton, NJ: Princeton University Press, 1975), p. 90.
15. Meyer and Acerra, *Marine et Révolution*, pp. 90–2.
16. Maximilien Sébastien Foy, *Histoire de la guerre de la péninsule sous Napoléon* (Paris: Baudouin, 1827), pp. 178–9.
17. Letter of 28 Thermidor Year VII (AN: AFIII/205).
18. Letter of 11 Germinal Year VII (AN: BB4/134).
19. Letter of 19 Nivôse Year VII (AN: BB3/157).
20. Narcisse Boutilier de Saint André, *Mémoires d'un père à ses enfants, 1793–1796* (Cholet: Editions du Bocage, 1994), pp. 48–53.
21. Bertaud, *La Révolution armée*, pp. 271–2.
22. Chevallier, *Souvenirs*, pp. 24–8.
23. Thomazi, *Les marins*, p. 18.
24. Letter from Morard de Galle to Minister, 19 Nivôse VII (AN: BB3/153).
25. Thomazi, *Les marins*, p. 17.
26. Quoted in Meyer and Acerra, *Marines et Révolution*, pp. 154–5.
27. Letter from Rear-Admiral Linois to Navy Minister, 7 Nivôse VIII (AN: BB4/132).
28. Letter from Commander of arms, 25 Vendémiaire VIII (AN: BB3:156).
29. Letter of 24 Thermidor VII (AN: BB3/155).
30. Letter from Admiral Martin, Commander of arms, Year VIII (AN: BB4/156).
31. Letter from Rear-Admiral Perrée to the Minister, 26 Frimaire VIII (AN: BB4/136).
32. Pierre-Edouard Plucket, *Journal de bord* (Paris: Editions de Paris, 1956), pp. 203–4.
33. Letter from Port Director of Brest, 3 Thermidor V (AN: AFIII/205).
34. Letter of 24 Thermidor VII (AN: BB3:155).
35. Report of Germinal VII (AN: BB3/158).
36. Letter from Town Commander to Minister, 1 Prairial VII (AN: BB3/154).
37. Letter from Port Director of Brest, Ventôse VIII (AN: BB4/138).
38. Letter of 19 Nivôse VII (AN: BB3/157).
39. Letter of 17 Pluviôse VII (AN: BB3/153).
40. Letter of 27 Frimaire VII (AN: BB3/159).
41. Guillaume-Marie Angenard, *Mémoires d'un capitaine corsaire* (Rennes: La Découvrance, 1996), p. 28.
42. Pierre Jurien de la Gravière, *Mémoires d'un amiral* (Paris: Editions du Musée de la Marine, 1977), p. 181.
43. Thomazi, *Les Marins*, pp. 258–9.
44. Chevallier, *Souvenirs*, p. 43.
45. Cormack, *Revolution and Political Conflict*, pp. 109–18; Donald Greer, *The Incidence of the Emigration during the French Revolution* (Cambridge, MA: Harvard University Press, 1951), p. 25.
46. Pierre Lévêque, 'Les officiers de marine du Premier Empire', in *Annales historiques de la Révolution française*, 316, 1999.
47. Thomazi, *Les Marins*, p. 270.

48. Jean Meyer, 'Le face à face des systèmes logistiques français et anglais en Méditerranée pendant les guerres de la Révolution et de l'Empire', in *Français et Anglais en Méditerranée de la Révolution française à l'indépendance de la Grèce, 1789–1830* (Vincennes: Service historique de la Marine, 1992), pp. 181–202, 182.
49. Plucket, *Journal*, pp. 203–4.
50. Gilbert Buti, 'Toulon de 1800 à 1815', in *Provence historique*, October–November–Décember 1989 (39) 158; Martine Acerra, *Rochefort et la construction navale française, 1661–1815* (Paris: Librairie de l'Inde, 1993).
51. Plucket, *Journal*, pp. 197–8.
52. Speech from Napoléon to the General Council of Workshops and Manufactures (*Conseil général des Fabriques et Manufactures*), 24 March 1811, quoted in Thomazi, *Les marins*, p. 243.
53. Napoleon, 'Correspondance avec Gentili', in *Bulletin de la Société des Sciences Historiques et Naturelles de la Corse*, quoted by Francis Pomponi, 'Corse et Sardaigne entre France et Angleterre, 1796–1805', in *Français et Anglais en Méditerranée*, pp. 231–50, 235.
54. Vigo-Roussillon, *Journal*, p. 61.
55. Meyer, 'Le face-à-face des systèmes logistiques', pp. 191–2.
56. Mackesy, *War in the Mediterranean*, pp. 32–7.
57. William Henry Flayhart, *Counterpoint to Tra: The Anglo-Russian Invasion of Naples (1805–1806)* (Gainesville, FL: University Press of Florida, 2004), pp. 40–52.
58. Savary, police reports for 4 July 1810, in Nicole Gotteri, *La police secrète du Premier Empire: Bulletins quotidiens adressés à Savary par l'Empereur de juin à décembre 1810* (Paris: Honoré Champion, 1997), vol. 1, p. 118.
59. Levavasseur, *Souvenirs*, pp. 121–2.
60. Sébastien Blaze, *Mémoires d'un apothicaire sur la guerre d'Espagne pendant les années 1808 à 1814* (Paris: Ladvocat, 1828), vol. 2, p. 232.
61. Blaze, *Mémoires*, vol. 2, p. 198.
62. Blaze, *Mémoires*, vol. 2, p. 64.
63. P. Martin, *Histoire de l'expédition française en Egypte* (Paris: Eberhart, 1815), vol. 1, p. 149.
64. Anne Brogini, *Malte, frontière de chrétienté (1530–1670)* (Rome: Editions de l'Ecole Française de Rome, 2006).
65. Joseph-Marie Moiret, *Mémoires sur l'expédition d'Egypte* (Paris: Belfond, 1984), p. 24.
66. Plucket, *Journal*, p. 30.
67. Plucket, *Journal*, p. 149.
68. Angenard, *Mémoires*, p. 31.
69. Michel Rodigneaux, *La guerre de course en Guadeloupe, XVIII–XIXe siècles* (Paris: L'Harmattan, 2006), p. 63.
70. Jean-François Landolphe, *Mémoires du capitaine Landolphe contenant l'histoire de ses voyages pendant trente-six ans* (Paris: Bertrand et Pillet, 1823), vol. 2, p. 10.
71. Plucket, *Journal*, pp. 148–9.
72. Plucket, *Journal*, p. 249.
73. Plucket, *Journal*, p. 149.
74. Angenard, *Mémoires*, pp. 31–2.

75. Plucket, *Journal*, p. 277.
76. Savary, police report, 5 June 1810, in Gotteri, *La police secrète*, vol. 1, pp. 31–2.
77. Angenard, *Mémoires*, pp. 131–2.
78. Angenard, *Mémoires*, pp. 133–4.
79. Plucket, *Journal*, p. 211.
80. Plucket, *Journal*, pp. 268–9.
81. Angenard, *Mémoires*, p. 33.

3 The Body in War

1. Alain Corbin, *Le temps et l'horreur: Essais sur le XIXe siècle* (Paris: Aubier, 1991), p. 96; Stéphane Audoin-Rouzeau, *14–18: Retrouver la guerre*, pp. 29–30.
2. Jean-François Lemaire, *Les blessés dans les armés napoléoniennes* (Paris: Lettrages-Distribution, 1990).
3. Claire Fredj, *'Le service de santé aux armées lors des expéditions outre-mer du Second Empire (Crimée, Cochinchine, Mexique)'*, thèse de doctorat d'histoire, directed by Daniel Nordman, Paris, EHESS, 2006.
4. Bertrand Taithe, *Defeated Flesh: Medicine, Welfare and Warfare in the Making of Modern France* (Manchester: Manchester University Press, 1999).
5. Sophie Delaporte, *'Le discours médical sur les blessures et les maladies pendant la Première Guerre Mondiale'*, thèse de doctorat d'histoire, directed by Stéphane Audouin-Rouzeau, Universitié de Picardie, 1998, 2 vols, and the same author's *Gueules cassées: Les blessés de la face de la Grande Guerre* (Paris: Noésis, 1996) and *Les médecins dans la grande guerre, 1914–1918* (Paris: Editions Bayard, 2003); Stéphane Audoin-Rouzeau, 'Massacres. Le corps et la guerre', in Alain Corbin, Jean-Jacques Courtine and Georges Vigarello (eds), *Histoire du corps* (Paris: Seuil, 2006), vol. 3, pp. 281–320.
6. Antoine de Baecque, *Le corps de l'histoire: métaphores et politique (1770–1800)* (Paris: Calmann-Lévy, 1993).
7. Poumiès de la Sibourie, *Souvenirs d'un médecin de Paris, 1789–1863* (Paris, 1910), p. 88.
8. J. A. Mangan, *Shaping the Superman: Fascist Body as Political Icon* (Portland: Frank Cass, 1999); Georges L. Mosse, *The Image of Man: The Creation of Modern Masculinity* (New York: Oxford University Press, 1996).
9. Christina S. Jarvis, *The Male Body at War: American Masculinity during World War II* (Dekalb: Northern Illinois University Press, 2004).
10. Kenneth Dutton, *The Perfectible Body: The Western Ideal of Male Physical Development* (New York: Continuum, 1995).
11. Larrey, *Mémoires et campagnes* (Paris: Tallandier, 2004), vol. 2, p. 779.
12. Larrey, *Mémoires et campagnes*, vol. 2, p. 786.
13. Vigo-Roussillon, *Journal*, p. 30.
14. Bourgogne, *Mémoires*, pp. 200–4.
15. Bourgogne, *Mémoires*, p. 200.
16. Sophie Delaporte, *'Le discours médical sur les blessures et les maladies pendant la Première Guerre Mondiale'*, Thèse de Doctorat d'histoire, Université de Picardie, 1998, 2 vols.
17. Bertaud, *La Révolution armée*, p. 248.

18. C. Alberge, *Vie et mort des soldats de l'an II à l'hôpital de l'Egalité de Pézenas*, in *Etudes sur Pézenas et sa région*, 2, 1971, p. 21.
19. M. Bouloiseau, *Malades et tire-au-flanc à l'armée de l'Ouest, ans II–III*, Actes du Congrès des Sociétés savantes de Toulouse, 1971.
20. F. H. Garrison, *Notes on the History of Military Medicine* (Washington DC: Association of Military Surgeons, 1922), pp. 169–70.
21. Vigo-Roussillon, *Journal*, p. 51.
22. Scheltens, *Mémoires d'un grenadier*, p. 84.
23. Jacquin, *Carnet de route*, p. 70.
24. Chevallier, *Souvenirs*, p. 119.
25. Faucheur, *Souvenirs*, p. 165.
26. Levavasseur, *Souvenirs*, p. 105.
27. H. Zinsser, *Rats, Lice and History* (Boston, MA: Little Brown:, 1935), pp. 161–4.
28. Antoine Bravard, letter to his friend, in Bouscayrol (ed.), *Cent lettres*, p. 123.
29. Fricasse, *Journal*, p. 57.
30. Brun de Villeret, *Cahiers du général Brun de Villeret, pair de France, 1773–1845* (Paris: Plon, 1953), p. 126.
31. Dominique Larrey, 'Mémoire sur la peste', *Description de l'Egypte* (Paris: Panckoucke, 1823), vol. 13, pp. 81–103, 81.
32. Dora B. Weiner, *The Citizen-Patient in Revolutionary and Imperial Paris* (Baltimore, MD: Johns Hopkins University Press, 1993), p. 284.
33. Pierre Millet, *Souvenirs de la campagne d'Egypte* (Paris: Emile Paul, 1903), pp. 61–2.
34. Louis Thurman, *Souvenirs* (Paris: Emile Paul, 1902), p. 76.
35. Charles François, *Journal du capitaine François dit le dromadaire d'Egypte* (Paris: Tallandier, 2003), p. 310.
36. J. Lasserre, 'A l'armée d'Egypte: Discipline, récompenses diverses et armes d'honneur', *Revue des études napoléoniennes*, 30, 1930, pp. 99–121, 106–7.
37. Antoine Métral, *Histoire de l'expédition des Français à Saint Domingue sous le Consulat de Napoléon Bonaparte* (Paris: Fanjat, 1825), p. 25.
38. Nicolas-Pierre Gilbert, *Histoire médicale de l'armée française à Saint Domingue* (Paris: Gabon, 1803), p. 55.
39. Dora B. Weiner, *The Citizen-Patient in Revolutionary and Imperial Paris* (Baltimore, MD: Johns Hopkins University Press, 1993), p. 284.
40. Antoine Jomini, *Histoire critique et militaire des guerres de la Révolution* (Bruxelles: Petit, 1842), vol. 4.
41. Christophe-Paulin de la Poix Fréminville, *Mémoires du chevalier de Fréminville (1787–1848)*, ed. Eugène Herpin (Paris: La Découvrance, 2006), p. 76.
42. Joseph Elysée Peyre-Ferry, *Journal des opérations militaires de l'armée française à Saint Domingue* (Paris: Les Editions de Paris, 2006), p. 179.
43. Faucheur, *Souvenirs*, pp. 285–6.
44. Louis Begos, *Souvenirs des campagnes du lieutenant colonel Louis Bégos, ancien capitaine adjudant-major au deuxième régiment suisse au service de France* (Lausanne: Librairie A. Delafontaine, 1859), p. 48.
45. René Desgenettes, *Histoire médicale de l'armée d'Orient* (Paris: Firmin Didot, 1845), p. 341–2.
46. Letter from Bonaparte to General Berthier, Cairo, 28 January 1799 (9 Pluviôse Year VII), in Napoléon Bonaparte, *Correspondance générale*, vol. 2, *La campagne d'Egypte et l'avènement*, ed. Thierry Lentz (Paris: Fayard, 2005), p. 820.

47. Vigo-Roussillon, *Journal*, p. 41.
48. Larrey, *Mémoires et campagnes*, vol. 2, p. 963.
49. Larrey, *Mémoires et campagnes*, vol. 2, p. 963.
50. Larrey, *Mémoires et campagnes*, vol. 2, p. 961.
51. Larrey, *Mémoires et campagnes*, vol. 2, p. 962.
52. Letter from Claude Simon to a friend, 28 March 1793, in Delorme (ed.), *Correspondence de Claude Simon*, p. 75.
53. Vigo-Roussillon, *Journal*, p. 40.
54. Lemaire, *Les blessés*, p. 287.
55. Sébasien Blaze, *Memoires d'un aide-major* (Paris: 1896, p. 3).
56. Jacquin, *Carnet de route*, pp. 70–1.
57. Kerkhove, *Observations médicales faites pendant la campagne de Russie en 1812* (Antwerp, 1837).
58. Serge Léon Louis Kourchnir, *'Considérations sur l'évolution du service de santé militaire de 1789 à 1814'* (Thèse de Doctorat d'histoire, Paris, 1955), p. 47.
59. Rothenberg, *Art of Warfare*, p. 237.
60. Scheltens, *Mémoires d'un grenadier*, p. 52.
61. Chevallier, *Souvenirs*, p. 110.
62. Jean-Paul Bertaud, *La Révolution armée*, p. 249.
63. BN, Lf 219/9, *Compte-rendu sur les hôpitaux établis à Besançon.*
64. Joliclerc, letter to his mother, 27 June 1793, in Joliclerc, *Lettres d'un volontaire*, p. 99.
65. Alexis Gosse, letter to his mother, 8 October 1794, in Bouscayrol (ed.), *Cent lettres*, p. 127.
66. Bassinet, letter to his father, 11 April 1794, *Cent lettres*, p. 226.

4 Troop Morale and Military Unity

1. John G. Fuller, *Troop Morale and Popular Culture in the British and Dominion Armies, 1914–1918* (Oxford: Clarendon Press, 1990).
2. Alan Forrest, *Napoleon's Men: The Soldiers of the Revolution and Empire* (London and New York: Hambledon and London, 2002).
3. François Cochet, *Survivre au front, 1914–1918: Les poilus entre contrainte et consentement* (Paris: 14–18 Editions, 2005).
4. Hew Strachan, 'Training, morale and modern war', in *Journal of Contemporary History*, 41(2), 2006, 211–27.
5. Stéphane Audoin-Rouzeau, *1914–1918: Les combattants des tranchées* (Paris: Armand Colin, 1986).
6. Marcel Reinhard, 'Nostalgie et service militaire pendant la Révolution', in *Annales historiques de la Révolution française*, 30, 1958.
7. Forrest, *Napoleon's Men*, pp. 40–42.
8. Samuel Lyman Atwood Marshall, *Men against Fire: The Problem of Battle Command* (New York: William Morrow and Co., 1947); M. Janowitz and E. A. Shils, 'Cohesion and disintegration in the Wehrmacht in World War II' (first published in 1948), in M. Janowitz (ed.), *Military Conflict: Essays in the Institutional Analysis of War and Peace* (Beverly Hills, CA: Sage Publications, 1975); Samuel A. Stouffer, *Studies in Social Psychology in World War Two: The American Soldier* (Princeton, NJ: Princeton University Press, 1949).

9. Janowitz and Shils, 'Cohesion and disintegration', p. 216.
10. Stephen D. Wesbrook, 'The potential for military disintegration', in Sam Charles Sarkesian (ed.), *Combat Effectiveness: Cohesion, Stress and the Volunteer Military* (Beverly Hills, CA: Sage Publications, 1980), pp. 244–78; C. Moskos, 'Behavior of combat soldiers in Vietnam', in Charles C. Moskos (ed.), *The American Enlisted Man: The Rank and File in Today's Military* (New York: Russell Sage Foundation, 1970), pp. 134–56.
11. Audoin-Rouzeau and Becker, 'Violence et consentement: la "culture de guerre" du premier conflit mondial', pp. 251–71.
12. Cochet, *Survivre au front.*
13. Cazals and Rousseau, *14–18*, pp. 141–8.
14. R. W. Little, 'Buddy relations and combat performance', in M. Janowitz (ed.), *The New Military: Changing Patterns of Organisation* (New York: Russell Sage Foundation, 1964), pp. 195–233.
15. Moskos, *American Enlisted Man*, p. 135.
16. Marshall, *Men Against Fire*, p. 161.
17. Fuller, *Troop Morale and Popular Culture*, pp. 22–31.
18. Moskos, 'Behavior of combat soldiers', pp. 135–6.
19. Moskos, *American Enlisted Man*, p. 135.
20. *Code-manuel du citoyen soldat* (1889), quoted in André Bach, *Fusillés pour l'exemple, 1914–1915* (Paris: Tallandier, 2003), p. 87.
21. Scheltens, *Mémoires d'un grenadier*, p. 44.
22. Chevallier, *Souvenirs*, pp. 247–8.
23. Louis Romand, *Mémoires de ma vie militaire, 1809–1815* (Besançon: F. Barthelet, 1981), p. 14.
24. Bourgogne, *Mémoires*, pp. 87–8.
25. Letter from François Lavaux to his father, 27 Prairial Year 7, in François Lavaux, *Mémoires* (Paris: Dentu, n.d. [*c.*1900], 4th edn), pp. 316–18.
26. Scheltens, *Mémoires*, p. 44.
27. Bourgogne, *Mémoires*, pp. 131–2.
28. Bourgogne, *Mémoires*, p. 132.
29. Maurin, 'Lettres d'un volontaire de l'an II', in *Nouvelle revue rétrospective*, January–June 1902, p. 85.
30. Letter of 27 December 1793, in Joliclerc, *Lettres*, p. 150.
31. Ch.-L. Chassin and L. Hennet, *Les volontaires nationaux pendant la Révolution*, 3 vols (Paris: Cerf, Noblet, 1899), vol. 1, p. 434.
32. J. Gibbons, *Roll On! Next War* (1935), p. 92, quoted in Fuller, *Troop Morale*, p. 35.
33. Bertaud, *La Révolution armée*, pp. 194–5.
34. Archives de la Guerre, XW97 (letter of Falize), quoted in Bertaud, *La Révolution armée*, p. 219.
35. Archives de la Guerre, XW49 (letter of 14 July 1794), quoted in Bertaud, *La Révolution armée*, p. 219.
36. Joliclerc, *Lettres*, pp. 141–3.
37. Letter of Tuzest, 13 Nivôse Year III, in Bouscayrol (ed.), *Cent lettres*, p. 254.
38. Letter of Villedieu, 2 Ventôse Year II, in Bouscayrol (ed.), *Cent lettres*, pp. 258–9.
39. Alexander L. George, 'Primary groups, organisation and military performance', in Roger W. Little (ed.), *Handbook of Military Institutions* (Beverly Hills, CA: Sage Publications, 1971), pp. 245–318.

40. Adolphe de Gauville, 'Un prisonnier de guerre en 1813', in *De la campagne de Saxe à la campagne de France: Lettres et souvenirs* (Paris: Teissèdre, 2000), pp. 27–43, 35–6.
41. Emmanuel Saint Fuscien, 'Place et valeur de l'exemple dans l'exercice de l'autorité et les mécanismes de l'obéissance dans l'armée française en 1914–1918', in Rémy Cazals, Emmanuel Picard and Denis Rolland (eds), *La grande guerre: Pratiques et expériences* (Toulouse: Privat, 2005), pp. 281–90, 282, 288.
42. Levavasseur, *Souvenirs militaires*, p. 71.
43. Lavaux, *Mémoires*, pp. 253–8.
44. Letter of 30 May 1794, in Joliclerc (ed.), *Lettres*, pp. 168–9.
45. Letter of 5 April 1795, in Joliclerc (ed.), *Lettres*, p. 196.
46. Lavaux, *Mémoires*, p. 287.
47. Vigo-Roussillon, *Journal de campagne*, p. 91.
48. Scheltens, *Souvenirs*, p. 108.
49. Levavasseur, *Souvenirs*, p. 56.
50. Fricasse, *Journal de marche*, pp. 95–6.
51. Fricasse, *Journal de marche*, pp. 95–103.
52. Joliclerc, *Lettres*, pp. 165–6.
53. Lavaux, *Mémoires*, p. 233.
54. Report by Carnot, 1 June 1793, quoted in Camille Rousset, *Les volontaires de 1791–1794* (Paris: 1870, 2nd edn), pp. 192–3.
55. Cochet, *Survivre au front*, pp. 205–6.
56. Lavaux, *Mémoires*, p. 237.
57. Charles Pierre Lubin Griois, *Mémoires du général Griois, 1792–1822* (Paris: Plon, 1909), vol. 1, p. 66.
58. Adolphe de Gauville, 'Un prisonnier de guerre', pp. 27–43, 33.
59. Levavasseur, *Souvenirs*, pp. 46–7.
60. Order of 8 January 1794, intermediate division, Réunion-sur-Oise, quoted by Lieutenant Claude Priard, *Les juges militaires sous la Révolution* (Vincennes: Commission française d'histoire militaire comparée, 1969).
61. Levavasseur, *Souvenirs*, p. 59.

5 From Individual Experience to Collective Identities

1. Heinz Gerhard Haupt, Michael G. Müller and Stuart Woolf (eds), *Regional and National Identities in Europe in the 19th and 20th Centuries* (Leiden: Kluwer Law International, 1998), p. 5.
2. Benedict Anderson, *Imagined Communities: Reflections on the Origin and Spread of Nationalism* (London: Verso, 2006), p. 7.
3. Peter McPhee, 'Frontiers, ethnicity and identity in the French Revolution: Catalans and Occitans', in Ian Coller, Helen Davies and Julie Kalman (eds), *French History and Civilisation: Papers from the George Rudé Seminar*. vol. 1 (Melbourne: George Rudé Society, 2005), pp. 30–7, especially 37.
4. Letter of Claude Cornet, 7 October 1794, in Bouscayrol (ed.), *Cent lettres*, pp. 246–7.
5. Joliclerc, *Lettres*, p. 201.
6. Faucheur, *Souvenirs*, pp. 194–5.

7. Michel de Certeau, Dominique Julia and Jacques Revel, *Une politique de la langue: la Révolution française et les patois* (Paris: Gallimard, 2002).
8. Eugen Weber, *Peasants into Frenchmen: The Modernization of Rural France, 1870–1914* (Stanford, CA: Stanford University Press, 1976), p. 297.
9. Letter from Harriet, head of the 1st Battalion of the Basque *chasseurs*, n.d., Year VIII, (Archives du Service Historique de l'Armée de Terre, Xb 11), quoted by Alan Forrest, *The Revolution in Provincial France: Aquitaine, 1789–1799* (Oxford: Clarendon Press, 2004, 1st edn: 1996), p. 308.
10. Letter of Moulinet, 16 April 1793, in Bouscayrol (ed.), *Cent lettres*, p. 89.
11. Faucheur, *Souvenirs*, p. 158.
12. Levavasseur, *Souvenirs*, p. 93.
13. Levavasseur, *Souvenirs*, p. 72.
14. Fricasse, *Journal de marche*, p. 8.
15. Stéphane Audoin-Rouzeau, 'The national sentiment of soldiers during the Great War', in Robert Tombs (ed.), *Nationhood and Nationalism in France, from Boulangism to the Great War (1889–1918)* (London: Harper Collins, 1991), pp. 89–100, 89, 99.
16. David Bell, *The Cult of the Nation in France: Inventing Nationalism, 1680–1800* (Cambridge, MA and London: Harvard University Press, 2003), pp. 83–106.
17. Bertaud, *La Révolution armée*, pp. 194–229; Bell, *Cult of the Nation in France*, p. 201.
18. Letter of Bravy Soulbost, Paris, 29 October 1792, in Bouscayrol (ed.), *Cent lettres*, pp. 84–5.
19. Letter of Jean Ataix, 16 May 1794, in Bouscayrol (ed.), *Cent lettres*, pp. 162–3.
20. Michael Broers, *The Politics of Religion in Napoleonic Italy: The War against God, 1801–1814* (London: Routledge, 2002), p. 28.
21. Joseph Laporte, *Mon voyage en Egypte et en Syrie: Carnets d'un jeune soldat de Bonaparte* (Paris: Presses Universitaires de France, 2008), pp. 37–40.
22. François, *Journal*, p. 223; Joseph-Marie Moiret, *Mémoires*, p. 36.
23. Scheltens, *Souvenirs*, pp. 39–40.
24. Levavasseur, *Mémoires*, p. 122.
25. Chevallier, *Souvenirs*, pp. 149–54, 164.
26. Chevallier, *Souvenirs*, pp. 129–31.
27. Faucheur, *Mémoires*, p. 184.
28. Scheltens, *Souvenirs*, p. 42.
29. Pierre Pluchon, *Nègres et juifs au XVIIIeme siècle; Le racisme au siècle des Lumières* (Paris, 1984).
30. Bourgogne, *Mémoires*, pp. 315–6.
31. Jean-Luc Quoy-Bodin, *L'armée et la franc-maçonnerie au déclin de la monarchie, sous la Révolution et l'Empire* (Paris: Economica, 1987), pp. 59–63.
32. Quoy-Bodin, *L'armée et la franc-maçonnerie*, pp. 115–19.
33. Quoy-Bodin, *L'armée et la franc-maçonnerie*, p. 166.
34. Levavasseur, *Mémoires*, p. 141.
35. Elzéar Blaze, *La vie militaire sous le Premier Empire ou moeurs de garnison, du bivouac et de la caserne* (Paris: A la librairie illustrée, 1837), p. 234.
36. Robert Guillemard, *Les amis en captivité, Orient de Malte ou aventures d'un sergent français*, 2 vols (Paris, 1827), vol. 1, pp. 82–3.
37. François Dumonceau, *Mémoires du general comte François Dumonceau* (Bruxelles: S. Puraye Brepols, 1958), vol. 1, p. 313–14.

38. Levavasseur, *Mémoires*, pp. 140–41.
39. Quoy-Bodin, *L'armée et la franc-maçonnerie*, pp. 174–5.
40. J.-N. Bouilly, *Mes récapitulations*, 3 vols (Paris: 1836–7), vol. 1, p. 363.
41. Scheltens, *Mémoires*, p. 30.
42. Joseph Dembowski, 'Voyage de retour de Saint Domingue en France', *Journal et Voyage à Saint Domingue*, Paris, Teissèdre, 1997, pp. 129–177 (pp. 167–168).
43. André Loez, 'L'espace public des tranchées: "Tenir" sous le regard des autres en 1914–1918', in Rémy Cazals, Emmanuelle Picard and Denis Rolland (eds), *La grande guerre: Pratiques et expériences* (Toulouse: Privat, 2005), pp. 259–68, 263–5.
44. Faucheur, *Souvenirs*, pp. 119–23.
45. Brun de Villeret, *Cahiers du général Brun*, p. 10.
46. Brun de Villeret, *Cahiers du général Brun*, p. 19.
47. Chevallier, *Souvenirs*, p. 166.
48. Scheltens, *Souvenirs*, p. 103.
49. Chevallier, *Souvenirs*, p. 146.
50. Levavasseur, *Mémoires*, p. 136.
51. Brun de Villeret, *Cahiers du générale Brun*, p. 24.
52. Faucheur, *Souvenirs*, p. 123.
53. Faucheur, *Souvenirs*, p. 311.
54. Levavasseur, p. 20.
55. Rafe Blaufarb, *The French Army, 1750–1820: Careers, Talent, Merit* (Manchester: Manchester University Press, 2005), p. 161.
56. Guillemard, *Mémoires*, p. 19.
57. Charles Ridel, *Les embusqués* (Paris: Armand Colin, 2007).
58. Bertaud, *La Révolution armée*, p. 119.
59. Joliclerc, *Lettres*, pp. 188–9.
60. Deborah Reed-Danahay, *Education and Identity in Rural France: The Politics of Schooling* (New York: Cambridge University Press, 1996), pp. 43–4.

6 War and the Economy

1. Letter from the District of Gaillac, 9 July 1793, in Joël Cornette, *Un Révolutionnaire ordinaire, Benoît Lacombe 1759–1819* (Paris: Champ Vallon, 1986), p. 221.
2. Letter from the District of Gaillac, 26 September 1793, in Cornette, *Un Révolutionnaire ordinaire*, p. 221.
3. François-Joseph Guélat, *Journal de François-Joseph Guélat (1791–1802): Mémoires d'un bourgeois de Porrentruy* (Delémont: Boéchat et fils éditeurs, 1906), p. 190.
4. Martyn Lyons, *Revolution in Toulouse: An Essay on Provincial Terrorism* (Berne: Peter Lang, 1978), p. 128.
5. P. H. David, *Un port de l'océan pendant la Révolution: La Rochelle et son district, 1791–1795* (La Rochelle: Pijolley, 1938), pp. 260–1.
6. Brun de Villeret, *Cahiers du général Brun*, pp. 9–10.
7. Lyons, *Revolution in Toulouse*, p. 128.
8. Dartigoeyte to the Comité de Salut Public, Toulouse, 27 Pluviôse Year II, in Alphonse Aulard (ed.), *Recueil des actes du Comité de Salut Public, avec la*

correspondance officielle des représentants en mission, 28 vols (Paris: Editions du CTHS, 1933), vol. 11, p. 40.

9. David, *Un port de l'océan*, p. 260.
10. Letter of 31 August 1795, in Joliclerc, *Lettres*, pp. 217–18.
11. Nicole Gotteri, *La police secrète du Premier Empire* (Paris: Champion, 1998), vol. 1, p. 120.
12. Barbé-Marbois, 'Mission dans la 13° division militaire en l'an IX', in Félix Rocquain (ed.), *L'état de la France au 18 Brumaire, d'après les rapports des conseillers d'état chargés d'une enquête sur la situation de la République* (Paris: Didier, 1874), p. 109.
13. Letter of Frédéric Tansard, Livorno, 18 November 1794 (ADI: 1J401).
14. Letter of Frédéric Tansard to his father, Livorno, 11 May 1796 (ADI: 1J401).
15. Georges Lefebvre, *Le Directoire* (Paris: A. Colin, 1971), p. 129.
16. Bourienne, *Mémoires*, vol. 7, p. 230.
17. Bourienne, *Mémoires*, vol. 7, p. 233.
18. Bourienne, *Mémoires*, vol. 7, p. 234.
19. Bourienne, *Mémoires*, vol. 7, p. 228.
20. François Georges Pariset, *Bordeaux au XVIIIe siècle* (Bordeaux: Fédération Historique du Sud-Ouest, 1968), p. 223.
21. Gabriel-Julien Ouvrard, *Mémoires de G.-J. Ouvrard sur sa vie et ses diverses opérations financières* (Paris: Moutardier, 1826, 3rd edn), vol. 1, pp. 2–3.
22. Letters from François Begouën to Nicolas Olive, 8 October 1797 and 30 January 1798, in Maurice Begouen Demeaux (ed.), *Mémorial d'une famille du Havre*, 2 vols (Paris: Société française d'Histoire d'Outre-Mer, 1982), vol. 1, pp. 142–3.
23. Ouvrard, *Mémoires de G.-J. Ouvrard*, vol. 1, pp. 5–6.
24. Demeaux, *Mémorial*, vol. 1, pp. 121–2.
25. François Begouën, note of 15 September 1792, in Demeaux, *Mémorial*, vol. 1, pp. 125–6.
26. François Begouën, note of 8 November 1792, in Demeaux, *Mémorial*, vol. 1, pp. 125–6.
27. Letter from François Begouën to Nicolas Olive, 26 July 1795, in Demeaux, *Mémorial*, vol. 1, p. 141.
28. Letter from François Begouën to Nicolas Olive, 26 July 1795, in Demeaux, *Mémorial*, vol. 1, pp. 148–9.
29. David, *Un port de l'océan*, p. 159.
30. David, *Un port de l'océan*, p. 278.
31. Patrick Boulanger, *Marseille, marché international de l'huile d'olive* (Marseille: Institut historique de Provence, 1986).
32. Michel Fontenay, 'Les derniers feux du "corso" chrétien à Malte (1679–1798)', in C. Villain-Gandossi, L. Durteste and S. Busuttil (eds), *Méditerranée, mer ouverte* (Paris: Editions de la Maison des Sciences de l'Homme, 1997), p. 226.
33. Charles Carrière and Marcel Courdurié, 'Un sophisme économique: Marseille s'enrichit en achetant plus qu'elle ne vend (Réflexions sur les mécanismes commerciaux levantins au XVIII° siècle', in *Histoire, Economie et Société*, 1984/1, pp. 7–51.
34. Charles Carrière, *Négociants marseillais au XVIIIème siècle: Contribution à l'étude des économies maritimes* (Marseilles: Institut Historique de Provence, 1973), vol. 1, p. 127.

35. Carrière, *Négociants marseillais au XVIIIème siècle*, vol. 1, p. 141.
36. Carrière, *Négociants marseillais au XVIIIème siècle*, vol. 1, p. 1043.
37. Vigo-Roussillon, *Journal*, p. 125.
38. Jean-Pierre Filippini, 'Livourne et l'Afrique du Nord au XVIIIème siècle', in *Revue d'histoire maghrébine*, 1, 1977, pp. 125–49.
39. Vigo-Roussillon, *Journal*, p. 125.
40. Charles Carrière, 'Les entrées de navires dans le port de Marseille pendant la Révolution', in *Provence historique*, 1957, pp. 200–25.
41. Carrière, *Négociants marseillais*, vol. 2, p. 1043.
42. Laure Junot, *Mémoires de Madame la duchesse d'Abrantès* (Tours: Maine, 1835), vol. 1, pp. 264–5.
43. Lucette Valensi, 'Les relations commerciales entre la régence de Tunis et Malte au XVIIIème siècle', in *Cahiers de Tunisie*, 43, 1963, pp. 71–83.
44. Daniel Panzac, *Les corsaires barbaresques: La fin d'une épopée (1800–1820)* (Paris: CNRS Editions, 1999), pp. 88–9.
45. Letter from Burgues-Missiessy to the Marseille Chambre de Commerce, 19 August 1806 (Archives de la Chambre de Commerce de Marseille, M Q5–1).
46. Letter from Chépy, Rhodes, 21 December 1797 (Archives du Ministère des Affaires Etrangères, Correspondance Commerciale et Consulaire: Rhodes, vol. 3, hereafter MAE, CCC).
47. Amaury Faivre d'Arcier, *Les oubliés de la liberté: Négociants, consuls et missionnaires français au Levant pendant la Révolution (1784–1798)* (Paris: Peter Lang, 2007), p. 165.
48. Vassilis Kremmydas, 'Capital et déploiement du commerce des Grecs: le cas de la marine marchande (fin XVIII°–début XIX° siècles)', in *Actes du 6° congrès international des études du Sud-Est européen* (Fondation nouvelle de la Recherche Scientifique: Athens, 1990), pp. 437–53.
49. Michel-Joseph Trullet, *Rapport sur le commerce des Idriotes et des Spetziotes*, 25 May 1803 (MAE, CCC, Naples de Romanie).
50. P. A. Hennique, *Les caboteurs et pêcheurs de la côte de Tunisie* (Paris: Gauthier-Villars, 1888), p. 82.
51. Jean-François Landolphe, *Mémoires du capitaine Landolphe contenant l'histoire de ses voyages pendant trente-six ans* (Paris: Bertrand et Pillet, 1823), vol. 2, p. 12.
52. Cornette, *Un Révolutionnaire ordinaire*, p. 236.
53. Silvia Marzagalli, *Les boulevards de la fraude: Le négoce maritime et le blocus continental (1806–1813)* (Lille: Presses Universitaires du Septentrion, 2000).
54. David, *Un port de l'océan*, p. 349.
55. David, *Un port de l'océan*, p. 349.
56. Letter of October 1800, in Cornette, *Un Révolutionnaire ordinaire*, p. 239.
57. Letter of 7 December 1800, in Cornette, *Un Révolutionnaire ordinaire*, p. 264.
58. Letter of 23 December 1800, in Cornette, *Un Révolutionnaire ordinaire*, p. 264.
59. Begouën Demeaux, *Mémorial d'une famille du Havre*, vol. 1, p. 151.
60. Letter of 9 June 1803, in Cornette, *Un Révolutionnaire ordinaire*, p. 265.
61. Letter of 29 June 1803, in Cornette, *Un Révolutionnaire ordinaire*, p. 265.
62. Benoît Lacombe, letter of 17 July 1803 (Register III, 53 and 54 of Lacombe's commercial correspondence), in Cornette, *Un Révolutionnaire ordinaire*, p. 239.

63. Letter of 31 October 1803 (III, 65) in Cornette, *Un Révolutionnaire ordinaire*, p. 242.
64. Letter of 25 January 1804 (III, 71), in Cornette, *Un Révolutionnaire ordinaire*, p. 242.
65. Letter of 23 March 1805, in Cornette, *Un Révolutionnaire ordinaire*, p. 243.
66. Cosme Ramaeckers, 'Voyages et campagnes en Espagne dans les années 1807–1808', in *Du Tage à Cabrera: Souvenirs de deux lieutenants et d'un caporal* (Paris: Teissèdre, 1999), p. 76.
67. Letter of 7 June 1805, in Cornette, *Un Révolutionnaire ordinaire*, p. 237.
68. Letter of 23 December 1800, in Cornette, *Un Révolutionnaire ordinaire*, p. 264.
69. Letter of 25 November 1811, in Cornette, *Un Révolutionnaire ordinaire*, p. 247.
70. Archives Municipales de Menton (I, 5), quoted in Jean-Louis Caserio, *La vie à Menton sous le Consulat et l'Empire*, vol. 1, *Aspects économiques* (Nice: Editions du Cabri, 1980), p. 85.
71. Caserio, *La vie à Menton*.
72. Ibid.
73. Archives Départementales des Alpes Maritimes (M 394), quoted in Caserio, *La vie à Menton*, p. 130.
74. Archives Municipales de Menton (D2, 54), quoted in Caserio, *La vie à Menton*, p. 25.
75. Daniel Ligou, *Montauban à la fin de l'Ancien Régime et aux débuts de la Révolution, 1787–1794* (Paris: Marcel Rivière, 1958), p. 592.
76. Fourcroy, 'Mission dans la 14° division militaire en floréal an IX', in Rocquain (ed.), *L'état de la France au 18 Brumaire, d'après les rapports des conseillers d'état chargés d'une enquête sur la situation de la République* (Paris: Didier, 1874), p. 208.
77. Najac, 'Mission dans la 19° division militaire en l'an IX', in Rocquain (ed.), *L'état de la France au 18 Brumaire*, p. 302.
78. H. Causse, 'Un industriel toulousain au temps de la Révolution et de l'Empire', in *Annales du Midi*, 69, 1957, pp. 121–33.
79. Français de Nantes, 'Mission dans la 8° division militaire en l'an IX', in Rocquain (ed.), *L'état de la France au 18 Brumaire*, pp. 45–7.
80. Barbé-Marbois, 'Mission dans la 13° division militaire en l'an IX', in Rocquain (ed.), *L'état de la France au 18 Brumaire*, p. 110.
81. Fourcroy, 'Mission dans la 14° division militaire en l'an IX', in Rocquain (ed.), *L'état de la France au 18 Brumaire*, p. 205.
82. Pétition du tribunal de commerce d'Angoulême au Conseil des Cinq Cents, 17 Prairial an VI, in Rocquain (ed.), *L'état de la France au 18 Brumaire*, pp. 394–5.
83. Lacuée, 'Mission dans la 1° division militaire', in Rocquain (ed.), *L'état de la France au 18 Brumaire*, p. 240.
84. Najac, 'Mission dans la 19° division militaire', in Rocquain (ed.), *L'état de la France au 18 Brumaire*, pp. 300–2.
85. Saint-Suzanne, 'Mission dans la 5° division militaire', in Rocquain (ed.), *L'état de la France au 18 Brumaire*, p. 353.
86. 'Observations sur la surcharge qu'éprouve le département de l'Aude dans la répartition des contributions directes', 1 Fructidor Year VI, in Rocquain (ed.), *L'état de la France au 18 Brumaire*, pp. 390–2, 391.

87. Raoul Hesdin, *The Journal of a Spy in Paris during the Reign of Terror (January–July 1794)* (London: John Murray, 1895), p. 3.
88. Lyons, *Revolution in Toulouse*, pp. 144–5.
89. *La fabrique lyonnaise de soieries et l'industrie de la soie en France, 1789–1889* (Lyon: Pitrat, 1889).
90. Gérard Thermeau, *Saint Etienne et son agglomération à l'aube de la révolution industrielle (1800–1815)* (Saint Etienne: Publications de l'Université de Saint Etienne, 2002), pp. 261, 274.
91. Ligou, *Montauban à la fin de l'Ancien Régime*, p. 414.
92. Fernand L'Huillier, *Recherches sur l'Alsace napoléonienne* (Strasbourg: Istra, 1947), p. 211.
93. Malcolm Crook, *Toulon in War and Revolution: From the Ancien Régime to the Restoration* (Manchester: Manchester University Press, 1991), p. 14.
94. Crook, *Toulon in War and Revolution*, p. 159.
95. Geoffrey Ellis, *Napoleon's Continental Blockade: The Case of Alsace* (Oxford: Clarendon Press, 1981), pp. 216–17.
96. Napoleon III, 'Speech of Bordeaux, 9 October 1852', *Le Moniteur universel*, 12 October 1852, in *Oeuvres de Napoléon III* (Paris: Amyot, 1856), vol. 3, pp. 341–4.

7 Civilians in the War

1. Bell, *First Total War*, pp. 11–12, 217.
2. Nicholas Atkin, *Daily Lives of Civilians in Wartime Twentieth Century Europe* (Westport, CT: Greenwood Press, 2008), pp. 1–3.
3. Maris A. Vinovskis, 'Have social historians lost the Civil War? Some preliminary demographic speculations', in Maris A. Vinovskis (ed.), *Towards a Social history of the American Civil War: Exploratory Essays* (New York: Cambridge University Press, 1990), pp. 1–30.
4. Célestin Guittard de Floriban, *Journal d'un bourgeois de Paris sous la Révolution*, ed. Raymond Aubert (Paris: France-Empire, 1974).
5. Claude Bailly, *Journal d'un artisan tourangeau, Claude Bailly, artisan sellier à Chinon au n° 27 de la rue Saint Etienne, 1789–1830* (Chinon: Editions de l'Office de tourisme de Chinon, 1989), p. 16.
6. Guittard de Floriban, *Journal d'un bourgeois de Paris*, p. 163.
7. Bailly, *Journal d'un artisan tourangeau*, p. 17.
8. Miot de Mélito, *Mémoires* (Paris: Michel Lévy, 1858), vol. 2, pp. 289–90.
9. Bailly, *Journal d'un artisan tourangeau*, p. 71.
10. Letter of Jean Tailhand, 8 December 1794, in Bouscayrol (ed.), *Cent lettres*, p. 65.
11. Fricasse, *Journal*, pp. 4–5.
12. Louise Eléonore Charlotte Adélaïde d'Osmond, Comtesse de Boigne, *Mémoires de Madame de Boigne*, 5 vols (Paris: Emile Paul, 1921–1923), vol. 1, p. 214.
13. Letter of Jean Ataix, 16 May 1794, in Bouscayrol (ed.), *Cent lettres*, p. 163.
14. Letter of Jacques Tuzest, 2 January 1795, in Bouscayrol (ed.), *Cent lettres*, p. 254.
15. Guittard de Floriban, *Journal d'un bourgeois de Paris*, pp. 306–8.

16. Bourrienne, *Mémoires*, vol. 3, pp. 232–6.
17. Constant, *Mémoires de Constant, premier valet de chambre de l'Empereur* (Paris: Ladvocat, 1830), vol. 5, p. 330.
18. Bourrienne, *Mémoires*, vol. 4, pp. 50–4.
19. Guittard de Floriban, *Journal d'un bourgeois de Paris*, pp. 444–5.
20. Georges Poisson, *Napoléon et Paris* (Paris: Berger-Levrault, 1964), p. 34.
21. A. M. Broadley, *The Journal of a British Chaplain in Paris during the Peace Negotiations of 1801–1802* (London: Chapman and Hall, 1913), pp. 197–8.
22. Joseph Clarke, *Commemorating the Dead in Revolutionary France: Revolution and Remembrance, 1789–1799* (Cambridge: Cambridge University Press, 2007), p. 244–6.
23. Jean-Paul Bertaud, *Quand les enfants parlaient de gloire: l'armée au cœur de la France de Napoléon* (Paris: Aubier, 2006), p. 57.
24. Georges Sand, *Histoire de ma vie* (Paris: 1855), vol. 1, p. 27.
25. Herbillon, *Quelques pages d'un vieux cahier: Souvenirs du général Herbillon (1794–1866)* (Paris: Berger-Levrault, 1928), p. 2.
26. Levavasseur, *Souvenirs*, p. 67.
27. Steven Englund, *Napoleon: A Political Life* (Cambridge, MA: Harvard University Press, 2005), pp. 261–2.
28. Miot de Mélito, *Mémoires*, pp. 283–93.
29. Howard Brown, 'The search for stability', in Howard Brown and Judith Miller (eds), *Taking Liberties: Problems of a New Order from the French Revolution to Napoleon* (Manchester: Manchester University Press, 2002), pp. 20–50, 33.
30. Forrest, *Conscripts and Deserters*, p. 144.
31. Georges Sand, *Histoire de ma vie* (Paris: Michel Lévy, 1856), vol. 4, pp. 158–9.
32. Scott Reynolds Nelson and Carol Sheriff, *A People at War: Civilians and Soldiers in America's Civil War, 1854–1877* (New York: Oxford University Press, 2008), p. 232.
33. Bailly, *Journal d'un artisan tourangeau*, p. 31.
34. Nicolas Ruault, *Gazette d'un parisien sous la Révolution: Lettres à son frère, 1783–1796* (Paris: Perrin, 1976), p. 325.
35. Guittard de Floriban, *Journal d'un bourgeois de Paris*, p. 277.
36. Ibid.
37. Raoul Hesdin, *The Journal of a Spy in Paris*, p. 12–13.
38. Ruault, *Gazette d'un parisien sous la Révolution*, p. 376.
39. Bailly, *Journal d'un artisan tourangeau*, p. 32.
40. Letter of Eloy Leclerc, 10 June 1794, in Bouscayrol (ed.), *Cent lettres de soldats de l'an II*, p. 102.
41. Martyn Lyons, *Revolution in Toulouse*, p. 126.
42. Hesdin, *Journal of a Spy in Paris*, pp. 12–13.
43. Bailly, *Journal d'un artisan tourangeau*, p. 36.
44. François Crouzet, *La grande inflation: La monnaie en France, de Louis XVI à Napoléon* (Paris: Fayard, 1993), pp. 380–559.
45. Letter of Alexis Gosse, 19 February 1795, in Bouscayrol (ed.), *Cent lettres de soldats de l'an II*, pp. 126–7.
46. Ruault, *Gazette d'un parisien sous la Révolution*, pp. 378–9.
47. Lyons, *Revolution in Toulouse*, p. 125; J. Coppolani, 'Bilan démographique de Toulouse de 1789 à 1885', 2nd series, 1965.

48. R. C. Cobb, 'Disette et mortalité: la crise de l'an III et de l'an IV à Rouen', in *Terreur et subsistances, 1793–1795* (Paris: Clavreuil, 1965).
49. Ruault, *Gazette d'un parisien sous la Révolution*, p. 380.
50. Letter of Marien Paravel, 28 December 1793, in Bouscayrol (ed.), *Cent lettres de soldats de l'an II*, p. 97.
51. François-Joseph Guélat, *Journal de François-Joseph Guélat (1791–1802): Mémoires d'un bourgeois de Porrentruy* (Delémont: Boéchat et fils éditeurs, 1906), p. 230.
52. Hesdin, *Journal of a Spy in Paris*, pp. 14–15.
53. Lyons, *Revolution in Toulouse*, p. 125.
54. François-Nicolas Mollien, *Mémoires d'un Ministre du Trésor public, 1780–1815* (Paris: Fournier, 1845), vol. 3, p. 135.
55. Antoine-Claire Thibaudeau, *Le Consulat et l'Empire*, 10 vols (Paris: Renouard, 1834–1835), vol. 3, p. 129.
56. Brillat Savarin, *Physiologie du goût ou méditations de gastronomie transcendante* (Paris: Charpentier, 1842), p. 116.
57. Speech by Barère, *Moniteur*, vol. 17, p. 474.
58. Declaration of Benoît Lacombe to the Municipal Council of Gaillac, 15 May 1793, in Joël Cornette, *Un Révolutionnaire ordinaire, Benoît Lacombe 1759–1819* (Paris: Champ Vallon, 1986), p. 214.
59. Cornette, *Un Révolutionnaire ordinaire*, p. 214.
60. Léon Brunchvicg, *Souvenirs de la Révolution à Nantes ou la mémoire d'un bleu* (Nantes: Vivant Editions, 1982), p. 118.
61. Soboul, *Les soldats de l'an II*, pp. 242–3.
62. Report from the Directory of the Tarn, 17 May 1793, in Cornette, *Un Révolutionnaire ordinaire*, p. 212.
63. Guélat, *Journal de François-Joseph Guélat*, p. 194.
64. Guitard de Floriban, *Journal d'un bourgeois de Paris*, p. 176.
65. Alain Lottin, *Boulonnais, noble et Révolutionnaire: Le journal de Gabriel Abot de Bazinghen (1779–1798)* (Arras: Presses de l'Université d'Artois, 1995), p. 248.
66. Fernand L'Huillier, *Recherches sur l'Alsace napoléonienne* (Strasbourg: Istra, 1947), p. 210.
67. Guittard de Floriban, *Journal d'un bourgeois de Paris*, p. 322.
68. Bailly, *Journal d'un artisan tourangeau*, p. 39.
69. Bailly, *Journal d'un artisan tourangeau*, p. 37.
70. Gabriel Désert, *La Révolution française en Normandie* (Toulouse: Privat, 1989), p. 202.
71. Guélat, *Journal de François-Joseph Guélat*, p. 235 (11 mars 1794).
72. Guélat, *Journal de François-Joseph Guélat*, p. 214.
73. Ibid.
74. Guélat, *Journal de François-Joseph Guélat*, p. 235.
75. Bailly, *Journal d'un artisan tourangeau*, p. 91.
76. Guélat, *Journal de François-Joseph Guélat*, 191.
77. Bailly, *Journal d'un artisan tourangeau*, p. 92.
78. Guittard de Floriban, *Journal d'un bourgeois de Paris*, p. 313.
79. Guittard de Floriban, *Journal d'un bourgeois de Paris*, p. 235.
80. Guittard de Floriban, *Journal d'un bourgeois de Paris*, pp. 299, 316.
81. Guélat, *Journal de François-Joseph Guélat*, pp. 234–5.

82. Letter from Jacques-François Begouën, 19 January 1814, in Maurice Begouën-Demeaux (ed.), *Mémorial d'une famille du Havre,* 2 vols (Paris: Société française d'Histoire d'Outre-Mer, 1982), vol. 1, p. 45.
83. Letter from Jacques-François Begouën, 15 February 1814, in *Mémorial d'une famille du Havre,* vol. 1, p. 46.
84. Peter McPhee, *Collioure, 1780–1815* (Melbourne: Melbourne University Press, 1989), p. 37.
85. Jacques Hantraye, *Les cosaques aux Champs-Elysées: L'occupation de la France après la chute de Napoléon* (Paris: Belin, 2005), pp. 99–107.
86. Letter from Jacques-François Begouën, 15 February 1814, in *Mémorial d'une famille du Havre,* vol. 1, p. 46.
87. Letter from Jacques-François Begouën, 16 February 1814, in *Mémorial d'une famille du Havre,* vol. 1, p. 46.
88. Letter of 16 February, in *Mémorial,* vol. 1, p. 48.
89. Paul Aymard, *Souvenirs d'un gamin de Lyon de 1814* (Lyon: Dessolins, 1871), pp. 5–7.
90. Letter of 28 March, in *Mémorial,* vol. 1, p. 55.
91. Letter of 29 March, in *Mémorial,* vol. 1, p. 55.
92. Comtesse de Boigne, *Mémoires,* vol. 1, p. 215.
93. Letter of 30 March, in *Mémorial,* vol. 1, p. 56.
94. Comtesse de Boigne, *Mémoires,* vol. 1, p. 216.
95. Edouard Lapène, *Campagnes de 1813 sur l'Ebre, les Pyrénées et la Garonne* (Paris: Anselin et Pochard, 1823), p. 336.
96. Edouard Lapène, *Campagnes de 1813 sur l'Ebre, les Pyrénées et la Garonne* (Paris: Anselin et Pochard, 1823), p. 337.
97. Letter from Desboiges to Puget *fils,* Strasbourg, 15 May 1814 (Archives Départementales de l'Isère, hereafter ADI: IJ260).
98. Letter from Dollet to Puget *fils*, Strasbourg, 13 July 1814 (ADI: 1J260).
99. Fourcroy, 'Mission dans la 16° division militaire', in Félix Rocquain (ed.), *L'état de la France au 18 Brumaire, d'après les rapports des conseillers d'état chargés d'une enquête sur la situation de la République* (Paris: Didier, 1874).
100. Dominic Lieven, *Russia against Napoleon: The Battle for Europe, 1807 to 1814* (London: Allen Lane, 2009), p. 478.
101. Thomas Dwight Veve, *The Duke of Wellington and the British Army of Occupation in France, 1815–1818* (Westport, CT: Greenwood Press, 1992), pp. 67–8.
102. 'Rapport de l'administration centrale du département des Alpes Maritimes au Corps Législatif', Year IX, in Rocquain (ed.), *L'état de la France,* p. 387.
103. Letter from Couzineau Huard to Puget *fils* in Marseille, Saumur, 11 August 1815 (ADI: 1J260).
104. Letter from Pottin to Puget *fils* in Marseille, Abbeville, 4 June 1814 (ADI: 1J260).
105. Comtesse de Boigne, *Mémoires*, vol. 1, p. 217.
106. Letter from Puget *fils*, Marseille, 1 April 1815 (ADI: 1J260).
107. Letter from Puget *père*, Paris, 3 April 1815 (ADI: 1J260).
108. Letter from Puget *père*, Paris, 25 April 1815 (ADI: 1J260).
109. Letter from Puget *père*, Paris, 13 May 1815 (ADI: 1J260).
110. Letter from Puget *père*, Paris, 20 June 1815 (ADI: 1J260).
111. Letter from Puget *père*, Paris, 24 June 1815 (ADI: 1J260).

112. Letter from Puget *père*, Paris, 27 June 1815 (ADI: 1J260).
113. Letter from Puget *père*, Paris, 28 June 1815 (ADI: 1J260).
114. Letter from Puget *père*, Paris, 30 June 1815 (ADI: 1J260).
115. Letter from Puget *père*, Paris, 2 July 1815 (ADI: 1J260).
116. Ibid.
117. Letter from Puget *père*, Paris, 10 July 1815 (ADI: 1J260).

Conclusion

1. Manfred F. Boemeke, Rogers Chickering and Stig Förster (eds), *Anticipating Total War*; Stig Förster and Jörg Nagler (eds), *On the Road to Total War*.
2. Thomas Dwight Veve, *The Duke of Wellington and the British Army of Occupation*, p. 68.
3. Marie-Cécile Thoral, *Les limites de la centralisation administrative: l'administration locale dans le département de l'Isère du Consulat à la Monarchie de Juillet* (Thèse de doctorat d'Histoire, Université de Grenoble, 2004, 3 volumes), vol. 3.
4. Isser Woloch, '"A sacred debt": Veterans and the State in Revolutionary and Napoleonic France', in David A. Gerber (ed.), *Disabled veterans in History* (Ann Arbor, MI: University of Michigan Press, 2000), pp. 145–62, 145.
5. Sudhir Hazareesingh, *The Saint Napoleon: Celebrations of Sovereignty in Nineteenth-Century France* (Cambridge, MA: Harvard University Press, 2004), pp. 78–104.
6. Natalie Petiteau, *Lendemains d'Empire: Les soldats de Napoléon dans la France du XIX° siècle* (Paris: La Boutique de l'Histoire, 2003).
7. *Almanach de la Famille militaire pour 1851* (Paris: Au bureau des Annales militaires, 1851), pp. 9–10.

Select Bibliography

Published documents

Almanach de la Famille militaire pour 1851 (Paris: Au bureau des Annales militaires, 1851).

Aulard, Alphonse ed., *Recueil des actes du Comité de Salut Public, avec la correspondance officielle des représentants en mission*, 28 vols (Paris: Editions du CTHS, 1933).

Bonaparte, Napoléon and Thierry Lentz ed., *Correspondance générale*, vol. 2, *La campagne d'Egypte et l'avènement* (Paris: Fayard, 2005).

Cornette, Joël ed., *Un Révolutionnaire ordinaire, Benoît Lacombe 1759–1819* (Paris: Champ Vallon, 1986).

Gotteri, Nicole *La police secrète du Premier Empire. Bulletins quotidiens adressés à Savary par l'Empereur de juin à décembre 1810* (Paris: Honoré Champion, 1997).

Rocquain, Félix *L'état de la France au 18 Brumaire, d'après les rapports des conseillers d'état chargés d'une enquête sur la situation de la République* (Paris: Didier, 1874).

Memoirs, diaries, letters

Angenard, Guillaume-Marie *Mémoires d'un capitaine corsaire* (Rennes: La Découvrance, 1996).

Aymard, Paul *Souvenirs d'un gamin de Lyon de 1814* (Lyon: Dessolins, 1871).

Bailly, Claude *Journal d'un artisan tourangeau, Claude Bailly, artisan sellier à Chinon au n° 27 de la rue Saint Etienne, 1789–1830* (Chinon: Editions de l'Office de tourisme de Chinon, 1989).

Begos, Louis *Souvenirs des campagnes du lieutenant colonel Louis Bégos, ancien capitaine adjudant-major au deuxième régiment suisse au service de France* (Lausanne: Librairie A. Delafontaine, 1859).

Blaze, Elzéar *La vie militaire sous le Premier Empire ou moeurs de garnison, du bivouac et de la caserne* (Paris: A la librairie illustrée, 1837).

Blaze, Sébastien *Mémoires d'un apothicaire sur la guerre d'Espagne pendant les années 1808 à 1814* (Paris: Ladvocat, 1828).

Bonaparte, Joseph *Mémoires et correspondance politique et militaire du roi Joseph* (Paris: Perrotin, 1855).

Bouilly, J.-N. *Mes récapitulations*, 3 vols (Paris: 1836–1837).

Bourgogne, Adrien *Mémoires* (Paris: Arléa, 1992).

Bouscayrol, René ed., *Cent lettres de soldats de l'an II* (Paris: Aux amateurs de livres, 1989).

Bricard, Louis-Joseph *Journal du canonnier Bricard, 1792–1802, Publié pour la première fois par ses petits-fils Alfred et Jules Bricard* (Paris, 1891).

Broadley, A. M. *The Journal of a British Chaplain in Paris during the Peace Negotiations of 1801–1802* (London: Chapman and Hall, 1913).

Brunchvicg, Léon *Souvenirs de la Révolution à Nantes ou la mémoire d'un bleu* (Nantes: Vivant editions, 1982).
Bussy, Jean-Marc 'Notes de Jean-Marc Bussy, appointé voltigeur. Campagnes d'Espagne et de Russie', in A. Jullien (ed.), *Soldats suisses au service étranger* (Geneva: A. Jullien Editeur, 1913), vol. 6, pp. 219–312.
Chevallier, *Souvenirs des guerres napoléoniennes* (Paris: Hachette, 1970).
Clausewitz, von Carl *On War* (London, 1968), p. 219.
Constant, *Mémoires de Constant, premier valet de chambre de l'Empereur* (Paris: Ladvocat, 1830).
d'Osmond, comtesse de Boigne, Louise Eléonore Charlotte Adélaïde *Mémoires de Madame de Boigne*, 5 vols (Paris: Emile Paul, 1921–1923).
de Bourrienne, Louis-Antoine Fauvelet *Mémoires de M. De Bourrienne, Ministre d'Etat: sur Napoléon, le Directoire, le Consulat, l'Empire et la Restauration*, 10 vols (Paris: Ladvocat, 1829).
de Gauville, Adolphe 'Un prisonnier de guerre en 1813', in *De la campagne de Saxe à la campagne de France. Lettres et souvenirs* (Paris: Teissèdre, 2000).
de la Gravière, Pierre Jurien *Mémoires d'un amiral* (Paris: Editions du Musée de la Marine, 1977).
de la Poix Fréminville, Christophe-Paulin and Herpin, Eugène ed., *Mémoires du chevalier de Fréminville (1787–1848)* (Paris: La Découvrance, 2006).
de la Sibourie, Poumiès *Souvenirs d'un médecin de Paris, 1789–1863* (Paris, 1910).
de Mélito, Miot *Mémoires* (Paris: Michel Lévy, 1858).
de Saint André, Narcisse Boutilier *Mémoires d'un père à ses enfants, 1793–1796* (Cholet: Editions du Bocage, 1994).
de Villeret, Brun *Cahiers du général Brun de Villeret, pair de France, 1773–1845* (Paris: Plon, 1953).
Delorme, Emmanuel ed., *Correspondance de Claude Simon* (Grenoble: Allier, 1899).
Dembowski, Joseph 'Voyage de retour de Saint Domingue en France', *Journal et Voyage à Saint Domingue*, Paris, Teissèdre, 1997, pp. 129–177 (pp. 167–168).
Demeaux, Maurice Begouen ed., *Mémorial d'une famille du Havre*, 2 vols (Paris: Société française d'Histoire d'Outre-Mer, 1982).
Desgenettes, René *Histoire médicale de l'armée d'Orient* (Paris: Firmin Didot, 1845).
Dumonceau, François *Mémoires du général comte François Dumonceau* (Bruxelles: S. Puraye Brepols, 1958).
Faucheur, Narcisse *Souvenirs des campagnes du sergent Faucheur* (Paris, 2004).
Foy, Maximilien Sébastien *Histoire de la guerre de la péninsule sous Napoléon* (Paris: Baudouin, 1827).
François, Charles *Journal du capitaine François dit le dromadaire d'Egypte* (Paris: Tallandier, 2003).
Fricasse, *Journal de marche d'un volontaire de 1792*, Brussels, n.d., 1st edn (Paris, 1882).
Gilbert, Nicolas-Pierre *Histoire médicale de l'armée française à Saint Domingue* (Paris: Gabon, 1803).
Griois, Charles Pierre Lubin, *Mémoires du général Griois, 1792–1822* (Paris: Plon, 1909).
Guélat, François-Joseph *Journal de François-Joseph Guélat (1791–1802): Mémoires d'un bourgeois de Porrentruy* (Delémont: Boéchat et fils éditeurs, 1906).
Guillemard, Robert *Mémoires de Robert Guillemard, sergent en retraite, de 1805 à 1823* (Paris: Delaforest, Bossange, Baudouin, 1826).

Guillemard, Robert *Les amis en captivité, Orient de Malte ou aventures d'un sergent français*, 2 vols (Paris, 1827).
Guittard de Floriban, Célestin and Aubert, Raymond ed., *Journal d'un bourgeois de Paris sous la Révolution* (Paris, France-Empire, 1974).
Herbillon, *Quelques pages d'un vieux cahier. Souvenirs du général Herbillon (1794–1866)* (Paris: Berger-Levrault, 1928).
Hesdin, Raoul *The Journal of a Spy in Paris During the Reign of Terror (January–July 1794)* (London: John Murray, 1895).
Jacquin, Francis-Joseph *Carnet de route d'un grognard de la Révolution et de l'Empire* (Paris: Clavreuil, 1960).
Joliclerc, E. *Joliclerc volontaire des armées de la Révolution: ses lettres (1793–1796)* (Paris: Perrin, 1905).
Junot, Laure *Mémoires de Madame la duchesse d'Abrantès* (Tours: Maine, 1835).
Kerkhove, *Observations médicales faites pendant la campagne de Russie en 1812* (Antwerp: 1837).
Landolphe, Jean-François *Mémoires du capitaine Landolphe contenant l'histoire de ses voyages pendant trente-six ans* (Paris: Bertrand et Pillet, 1823).
Lapène, Edouard *Campagnes de 1813 sur l'Ebre, les Pyrénées et la Garonne* (Paris: Anselin et Pochard, 1823).
Laporte, Joseph *Mon voyage en Egypte et en Syrie. Carnets d'un jeune soldat de Bonaparte* (Paris: Presses Universitaires de France, 2008).
Larrey, Dominique 'Mémoire sur la peste', *Description de l'Egypte* (Paris: Panckoucke, 1823), vol. 13, pp. 81–103.
Larrey, Dominique *Mémoires et campagnes* (Paris, Tallandier: 2004).
Lasserre, 'A l'armée d'Egypte: Discipline, récompenses diverses et armes d'honneur', *Revue des études napoléoniennes*, 30, 1930, pp. 99–121.
Lavaux, François *Mémoires* (Paris: Dentu, n.d. [around 1880]).
Levavasseur, Octave *Souvenirs Militaires* (Paris: Plon, 1914).
Lombard, Jean *Un volontaire de 1792* (Paris: Savine, 1892).
Lottin, Alain *Boulonnais, noble et Révolutionnaire. Le journal de Gabriel Abot de Bazinghen (1779–1798)* (Arras: Presses de l'Université d'Artois, 1995).
Martin, P. *Histoire de l'expédition française en Egypte* (Paris: Eberhart, 1815).
Maurin, 'Lettres d'un volontaire de l'an II', *Nouvelle Revue Rétrospective*, January–June 1902, p. 85.
Métral, Antoine *Histoire de l'expédition des Français à Saint Domingue sous le Consulat de Napoléon Bonaparte* (Paris: Fanjat, 1825).
Millet, Pierre *Souvenirs de la campagne d'Egypte* (Paris: Emile Paul, 1903).
Moiret, Joseph-Marie *Mémoires sur l'expédition d'Egypte* (Paris: Belfond, 1984).
Mollien, François-Nicolas *Mémoires d'un Ministre du Trésor public, 1780–1815* (Paris: Fournier, 1845).
Ouvrard, Gabriel-Julien *Mémoires de G.-J. Ouvrard sur sa vie et ses diverses opérations financières* (Paris: Moutardier, 1826, 3rd edn).
Peyre-Ferry, Joseph Elysée *Journal des opérations militaires de l'armée française à Saint Domingue* (Paris: Les editions de Paris, 2006).
Plucket, *Journal de bord du corsaire Plucket* (Paris: Les éditions de Paris, 1956).
Ramaeckers, Cosme and Anon., *Du Tage à Cabrera. Souvenirs de deux lieutenants et d'un caporal* (Paris: Teissèdre, 1999).
Romand, Louis *Mémoires de ma vie militaire, 1809–1815* (Besançon: F. Barthelet, 1981).

Ruault, Nicolas *Gazette d'un parisien sous la Révolution. Lettres à son frère, 1783–1796* (Paris: Perrin, 1976).
Sand, Georges *Histoire de ma vie* (Paris: Michel Lévy, 1856).
Savarin, Brillat *Physiologie du goût ou méditations de gastronomie transcendante* (Paris: Charpentier, 1842).
Scheltens, Henri *Mémoires d'un grenadier de la Garde* (Paris: Editions du grenadier, 2004).
Thibaudeau, Antoine-Claire *Le Consulat et l'Empire*, 10 vols (Paris: Renouard, 1834–1835).
Vigo-Roussillon, François *Journal de campagne* (Paris: Editions France Empire, 1981).

Key secondary literature

Acerra, Martine *Rochefort et la construction navale française, 1661–1815* (Paris, Librairie de l'Inde: 1993).
Acerra, Martine and Jean Meyer, *Marines et Révolution* (Rennes: Ouest-France, 1988).
Alberge, C. *Vie et mort des soldats de l'an II à l'hôpital de l'Egalité de Pézenas*, in *Etudes sur Pézenas et sa région*, 2, 1971.
Anderson, Benedict *Imagined communities: Reflections on the Origin and Spread of Nationalism* (London: Verso, 2006).
Atkin, Nicholas *Daily Lives of Civilians in Wartime Twentieth Century Europe* (Westport, CT: Greenwood Press, 2008).
Audoin-Rouzeau, Stéphane *Combattre (1914–1918)* (Amiens: CRDP, 1995).
Audoin-Rouzeau, Stéphane 'Massacres: Le corps et la guerre', in Alain Corbin, Jean-Jacques Courtine, Georges Vigarello (eds), *Histoire du corps* (Paris: Seuil, 2006), vol. 3, pp. 281–320.
Audoin-Rouzeau, Stéphane and Annette Becker, 'Violence et consentement: la culture de guerre du premier conflit mondial', in Jean-Pierre Rioux and Jean-François Sirinelli (eds), *Pour une histoire culturelle* (Paris: Le Seuil, 1997), pp. 251–71.
Bach, André *Fusillés pour l'exemple, 1914–1915* (Paris: Tallandier, 2003).
Barrois, Claude *Psychanalyse du guerrier* (Paris: Hachette, 1993).
Battesti, Michèle *Trafalgar: Les aléas de la stratégie navale de Napoléon* (Paris: Economica, 2004).
Becker, Annette and Audoin-Rouzeau, Stéphane, *14–18: Retrouver la guerre* (Paris: Gallimard, 2000).
Bell, David *The Cult of the Nation in France: Inventing Nationalism, 1680–1800* (Cambridge, MA and London: Harvard University Press, 2003).
Bell, David *The First Total War: Napoleon's Europe and the Birth of Warfare as we Know it* (Boston, MA and New York: Houghton Mifflin Company, 2007).
Bertaud, Jean-Paul *La Révolution armée. Les soldats-citoyens et la Révolution française* (Paris: Robert Laffont, 1979).
Bertaud, Jean-Paul *Quand les enfants parlaient de gloire: l'armée au cœur de la France de Napoléon* (Paris: Aubier, 2006).
Black, Jeremy *The Age of Total War, 1860–1945* (Westport, CT: Praeger Security International, 2006).

Blaufarb, Rafe *The French Army, 1750–1820: Careers, Talent, Merit* (Manchester: Manchester University Press, 2002).

Bodinier, Gilbert 'Du soldat républicain à l'officier impérial: convergences et divergences entre l'armée et la société', in André Corvisier (ed.), *Histoire militaire de la France*, vol. 2, Jean Delmas (ed.), *De 1715 à 1871* (Paris: Presses Universitaires de France, 1992).

Bonnette, P. 'Le calvaire médical de Saint Domingue et de la Guadeloupe', *Hippocrate*, 6, 1938, pp. 470–90.

Bouloiseau, M. *Malades et tire-au-flanc à l'armée de l'Ouest, ans II–III*, Actes du Congrès des Sociétés savantes de Toulouse, 1971.

Bourke, Joanna *An Intimate History of Killing: Face to Face Killing in Twentieth-Century Warfare* (New York: Basic Books, 1999).

Brice, Raoul Marie and Bottet, Maurice *Le corps de santé militaire en France. Son évolution, ses campagnes: 1708–1882* (Paris: 1907).

Broers, Michael *Europe under Napoleon, 1799–1815* (New York: Edouard Arnold, 1996).

Broers, Michael *The Politics of Religion in Napoleonic Italy: The War Against God, 1801–1814* (London: Routledge, 2002).

Brown, Howard 'The search for stability', in Howard Brown and Judith Miller (eds), *Taking Liberties: Problems of a New Order from the French Revolution to Napoleon* (Manchester: Manchester University Press, 2002), pp. 20–50.

Buti, Gilbert 'Toulon de 1800 à 1815', in *Provence historique*, 39, October–November–Décember 1989, p. 158.

Camon, Hubert *La guerre napoléonienne. Les batailles* (Paris: Chapelot, 1910).

Carrière, Charles 'Les entrées de navires dans le port de Marseille pendant la Révolution', in *Provence Historique*, 1957, pp. 200–25.

Carrière, Charles *Négociants marseillais au XVIIIème siècle. Contribution à l'étude des économies maritimes* (Marseille: Institut Historique de Provence, 1973).

Caserio, Jean-Louis *La vie à Menton sous le Consulat et l'Empire*, vol. 1, *Aspects économiques* (Nice: Editions du Cabri, 1980).

Causse, H. 'Un industriel toulousain au temps de la Révolution et de l'Empire', in *Annales du Midi*, 69, 1957, pp. 121–33.

Cazals Rémy and Frédéric Rousseau, *14–18: Le cri d'une génération* (Toulouse: Privat, 2003).

Chassin, Charles-Louis *La Vendée patriote*, 4 vols (Paris, 1893–1895).

Chassin Charles-Louis and L. Hennet, *Les volontaires nationaux pendant la Révolution*, 3 vols (Paris: Cerf, Noblet, 1899).

Chevallier, A. G. 'Hygienic problems in the Napoleonic armies', in *Ciba Symposia*, 1941.

Chickering, Roger 'Total war: The use and abuse of a concept', in Manfred F. Boemeke, Chickering Roger and Stig Förster (eds), *Anticipating Total War: The German and American Experiences, 1871–1914* (Cambridge: Cambridge University Press, 1999), pp. 13–28.

Clarke, Joseph *Commemorating the Dead in Revolutionary France: Revolution and Remembrance, 1789–1799* (Cambridge: Cambridge University Press, 2007).

Cobb, Richard C. *The Police and the People: French Popular Protest, 1789–1820* (Oxford: Oxford University Press, 1972).

Cochet, François *Survivre au front, 1914–1918. Les poilus entre contrainte et consentement* (Paris: 14–18 Editions, 2005).

Cole, Juan *Napoleon's Egypt: Invading the Middle East* (New York: Palgrave Macmillan, 2008).
Colin, Jean *Les transformations de la guerre* (Paris: Flammarion, 1911).
Cormack, William *Revolution and Political Conflict in the French Navy, 1789–1794* (New York: Cambridge University Press, 1995).
Crépin, Annie *La conscription en débat ou le triple apprentissage de la nation, de la citoyenneté, de la République (1798–1889)* (Arras: Presses de l'Université d'Artois, 1998).
Crépin, Annie *Défendre la France. Les Français, la guerre et le service militaire de la guerre de Sept ans à Verdun* (Rennes: Presses Universitaires de Rennes, 2005).
Crocq, Louis *Les traumatismes psychiques de guerre* (Paris: Odile Jacob, 1999).
Crook, Malcolm *Toulon in war and revolution: from the Ancien Régime to the Restoration, 1750–1820* (Manchester: Manchester University Press, 1991).
Crouzet, François *La grande inflation. La monnaie en France, de Louis XVI à Napoléon* (Paris: Fayard, 1993).
David, P. H. *Un port de l'océan pendant la Révolution. La Rochelle et son district, 1791–1795* (La Rochelle: Pijolley, 1938).
d'Arcier, Amaury Faivre *Les oubliés de la liberté. Négociants, consuls et missionnaires français au Levant pendant la Révolution (1784–1798)* (Paris: Peter Lang, 2007).
de Baecque, Antoine *Le corps de l'histoire: métaphores et politique (1770–1800)* (Paris: Calmann-Lévy, 1993).
de Certeau, Michel Dominique Julia and Jacques Revel, *Une politique de la langue: la Révolution française et les patois* (Paris: Gallimard, 2002).
Desbois, Evelyne 'Vivement la guerre qu'on se tue! Sur la ligne de feu en 14–18', in Terrain, 19, October 1992, pp. 65–80.
Dubois, Laurent *Avengers of the New World: The Story of the Haitian Revolution* (Cambridge, MA: Belknap Press of Harvard University Press, 2005).
Dutton, Kenneth *The Perfectible Body: The Western Ideal of Male Physical Development* (New York: Continuum, 1995).
Ellis, Geoffrey *Napoleon's Continental Blockade: The case of Alsace* (Oxford: Clarendon Press, 1981).
Englund, Steven *Napoleon: A Political Life* (Cambridge, MA: Harvard University Press, 2005).
Filippini, Jean-Pierre 'Livourne et l'Afrique du Nord au XVIIIème siècle', *Revue d'histoire maghrébine*, 1, 1977, pp. 125–49.
Finley, Milton *The Most Monstrous of Wars: The Napoleonic Guerrilla in Southern Italy, 1806–1811* (Richmond, VA: University of South Carolina Press, 1994).
Flayhart, William Henry *Counterpoint to Trafalgar: The Anglo-Russian Invasion of Naples (1805–1806)* (Gainesville, FL: University Press of Florida, 2004).
Forrest, Alan *Conscripts and Deserters: The Army and French Society during the Revolution and Empire* (Oxford: Oxford University Press, 1998).
Forrest, Alan *Napoleon's Men, The soldiers of the Revolution and Empire* (London and New York: Hambledon Continuum, 2002).
Forrest, Alan *The Revolution in Provincial France: Aquitaine, 1789–1799* (Oxford: Clarendon Press, 2004).
Förster Stig and Jörg Nagler, eds, *On the Road to Total War: The American Civil War and the German Wars of Unification, 1861–1871* (Cambridge: Cambridge University Press, 1997).

Fuller, John G. *Troop Morale and Popular Culture in the British and Dominion Armies, 1914–1918* (Oxford: Clarendon Press, 1990).
Garrison, F. H. *Notes on the History of Military Medicine* (Washington DC: Association of military surgeons, 1922).
George, Alexander L. 'Primary groups, organisation and military performance', in Roger W. Little (ed.), *Handbook of Military Institutions* (Beverly Hills, CA: Sage Publications, 1971), pp. 245–318.
Gerbod, Paul 'L'éthique héroïque en France (1870–1914)', in *Revue historique*, 54, October–December 1982, pp. 268, 409–29.
Guiomar, Jean-Yves *L'invention de la guerre totale, XVIII-XX siècles* (Paris: Le Félin, 2004).
Hagemann, Karen Alan Forrest and Jane Rendall, eds, *Soldiers, Citizens and Civilians: Experiences and Perceptions of the French Wars, 1790–1820* (Basingstoke: Palgrave Macmillan, 2009).
Hantraye, Jacques *Les cosaques aux Champs-Elysées. L'occupation de la France après la chute de Napoléon* (Paris: Belin, 2005).
Haupt, Heinz Gerhard, Michael G. Müller and Stuart Woolf, eds, *Regional and National Identities in Europe in the 19th and 20th centuries* (Leiden: Kluwer Law International, 1998).
Hazareesingh, Sudhir *The Saint Napoleon: Celebrations of Sovereignty in Nineteenth Century France* (Cambridge, MA: Harvard University Press, 2004).
Hopkin, David M. *Soldier and Peasant in French Popular Culture, 1766–1870* (London: Royal Historical Society, 2002).
Janowitz M. and E. A. Shils, 'Cohesion and disintegration in the Wehrmacht in World War II' (first published in 1948), in M. Janowitz (ed.), *Military Conflict: Essays in the Institutional Analysis of War and Peace* (Beverly Hills, CA: Sage publications, 1975).
Jarvis, Christina S. *The Male Body at War: American Masculinity During World War II* (Dekalb: Northern Illinois University Press, 2004).
Jeismann, Michael *La patrie de l'ennemi. La notion d'ennemi national et la représentation de la nation en Allemagne et en France de 1792 à 1918* (Paris: CNRS Editions, 1997).
Kourchnir, Serge Léon Louis *Considérations sur l'évolution du service de santé militaire de 1789 à 1814* (Thèse de Doctorat d'histoire, Paris, 1955).
Lafon, Jean-Marc *L'Andalousie et Napoléon. Contre-insurrection, collaboration et résistances dans le midi de l'Espagne (1808–1812)* (Paris: Nouveau Monde éditions, 2007).
Laurens, Henry *L'expédition d'Egypte, 1798–1801* (Paris: Seuil, 1997).
Lebigot, François 'La folie et la guerre de 1914–1918', in *Médecine et armées*, 23, 2, 1995, pp. 203–6.
Leggiere, Michael *The Fall of Napoleon: The Allied Invasion of France, 1813–1814* (New York: Cambridge University Press, 2007).
Lemaire, Jean-François *Les blessés dans les armés napoléoniennes* (Paris: Lettrages-Distribution, 1990).
Lévêque, Pierre *Les officiers de marine du Premier Empire* (Paris: Editions du Service historique de la Marine, 2003), 2 vols.
L'Huillier, Fernand *Recherches sur l'Alsace napoléonienne* (Strasbourg: Istra, 1947).
Lieven, Dominic *Russia Against Napoleon: The Battle for Europe, 1807 to 1814* (London: Allen Lane, 2009).

Ligou, Daniel *Montauban à la fin de l'Ancien Régime et aux débuts de la Révolution, 1787–1794* (Paris: Marcel Rivière, 1958).

Little, R. W. 'Buddy relations and combat performance', in M. Janowitz (ed.), *The New Military: Changing Patterns of Organisation* (New York: Russel Sage Foundation, 1964), pp. 195–233.

Loez, André 'L'espace public des tranchées. "Tenir" sous le regard des autres en 1914–1918', in Rémy Cazals, Emmanuelle Picard and Denis Rolland (eds), *La grande guerre. Pratiques et expériences* (Toulouse: Privat, 2005), pp. 259–68.

Lynn, John *The Bayonets of the Republic: Motivation and Tactics in the Army of Revolutionary France, 1791–1794* (Urbana, IL: University of Illinois Press, 1984).

Lyons, Martyn *Revolution in Toulouse: An Essay on Provincial Terrorism* (Berne: Peter Lang, 1978).

Marshall, Samuel Lyman Atwood, *Men Against Fire: The Problem of Battle Command* (New York: William Morrow and Co., 1947).

Martin, Jen-Clément *La Vendée et la France* (Paris: Seuil, 1987).

Marzagalli, Silvia *Les boulevards de la fraude. Le négoce maritime et le blocus continental (1806–1813)* (Lille: Presses Universitaires du Septentrion, 2000).

McPhee, Peter *Collioure, 1780–1815* (Melbourne: Melbourne University Press, 1989).

McPhee, Peter 'Frontiers, ethnicity and identity in the French Revolution: Catalans and Occitans', in Ian Coller, Helen Davies and Julie Kalman (eds), *French History and Civilisation.* Papers from the George Rudé Seminar. Volume 1, 2005, Melbourne, George Rudé Society, 2005.

Mackesy, Piers *The War in the Mediterranean, 1803–1810* (London, 1957).

Meyer, Jean 'Le face à face des systèmes logistiques français et anglais en Méditerranée pendant les guerres de la Révolution et de l'Empire', in *Français et Anglais en Méditerranée de la Révolution française à l'indépendance de la Grèce, 1789–1830* (Vincennes: Editions du Service historique de la Marine, 1992), pp. 181–202.

Moskos, C. 'Behavior of combat soldiers in Vietnam', in Charles C. Moskos (ed.), *The American Enlisted Man: The Rank and File in Today's Military* (New York: Russel Sage Foundation, 1970), pp. 134–56.

Mosse, George L. *Fallen Soldiers: Reshaping the Memory of the World Wars* (Oxford, Oxford University Press, 1990).

Mosse, Georges L. *The Image of Man: The Creation of Modern Masculinity* (New York: Oxford University Press, 1996).

Nef, John U. *La route de la guerre totale* (Paris: Armand Colin, 1949).

Nelson Scott Reynolds and Carol Sheriff, *A People at War: Civilians and Soldiers in America's Civil War, 1854–1877* (New York: Oxford University Press, 2008).

Panzac, Daniel *Les corsaires barbaresques. La fin d'une épopée (1800–1820)* (Paris: CNRS Editions, 1999).

Petiteau, Natalie *Lendemains d'Empire. Les soldats de Napoléon dans la France du XIX° siècle* (Paris: La Boutique de l'Histoire, 2003).

Poisson, Georges *Napoléon et Paris* (Paris: Berger-Levrault, 1964).

Pomponi, Francis 'Corse et Sardaigne entre France et Angleterre, 1796–1805', in *Français et Anglais en Méditerranée de la Révolution française à l'indépendance de la Grèce, 1789–1830* (Vincennes: Editions du Service historique de la Marine, 1992), pp. 231–50.

Priard, Lieutenant Claude *Les juges militaires sous la Révolution* (Vincennes: Commission française d'histoire militaire comparée, 1969).

Prost, Antoine 'Les limites de la brutalisation: tuer sur le front occidental en 14–18', *Vingtième siècle. Revue d'Histoire*, 5, January–March 2004, pp. 5–20.

Quoy-Bodin, Jean-Luc *L'armée et la franc-maçonnerie au déclin de la monarchie, sous la Révolution et l'Empire* (Paris: Economica, 1987).

Reed-Danahay, Deborah *Education and Identity in Rural France: The Politics of Schooling* (New York: Cambridge University Press, 1996).

Reinhard, Marcel 'Nostalgie et service militaire pendant la Révolution', *Annales historiques de la Révolution française*, 30, 1958, pp. 1–15.

Richard, C. *Le Comité de salut public et les fabrications de guerre sous la Terreur* (Paris, 1921).

Rodigneaux, Michel *La guerre de course en Guadeloupe, XVIII-XIXe siècles* (Paris: L'Harmattan, 2006).

Rothenberg, Gunther *The Art of Warfare in the Age of Napoleon* (Bloomington, IN: Indiana University Press, 1980).

Rousset, Camille *Les volontaires de 1791–1794* (Paris: 1870, 2nd edn).

Saint Fuscien, Emmanuel 'Place et valeur de l'exemple dans l'exercice de l'autorité et les mécanismes de l'obéissance dans l'armée française en 1914–1918', in Rémy Cazals, Emmanuel Picard and Denis Rolland (eds), *La grande guerre. Pratiques et expériences* (Toulouse: Privat, 2005), pp. 281–90.

Scott, William *Terror and Repression in Revolutionary Marseilles* (New York: Barnes and Noble, 1973).

Secher, Reynald *Le génocide franco-français: la Vendée* (Paris: Presses Universitaires de France, 1986).

Soboul, Albert *Les soldats de l'an II* (Paris: Club français du livre, 1959).

Soboul, Albert *Les Sans-culottes parisiens en l'an II* (Paris: Seuil, 1968).

Strachan, Hew 'Training, morale and modern war', in *Journal of contemporary history*, 41, 2, 2006, pp. 211–27.

Stouffer, Samuel A. *Studies in Social Psychology in World War Two: The American Soldier* (Princeton, NJ: Princeton University Press, 1949).

Thomazi, Auguste *Les marins de Napoléon* (Paris, 1978).

Thoral, Marie-Cécile *L'ascension du pouvoir local au XIX° siècle: le département de l'Isère face à la centralisation napoléonienne* (Rennes: Presses Universitaires de Rennes, 2010).

Tombs, Robert ed., *Nationhood and Nationalism in France, from Boulangism to the Great War (1889–1918)* (London: Harper Collins, 1991).

Veve, Thomas Dwight *The Duke of Wellington and the British Army of Occupation in France, 1815–1818* (Westport, CT: Greenwood Press, 1992).

Villain-Gandossi, C., L. Durteste and S. Busuttil, eds, *Méditerranée, mer ouverte* (Paris: Editions de la Maison des Sciences de l'Homme, 1997).

Weber, Eugen *Peasants into Frenchmen: The Modernization of Rural France, 1870–1914* (Stanford, CA: Stanford University Press, 1976).

Wesbrook, Stephen D. 'The potential for military disintegration', in Sam Charles Sarkesian (ed.), *Combat Effectiveness: Cohesion, Stress and the Volunteer Military* (Beverly Hills, CA: Sage Publications, 1980), pp. 244–78.

Weiner, Dora B. *The Citizen-Patient in Revolutionary and Imperial Paris* (Baltimore, MD: Johns Hopkins University Press, 1993).

Winter, Jay 'Shell-shock and the Cultural History of the Great War', *Journal of Contemporary History*, 35, 1 (special issue) January 2000, pp. 7–11.
Woloch, Isser '"A sacred debt": Veterans and the State in Revolutionary and Napoleonic France', in David A. Gerber (ed.), *Disabled Veterans in History* (Ann Arbor, MI: University of Michigan Press, 2000), pp. 145–62.
Zinsser, H. *Rats, Lice and History* (Boston, MA: Little Brown, 1935).

Index